Splinters of a Nation

GERMAN POW CAMPS IN UTAH

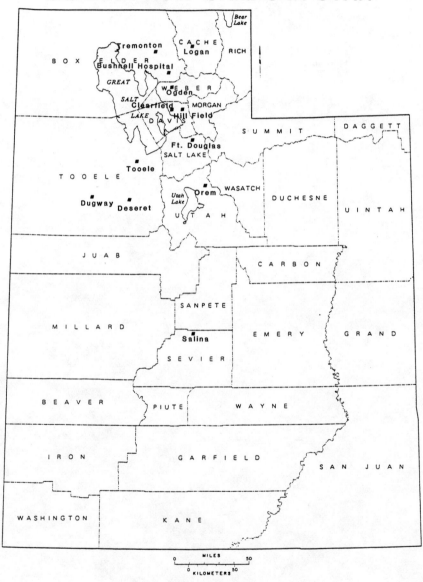

German POW camps in Utah

Splinters of a Nation

German Prisoners of War in Utah

Allan Kent Powell

University of Utah Press
Salt Lake City
1989

Volume 6
in the Utah Centennial Series
Charles S. Peterson, Series Editor

The paper in this book meets the standards
for permanence and durability established by the
Committee on Production Guidelines for Book
Longevity of the Council on Library Resources

Library of Congress Cataloging-in-Publication Data

Powell, Allan Kent.
    Splinters of a nation : German prisoners of war in Utah / Allan
Kent Powell ; with a foreword by Charles S. Peterson.
        p.   cm. — (Utah centennial series ; v. 6)
    Bibliography: p.
    Includes index.
    ISBN 0-87480-330-6
    1. World War, 1939-1945—Prisoners and prisons, American. 2.
Prisoners of war—Germany—History—20th century. 3. Prisoners of
war—Utah—History—20th century. 4. Prisoners of war—Italy—
History—20th century. 5. World War, 1914-1918—Prisoners and pri-
sons, American. 6. World War, 1939-1945—Prisoners and prisons,
German. 7. Prisoners of war—United States—History—20th century. I. Title. II. Series.
D805.U5P69   1989
940.54'727309792—dc20   89-4787
                                                              CIP

For Brenda
Whose cheerfulness and enthusiasm for life touches so many

Contents

Foreword

No event did more to upend and reorder world affairs than World War II. Sparks from its collisions flashed around the globe leaving conflagrations great and small. Few places were totally untouched and many were never the same again. Among the places that underwent profound change were the states of America including Utah.

At the continental interior of the lower forty-eight states, Utah had long been sheltered. The first Euroamerican explorers and geographers passed it by or failed to recognize its inward-flowing drainages. The territory and state became a refuge and a retreat for those who, like the Mormons, chose its isolation in a determined effort to remain untouched by the world. It is true that politics, railroads, mining, new immigration and, in time, tourism, resource-managing agencies, and depression changed the interests of many Utahns and built a more complex society. Yet, content with life's routines and pleased with its prospects, Utahns at the end of the third decade of the twentieth century still enjoyed a degree of innocence as Hitler stepped forward and war loomed.

World War II and the interventionist world that it introduced shattered isolation. Indeed, it may be argued that the war was the most significant event in the state's past one hundred years. Always after, Utah interacted with the nation and with the counties and peoples of the world at a quickened tempo. The "Crossroads of the West" that for a generation had been little more than a matter of promotional hyp became and remain a Utah reality. Ordinance and supply depots mushroomed as national security demanded

that installations be placed well to the interior of coasts and boundaries. War plants were built as part of a decentralized production
strategy. Nearly 65,000 young Utahns served in the military, mul-
tiplying the number for whom the larger world became a reality.
Other thousands were stationed in Utah or passed through it, going
and coming to assignments in the Pacific theater. For many Americans the experience of those years represented their only impression of Utah.

One of the far-flying sparks that helped to change the face of
Utah was the prisoner of war experience told here in *Splinters of
a Nation* by Utah historian Kent Powell. Bringing several thousand
veterans of Nazi Germany and Fascist Italy to the hamlets and farms
of the state, the POW program gave an immediacy to both the war
and the processes by which the world was being rearranged. Indeed, no aspect of change impacted more directly on the
homefront unless possibly the direct pain of separation as men and
women went to war. As early as the 1930s, the Civilian Conservation Corps had brought thousands of young men into the state,
and military installations during World War II provided a local van-
tage point from which Utahns got personal impressions of the war.
But training, conservation work, and manning wartime military
operations were carried on largely out of the public view. By contrast, POW crews worked on individual farms, making contact with
thousands of Utahns on an individual basis.

Powell's book appears as we begin the commemoration of the
fiftieth anniversary of World War II. Depending heavily upon oral
histories and personal contacts, *Splinters of a Nation* reflects the
former prisoner of war's point of view and offers Utahns and Americans a glimpse into the lives and thoughts of people who suffered
imprisonment. In this regard, the comparative chapters dealing
with World War I Germans, World War II Germans and Italians,
and American soldiers held in Axis prisons are broader in their examination and more tolerant in spirit than a straightforward account
of "Nazi" prisoners of war might have been. *Splinters of a Nation's*
discussion of prisoners of war in Utah and its account of civilians
interacting with German and Italian prisoners make it the first book
ever to deal with the experience of World War II for individual
Utahns. With regards to war it illustrates that even in the best of
circumstances individuals are still the victims of war. Yet even vic-

tims had some individual choice in how they coped with their circumstances.

In addition, Powell's book is a lens through which we look at the Utah experience as well as one through which we see an American experience and a world experience. In another way it is a yardstick against which the nation's response to humanity may be measured, providing, if nothing else, a second viewpoint as we consider the wartime treatment of Japanese. In it we read of how the self-interest of a nation, which itself had POWs whose lives were at stake, responded to international laws and conventions governing the treatment of prisoners. It reflects also a view of tragedy as a system, however humane the policy behind it, responded to wartime tension and the frailties of a single person to bring disaster. Finally, it provides an intimate view of an important dimension of one state's role in World War II.

Powell's previous work includes study of labor in Utah's coalfields and of German immigration to Utah. He has been a key figure in the historical preservation movement throughout the state, coordinating field services for the Division of State History, where he has been employed for twenty years. Few people know state history better than he or better understand its larger portents. He has taught at various institutions throughout the state and is active professionally. He is author and editor of several earlier books including his *The Next Time We Strike: Labor in Utah's Coal Fields, 1903–1933,* a sensitive study of the peculiar mix of conservatism and radical impulses that have characterized labor in Utah. He has also edited two outstanding county histories.

In the present monograph Powell brings a long-term interest in the subject of prisoners of war to fruition. His account of a world turned upside down helps us understand that wars are fought not just by nations but that states (as part of the federal union) and individuals, too, act and are acted upon. It was a different world Utahns and citizens of other states looked out upon in 1945 at the war's end. That this was so was in some part the result of the prisoner-of-war experience. The editor and the University of Utah Press hope *Splinters of a Nation* will be a point of departure from which complexity's importance may be more fully understood as the centennial of statehood is approached.

Charles S. Peterson

Acknowledgments

Researching, writing, and producing this study has been possible because of the encouragement and assistance of many people. Special thanks go to Charles S. Peterson for his suggestions and for his continual support since my freshman days at the College of Eastern Utah. Other readers have spent long hours going over the manuscript to offer valuable comments and recommendations. They include Helen Zeese Papanikolas, Philip F. Notarianni, Richard C. Roberts, and Arnold Krammer. I am grateful for their help, but acknowledge my sole responsibility for any errors or omissions within the book.

I appreciate the encouragement of Sharon Arnold that I prepare a manuscript about the German prisoners of war in Utah and submit it to the University of Utah Press. David Catron, director of the University of Utah Press, has continued the encouragement through the completion of the book.

My research was facilitated by a number of people. The staffs of the Modern Military Records Branch and the Photograph Branch of the National Archives made valuable documents and pictures available. The Dienst Stelle fuer die Benachrichtigung der Naechsten Angehoerigen von Gefallen der ehemaligen deutschen Wehrmacht, located in West Berlin, made available personnel files of a number of former German prisoners of war who were in Utah and also provided me with the addresses of living former prisoners of war. Without this generous help, I would have been unable to locate many of the men that I interviewed, including the five men wounded at the Salina camp in Utah.

I am indebted to the Utah Endowment for the Humanities for a small grant to the Utah German-American Society for a series of lectures about the German POW experience. The lectures were especially rewarding in the number of people who came forward to offer documents, stories, and the names of former German prisoners.

Gregory Thompson and his staff at the University of Utah Marriott Library Special Collections were very gracious in making their holdings available. Jeffery Simmonds at the Utah State University Merrill Library Special Collections provided access to documents collected by Ralph A. Busco. Jeffery Johnson assisted with records at the Utah State Archives and introduced me to his father, Floyd Johnson, for whom the Salina prisoners of war worked in Aurora, Utah. John Sillito introduced me to manuscripts on the Ogden Defense Depot at the Weber State College Library. Joyce Fencl, public affairs director, provided access to photographs and documents at the Ogden Defense Depot. Thanks are due Kathy Bradford and Larry Douglass for making available a number of interviews they conducted for the Brigham City Museum. Jay Haymond and the staff of the Utah State Historical Library were generous in their help, especially Christine Gustin who transcribed many of the oral history interviews conducted in English for this study. Melvin T. Smith, former director of the Utah State Historical Society, offered encouragement in the initial stages of this project. Max J. Evans, present director, has supported its completion. I appreciate the many positive contributions by my other colleagues at the Utah State Historical Society.

In Germany my dear friends Christa Breidenstein of Kassel, Gerard Habimana of West Berlin, and Paul and Margret Wollborn of Ahnatal, opened their homes to me and assisted my efforts in countless ways. Another long-time friend, Linda S. Baumgart, introduced me to a statement from Gail Sheehy's book, *Passages*, which expresses fully my debt as a historian and as a fellow human being to those people who have shared with me so much. "I count my own fortune now in the treasury of lives opened to me in trust. They live in me, resonate in me, teach me every day that no age or event can of itself prevent the human spirit from outstretching its former boundaries." Among those people whose stories are the foundation for this book and who have enriched my life in ways they will never know are Karl Altkruger, Josef Becker, Stanley Blackhurst, Emil Blau, Richard Boettger, Wallace Butterfield, Edith Cannon, Benjamin Gabaldon, Brunhilde Poes Glasgow, Gene White Gonzalez, Ernst Hinrichs, Georg Hirschmann, Lawrence Hood, Paul Hupfner, Willi Klebe, Eric Kososik, Dieter Lampe, Otto Liebergesell, Ernst Luders, Ray Matheny, Gene Miconi, Leonhard Mombar, Lorraine N. Nelson, Beatrice Gappmayer Pyne, Heinz Siegel, Harvey Sundstrom, Morris Taylor, Kurt Treiter, Frederick Weber, Rudolf Weltin, and Cobie Van der Puhl Wilson.

The help and encouragement of my family has been a constant source of strength. My deepest thanks to my parents, Leland and Luella Powell; my children, Lee, Liesel, and Adrianna; and especially my wife Brenda, to whom this book is most appropriately dedicated.

We are a part of our people, a
splinter of
the nation which because of the war
has been
separated into a foreign land

Unknown German prisoner of war at Ogden, Utah
November 1945

Introduction

The shots that shattered the silence of the midsummer night in the central Utah town of Salina woke nearly every one of the town's 2,000 residents. Many feared that the recently arrived German prisoners of war were escaping from their compound in the old Civilian Conservation Corps camp east of Main Street. The danger was real if the American guards had been overpowered. What resistance could sleep-drugged men and women have offered against these soldiers of Hitler's army, veterans of the battlefields of North Africa and Europe, especially when their own sons were scattered around the world fighting the Japanese in the Pacific and occupying Germany following the fall of Berlin and the capitulation of the Nazi government two months earlier? But before the night of July 8, 1945, was over, most of Salina learned that a crazed American soldier had poured 250 rounds from a machine gun into the tents of the sleeping prisoners. Nine men were killed and nineteen were wounded. They were part of the company of 250 men sent from Florence, Arizona, the previous month to assist the farmers of Sevier and Sanpete counties with their sugar beets.

The shooting at Salina received national and international attention as newspapers reported the tragedy. Americans realized that even in the face of the terrible atrocities in the concentration camps of Nazi Germany and Japanese POW camps, their own innocence had been touched by the dishonorable actions of one man whose hate and instability led to tragedy. The incident was the worst of its kind to occur during the entire sojourn of more than 371,000

German and 51,000 Italian prisoners of war who were in the United States between 1943 and mid-1946.

Salina was another in a long line of tragedies that have marked the state's history of settlement, relations with Indians and non-Mormon outsiders, industrial development, and the impact of the federal government in Utah. It followed such tragedies as the deaths of over 200 Mormon handcart pioneers in the early snows of 1856; the massacre of 120 California-bound emigrants by Mormons and Indians at Mountain Meadows in September 1857; the killing of more than 250 Indians on the Bear River in January 1863; and the deaths of 200 coal miners at Scofield on May 1, 1900, and 172 miners at Castle Gate on March 8, 1924, in two of the nation's worst mining disasters.

Salina was symbolic of how World War II drew Utah into a new federal and military relationship through the prisoners of war who were sent to the state and the impact that the war had in the interior valleys of the West. This federal relationship had begun in 1862 with the founding of Fort Douglas initially to keep a close watch on Mormon Utah during the Civil War. If Fort Douglas was at first a symbol of federal control over Utah, in time it became an important cog in the federal administration of the West. Headquarters for the Ninth Army Service Command was established at Fort Douglas in January 1942 and, during World War II, was responsible for military affairs, including administration of POW camps, in states west of the Rocky Mountains. In the words of Leonard J. Arrington and Thomas G. Alexander, Fort Douglas was during World War II "the military nerve center of the western United States."[1]

If Fort Douglas was the military nerve center of the western United States, the huge supply depots at Ogden, Tooele, and Clearfield were vital centers for equipping the military effort against the Japanese in the Pacific. Obviously, Utah was an important part of a global war. The state benefited economically from this role, not only during World War II but also in the postwar years, since defense industries have remained a critical part of the state's economy. The POW experience can be viewed as a part of this federal/state relationship in which a national policy and resources were successfully implemented to serve local and state needs. Under such conditions, the Salina shooting went beyond being a local or even state tragedy; it demonstrated how individuals and a nation reacted to the violence and injustices of war, for it had struck innocent foreigners, albeit former enemies.

Yet Salina was not typical or representative of the POW experience in the United States. Americans had adhered to both the letter and the spirit of the Geneva Convention in their treatment of the prisoners of war. The Germans were given excellent food, were well clothed and housed, were provided opportunities for education and recreation, and, through the money they earned, were able to purchase small luxuries at the camp canteens.

Work was, without question, a matter of forced labor. The no-work, no-eat policy was articulated among the American administrators and prisoners alike. When POW labor was acknowledged with some gesture of thanks and respect, when the work seemed directed to a meaningful end, and when the opportunities provided seemed to outweigh the drudgery and effort, then prisoners were productive, sometimes they were almost content, looking at the arbitrariness of the work with the same resignation they had viewed their assignments as soldiers. But if their tasks seemed to be make-work projects in which no one showed interest and for which no one benefited, or if they lacked positive interaction with Americans or even other prisoners, then work performance was generally poor, theft and waste widespread, and hostilities toward their captors more likely to surface.

In an exhaustive 1970 dissertation, "The Administration and Operation of Prisoner of War Camps during World War II," historian Edward J. Pluth states that America's POW program reflected a long-term effort to define and protect the rights of prisoners of war. Perhaps most revealing was that in contrast to centuries of mistreatment by captors of their prisoners of war, "the American experience showed that prisoners can be well treated and still used to the advantage of the capturing power."[2]

Former prisoners of war were universal in their praise for the excellent treatment under the Americans except for a month or two right after Germany's defeat. But not all Americans agreed with the policy. Some rankled against the proper, if not luxurious, treatment that the prisoners enjoyed. Other critics found that the opportunity to reeducate the prisoners and to prepare them for rebuilding a democratic postwar Germany was being overlooked by shortsighted administrators primarily concerned with prisoner security and employment.

Despite minor shortcomings, the treatment of German prisoners of war in America was commendable, and, in the long run, advantageous in the dividends that came through the reduced security needs and the positive feelings about the United States that the former prisoners carried back to Europe and have maintained for nearly a half-century.

There were other benefits to Americans in the POW presence. Prisoners aided the war effort and helped provide an economic windfall for many American farmers and employers. But just as important were the personal contacts and friendships that developed between prisoners and captors. These contacts gave Americans a unique wartime opportunity to learn tolerance and appreciation for those who were different. The experience undoubtedly helped America shed some of the bonds of nativism with which it had been shackled for much of its history, to better accept the immigrants in their midst and perhaps cope more easily with its burden of racial inequality in the decades following the war.

A major focus throughout this study is the treatment of the German prisoners of war in the United States during World War II, with specific emphasis on Utah. This accounting, however, can be better understood in the context of the experience of other military prisoners who shared the same fate. Three groups, covered in separate chapters, offer an interesting and insightful comparison with World War II German prisoners: German prisoners captured on board naval vessels by American forces at the outbreak of World War I who were sent to Fort Douglas, Utah, in 1917; American and specifically Utah prisoners of war held in POW camps in Germany until 1945; and the Italian prisoners of war, allies of the Germans at the time of their capture, who were also sent to the United States.

As mentioned earlier, Utah's experience in World War II was something of a reenactment of its experience with international immigration and emigration in earlier decades. Although there are vast differences between the status of prisoners of war and that of emigrants, World War II did have a broadening impact on what had been an isolated and somewhat self-contained state. Included in the ranks of the German prisoners were Austrians, Frenchmen,

Belgians, Dutchmen, Yugoslavians, Rumanians, Czechs, Poles, Russians, and Mongolians. Wartime labor demands also meant the recruitment of Mexican nationals and Filipinos as farm workers and American Hispanics as coal miners as well as the movement of American citizens from all over the country for work at military installations. A treatment of a people that had tragic consequences was the relocation to Utah of 8,130 Japanese Americans who were confined at Topaz in Millard County from September 11, 1942, until the camp closed on October 31, 1945. The Japanese Americans sent to Topaz were victims of a wartime hysteria that justified sacrificing constitutional rights to a questionable national emergency. Rather than the selective arrest of German men as enemy aliens that occurred during World War I, the internment of Japanese Americans from the West Coast in World War II included not only men but also women, children, and the aged. With over 8,000 Japanese Americans and 8,000 German and 7,000 Italian prisoners of war sent to Utah between 1942 and 1945, the total of 23,000 individuals kept behind barbed wire was a significant number in a state whose population in 1945 approached only 600,000.

The chapters that follow are based on contemporary documents, interviews with former prisoners of war and involved American citizens, and the publications of other students of the German POW experience in America. The narrative traces the prisoners' capture in North Africa, Italy, and France; their initial contact with American soldiers, the fears, apprehension, and excitement for their future—especially when they learned they were going to the United States; the passage by ship; their processing through the ports of disembarkation at Boston, New York City, and Norfolk; and the train ride to their first camp. An examination of the policies which directed American treatment of the prisoners is followed by a sketch of the conditions in the POW camps, including housing, food, clothing, discipline, canteen privileges, mail, reeducation efforts, and transfers. The twelve camps where German prisoners of war were kept in Utah are introduced and an analysis is offered of how the prisoners conducted themselves as captured soldiers of Nazi Germany. The ardent faith of prisoners captured early in the war in North Africa is contrasted with growing defeatism as the Americans swept across France into Germany. Aspects of prisoner conduct include escape attempts by a few individuals and the emergence of a strong animosity by Austrian prisoners toward their former German comrades.

During the prisoners' stay in America, the hours and days were occupied by work and free-time activities. POW labor became a highly prized opportunity for Utah's sugar beet farmers and fruit growers because military service and high-paying jobs in war industries had drastically reduced the number of available agricultural workers. Although farmers were required to pay the prevailing wage for prisoner labor, they clamored to keep the Germans in this country at least through the 1946 harvest. Other prisoners were employed at Utah military installations, with the largest number assigned to the Ogden Defense Depot, where they worked in warehouses, repair shops, and offices. One primary advantage for those assigned to the military installations was the enhanced opportunity for free-time activities that included sports, hobbies, music and theatrical groups, libraries, classes, and movies. Although these activities were not totally absent from the smaller agricultural work camps, the lack of facilities and equipment was a problem. But if free-time activities were not as diverse in the agricultural camps, the prisoners engaged in farm work did have a greater opportunity to see and experience America and Americans up close as they worked the fields and orchards and met the farmers and their families, who were both curious about and appreciative of the prisoners. The gestures of goodwill expressed by both sides were fondly remembered long after the prisoners returned to their homeland. There were also opportunities for interaction with civilians at Ogden, Bushnell Hospital, and Fort Douglas who either worked at or visited these locations. Despite official policy to the contrary, friendships developed and a few romances blossomed between Americans and the German prisoners. And American children sparked feelings of a common humanity, reminding the prisoners of their own families at home.

Work and other activities filled the prisoners' time, but home filled their thoughts. It is difficult to convey in words the homesickness and longing felt by the prisoners—feelings that were intensified by anxiety about their homes and families as Germany became a battleground. At the war's end, tormented by fears of what the Allied bombing had done and what Russian occupation of their villages and cities would mean, the German prisoners were frustrated by seemingly endless delays in their departure from the United States. For nearly half of the 371,000 prisoners, the situation became nearly unbearable when, after returning across the Atlantic, they were sent to work camps in France, Belgium, and England, where some stayed an additional two years before finally reaching German soil.

Once home, the former prisoners began to restructure their own lives and joined with millions of others in the rebuilding of Germany. They were at an advantage over their neighbors, for they returned from America well fed and in good health, some well supplied with American cigarettes and other items which were valued commodities on the black market and others with acquaintances and friends in America on whom they could call for assistance.

But did any German prisoners of war remain in the United States? All prisoners were required to return to Germany; and although many considered returning to America to live, only a few, no more than 2 percent, actually did. Three who returned to Utah were Eric Kososik, Otto Liebergesell, and Frederick Weber. Their stories are told on later pages. Others have returned as visitors and some have maintained or reestablished old friendships with American civilians they met while here.

In reflecting on the prisoners of war, it is important to keep in focus the contexts in which their experience took place. The broad context of World War II is obvious since it was the reason men became soldiers and soldiers became prisoners sent to the United States. Today it is easy to look back on the war and see its inevitability given the rise of Adolf Hitler to power, his seemingly insatiable demands for territory and concessions, and his mistreatment of human beings as his diabolical programs were implemented. But for many, and especially for German citizens, the wickedness and the misdirection of the Nazi regime were not apparent in the early days and, for some, never accepted even after the war was lost. Hence, the POW experience must also be viewed through a veil of nationalism. Patriotism or nationalism was the primary reason Germans became soldiers, and although some were infected by the disease of nazism, it is important to draw a line between nationalism and nazism. This question will be explored later, but the reader is advised to keep in mind the distinction and know that the actions and attitudes of the prisoners of war were shaped by many influences, two of which were the Nazi ideology dominant in Germany and the love of country that burned with the same intensity for German soldiers as it did for American soldiers and their Allies.

The patriotism of German soldiers grew out of strong ties to the family. Another factor which shaped the prisoners' life in the United States was a concern for what was happening to families and homes. Despite their personal well-being in the United States, it was difficult for prisoners to live with the fear that their homes were being destroyed and their loved ones killed as the war was brought home to Germany. Many of them demonstrated a large measure of selflessness and humanity in the way their thoughts and concerns transcended the physical comfort of America to keep fresh in their minds the ordeal of war as it bore upon their families and friends and destroyed forever the world they had known.

Although the German prisoners were considered by American authorities to be generally apathetic toward politics, many returned to Germany with an appreciation for democracy and some understanding that if Germany were to rise from its second defeat in fewer than three decades, it would have to be from a new foundation based on democratic principles and not the traditional authoritarianism and militarism of the past. Nearly fifty years after World War II, democracy has succeeded in West Germany, one of America's most loyal allies. Returning prisoners of war appear to have carried the seeds of democracy and an appreciation of America, which contributed to the rebuilding of Germany as a pro-American democracy.

Nevertheless, German POW experience played out on a stage of preconceptions about the United States that, by and large, bespoke a land of unlimited opportunity, wide-open spaces, noble savages, brutal gangsters, and epic adventure. Whereas the French and English were historical enemies of the Germans, Americans, despite their participation in World War I, were not. Hundreds of thousands of Germans had immigrated to the United States, and most prisoners of war arrived with knowledge of someone who had come to America before immigration restriction acts, worldwide depression, and the ascent of Adolf Hitler limited the outflow of Germans to America.

American movies played in Germany; and German film makers produced cowboy westerns in Europe, which became so popular that by World War I the western film was a well-known and widely accepted part of European popular culture. The seventy books about the American West written by Karl May between 1875 and his death in 1912 enjoyed tremendous popularity in Germany during the 1920s and 1930s. Born near Dresden, Karl May never visited America, but his image of the American West became that of millions of Europeans. He was a favorite author of Adolf Hitler's, and the heroes he portrayed were "all models of Teutonic virtue, . . . reincarnated Germanic Galahads, bent on clearing the west of desperados and bad Indians, and glorying in their missions of mercy."[3]

As German prisoners of war learned America was their destination, they spoke of going to the land of Winnetou, Old Shatterhand, Old Firehand, and Old Surehand. Undoubtedly some dreamed that their American adventure would be comparable with that of Karl May's characters. America, then, was not a place the incoming Germans feared or despised. Through movies, books, and the experiences of others, America held a special attraction for many, but this attraction was in counterpoint to their status both as soldiers of the Third Reich and as prisoners of war. The experience of America would prove to be different from the preconceptions the prisoners held, yet it was still an adventure, and one that, for most, took on undertones of nostalgia as memories dimmed of war's ugliness and the pangs of homesickness and confinement receded.

Nearly two dozen articles about the POW experience in individual states or localities have appeared in state historical journals and regional publications throughout the United States. One of the first was written by Ralph Busco and Douglas Alder, "A History of the Italian and German Prisoner of War Camps in Utah and Idaho during World War II," which appeared in 1971 in the *Utah Historical Quarterly.* On a broader scale, Arnold Krammer's *Nazi Prisoners of War in America*, published in 1979, gives an excellent summary of the experience on a national scale. Both studies have been invaluable.

A conscious effort in this undertaking has been to present the POW experience through the words of the former prisoners as completely as language, cultural, and age barriers permit. In this endeavor I interviewed twenty-five former prisoners of war. The interviews contain vivid memories of their experience, but time has healed many wounds and most do not show the bitterness that must have existed for many as they returned to their war-torn homeland and began the long process of rebuilding their homes and lives. In this regard, the account by a victim of the Salina shooting, Dieter Lampe, "The Salvo from Salina," offers an insightful glimpse of the frustration he experienced just after the war; and when it is compared with his 1987 interview, the two provide—as Lampe freely admits—an excellent example of the transformation that occurred in his own life.

Because of the international missionary program of the Church of Jesus Christ of Latter-day Saints, Mormon Utahns have always been interested in other peoples and cultures. An interesting facet of the POW experience was how simple acts of charity by Utahns were long remembered after the prisoners returned home. Farmers provided prisoners with extra food, or supplied them with much-desired cigarettes, or simply acknowledged them as fellow human beings; and after the prisoners returned to their homes, countless families sent hundreds of packages of food and clothing to the men who had come to America as their enemies but left as friends.

These acts of kindness were not confined to Mormons or to Utah, for such acts were common throughout the United States. But these friendships and other demonstrations of goodwill have made my work in researching and writing this book more pleasant in that Utahns have shared with me letters from former prisoners of war as well as addresses of those with whom they had maintained contact. Most former prisoners whom I contacted about this project were both anxious to tell their stories and to reciprocate for the kindnesses they found here in Utah and America. Still, there were a few who refused to meet me or to be interviewed, most claiming illness or a dimming of memory over the years since their captivity so that there was nothing to recall about their experience in America. For some, their memories were wrapped in the larger story of combat, dead family members, destroyed homes, and a lost homeland which they were reluctant to recall. Some wanted to help but were unable. One former prisoner of war, who lived in Munich and was dying of cancer, had planned to spend several days with me recounting his story. Yet his pain was so intense that I was left with little of his story that I could use. I was left, however, with the conviction that it was important to document now the experiences of both the former prisoners of war and those with whom they had come in contact before their stories were lost. Indeed, a primary objective of this book is to encourage others to come forward with their stories and to weigh their experiences against those of the individuals chronicled in the following pages.

Roll call for German naval prisoners of war at Fort Douglas, 1917–18. (National Archives photo)

German naval prisoners of war doing gymnastic exercises at Fort Douglas, 1917–18. (National Archives photo)

ONE

The Kaiser's Men: German Prisoners of War in Utah during World War I

Utahns took little notice during the summer of 1914 as certain events occurred in Europe. The assassination of the Austrian archduke, Francis Ferdinand, in Sarajevo, Serbia, in late June 1914 and the subsequent mobilization of the Russian army to assist its Slavic brothers if Austria carried out its threat of a military attack on Serbia were remote and seemingly unimportant events to most Utahns and Americans. Even when Germany invaded Belgium in August 1914 on its way into France, few people expected that this latest European conflict would last more than a few months or that within three years the United States would be participating in a world conflict, with their sons and brothers manning the muddy trenches and fighting in the blood-soaked forests and fields of eastern France. But the United States entered the war in the spring of 1917; and as young men from Salt Lake City, Ogden, and the towns and villages of Utah either joined the army or registered for the country's first draft since the Civil War, preparations were underway to bring to Fort Douglas, Utah, more than 500 German naval personnel captured by American forces stationed in Guam and Hawaii.

Quick action was taken in sending the German naval prisoners of war to Fort Douglas, but the transfer to the United States of captured German soldiers from the battlefields of Europe presented a more complex situation. Newspaper editorials and letters to Congress and executive agencies demanded that German prisoners of war be sent to the United States, arguing that the army would not then be burdened with supporting them so far from its base of supplies; soldiers could be relieved from guard duties and reassigned to frontline fighting units; prisoners would be utilized as much-needed laborers in the United States; the danger of submarine attack on transport ships returning to the United States with prisoners on board would be lessened; American prisoners would be well treated by their captors; and immigration would be encouraged after the war.[1]

On June 5, 1918, Gen. Peyton C. March, Chief of Staff, instructed Gen. John J. Pershing that all American-held prisoners were to be sent to the United States. Pershing requested that the plan be reconsidered in light of commitments he had made to Great Britain and France for providing prisoners of war to meet their critical labor shortages. Before any final arrangement was decided, however, fighting ended and the planned transfer of prisoners was dropped.[2] But the German naval and merchant marine personnel who had been captured in isolated tide pools of the world conflict and were being held as prisoners on American soil had to be cared for and the anti-German sentiment in the United States had demanded that "enemy aliens" be locked up.

The World War I experience by the United States in handling the naval prisoners of war was important as a small-scale exercise in how the country would deal with the masses of prisoners sent to America during World War II. During World War I, approximately 6,000 prisoners were held in four camps in the United States. Of these prisoners, 1,356 were naval personnel and included 517 men from the crews of the *Cormoran, Geier,* and *Locksun* who were interned in Utah. There were 1,800 merchant crewmen who had been on German luxury liners or German cargo ships in American ports when the United States went to war in April 1917. Another 500 merchant crewmen were brought to the United States from Panama and the Philippines. And, finally, there were 2,300 "enemy aliens"—civilians arrested on suspicion of questionable activities in support of the enemy or against the United States.

The selection of Fort Douglas as an internment camp for the naval personnel proved to be an advantage a quarter of a century later when the World War II prisoners arrived; Utah was one of three states that had had previous experience in handling prisoners of war. The wartime contact with foreign nationals between 1917 and 1920—added to the state's earlier experience with immigrants—

would offer some indication of what might be expected from German American residents when Germany and the United States stood again as enemies between 1941 and 1945.

The four camps in which the sailors from captured naval vessels, merchant crewmen, and enemy aliens were held included Fort Douglas, Utah; Fort McPherson and Fort Oglethorpe, Georgia; and Hot Springs, North Carolina. Fort Douglas was designated as War Prison Barracks Three. In addition to the crews of the *Cormoran*, *Geier*, and *Locksun*, all civilian enemy aliens arrested west of the Mississippi River were sent to Fort Douglas. Fort Oglethorpe, located across the state line from Chattanooga, Tennessee, held all civilian enemy aliens arrested east of the Mississippi River. Fort McPherson held approximately 850 sailors from three German naval vessels—*Kron Prinz Wilhelm*, *Appam*, and *Etiel Frederic*—captured in the Atlantic region. (Later, on March 28, 1918, the naval prisoners at Fort Douglas were transferred to Fort McPherson, thereby consolidating all naval prisoners of war at the Georgia camp.) The camp in Hot Springs, a resort town in the Blue Ridge Mountains, was where the 2,300 merchant crewmen were assembled.

An announcement was made on May 2, 1917, that Fort Douglas was to be the site of one of the internment camps for German prisoners of war taken from naval vessels seized when the United States entered the war. Work began immediately on the fifteen-acre camp located just west of the fort on ground now occupied by the University of Utah's Jon M. Huntsman Center and parking lot.[3] Forty days after the announcement, 321 German prisoners arrived at Salt Lake City's Denver & Rio Grande Railroad depot. The men were from the SMS *Cormoran*, a German auxiliary cruiser that had been held at Guam for twenty-three months, since December 15, 1914, when the ship entered the harbor of Apra in an unsuccessful effort to secure enough coal and provisions to reach the nearest German port in East Africa. While the *Cormoran* was at Guam, its captain, Adelbert Zuckerschwerdt, received orders from Germany that in case of war with the United States, he was to destroy his vessel rather than allow it to be taken. Accordingly, when diplomatic relations were broken off between Germany and the United States, final preparations were completed including putting gasoline into the ship's machinery, boiler, and bilges. The preparations

Interior of barracks for German naval prisoners of war at Fort Douglas, 1917–18. (National Archives photo)

Mess hall for German naval prisoners of war at Fort Douglas, 1917–18. (National Archives photo)

Shower room for German naval prisoners of war at Fort Douglas,
1917–18. (National Archives photo)

Exterior of German prisoner of war officers' quarters at Fort Douglas,
1917–18. (National Archives photo)

Kiosk at Fort Douglas where German prisoners of war learned of camp
activities and read newspaper articles, August 1917. (Shipler Collection,
Utah State Historical Society)

German naval prisoners performing as members of the Vater Jahn Gymnastics Club, Fort Douglas, August 1917. (Shipler Collection, Utah State Historical Society)

German naval prisoners of war outside their Fort Douglas barracks, August 1917. (Shipler Collection, Utah State Historical Society)

were thorough. When a United States naval officer boarded the ship to announce that the crewmen were now war prisoners of the United States, the ship exploded and sunk in minutes. The sailors plunged into the sea, where "battling against the water most of them were compelled to shed even their clothing in order to remain afloat until they could be picked up. . . . And when they were finally pulled up and taken ashore, were absolutely naked."⁴ Some men were in the water more than half an hour. Five men and two officers drowned. The survivors lost everything they had with the exception of items taken ashore by the officers before the explosion.

Sent by troop transport under the guard of sixty marines, the prisoners arrived in San Francisco on June 8, 1917, and were placed on board a special train that arrived in Salt Lake City at 1:20 A.M. two days later, where responsibility for the prisoners was transferred to the Fort Douglas army authorities assisted by thirty policemen under the command of Salt Lake City Chief of Police J. Parley White. Officials attempted to keep secret the time of arrival of the prisoners. They were unsuccessful. "Several hundred civilians . . . had gathered at the station and braved the lateness of the hour and the chill of the night winds to see the prisoners arrive."⁵

The spectators were not allowed to view the prisoners, however. The platform was cleared by army guards from the camp and the local police. A group of newspaper reporters was allowed to remain on the platform, but with their backs to the wall of the depot and under the watchful eye of a sentry charged with preventing any overly enthusiastic newspaperman from crossing the boundary or interfering with the arrival of the prisoners and their transfer to the camp. A German warrant officer, clad in a blue uniform, and armed with a bundle of papers, preceded his fellow prisoners off the train and took his position behind a table. The prisoners filed off the train in orderly fashion, formed in double ranks, waited for their names to be called, then moved across the platform to form a new line. The entire process took over two hours. Each prisoner was thoroughly searched—which took the rest of the night—and, under heavy guard, loaded into seven streetcars that, with an escort of automobiles, rattled up South Temple Street to the unfinished compound. Chief White, who had some responsibility for guarding the Germans gave his men orders to "shoot to kill any man who attempts to escape."[6]

Ten days later, on June 20, 1917, ten more Germans arrived in Salt Lake City, this time at the Union Pacific Railroad station. These men, too, were from the *Cormoran*, including one Lt. I. von Elpons, described by Utah newspapers as a baron. Arriving also—but not as a prisoner of war—was the baron's wife, Ilse. This time, authorities were less apprehensive about the transfer of prisoners from the railroad station to the prison camp. The press was allowed to photograph the prisoners for the first time, and the *Salt Lake Tribune* photographs include one of wounded prisoners on crutches, a group picture as the men boarded the streetcar for Fort Douglas, and pictures of "Baron and Baroness I. von Elpons." Nevertheless, no civilians, including newspaper reporters, were permitted to converse with the prisoners; all information was provided through U.S. Army Capt. Norris Stayton, who had had charge of the prisoners from San Francisco to Salt Lake City.

When the sailors from the *Cormoran* arrived, the camp was not fully ready to receive prisoners. Camp officials had been given just over a month to construct barracks and make other necessary preparations. The prisoners had arrived nearly a week before they were expected. Panicked, lest more prisoners were on their way, Col. Arthur Williams, in command at Fort Douglas, wired his superior not to send any more prisoners until the camp was ready for them.

Where the arrival and processing of the 321 naval prisoners had been carried out with a thoroughness and seriousness that certainly impressed local citizens and perhaps even the German prisoners themselves, the arrival of the 10 prisoners had the trappings of a comic opera. The Baroness Ilse von Elpons was beautiful, aristocratic, and a fascinating enemy celebrity. Her story was given full play by Salt Lake City's news media. The American-born daughter of Jacob Niess, publisher of a German language newspaper in Denver, she had met the German naval lieutenant, Baron I. von Elpons, after the *Cormoran* had stopped in San Francisco several years before. They had married, and while on their honeymoon near San Francisco, von Elpons was arrested and transported to Salt Lake City along with the other nine prisoners. Accompanying him to Salt Lake City, the baroness was housed at U.S. Govern-

ment expense in the Wilson Hotel while her husband was in the
POW camp. A *Salt Lake Tribune* reporter described her as "the vi-
vacious heroine of the party, aristocratic in her bearing to her very
finger tips, aside from her husband . . . the most cool and collected
personage in the party." Von Elpons's wife seemed unconcerned
that her husband was about to enter a POW camp. Rather, "the baroness came to Salt Lake very much as would the wife of a college
professor or someone bent solely on sightseeing." But her loyalty
to Germany ran deep as she boasted, "My heart is with Germany."
She also confirmed what many Americans believed about their German American neighbors when she declared, "It takes more than
one generation to make an American." Still, even with her strong
feelings for Germany, she averred she "would not lift a finger to
injure the United States. My love for Germany is more of a hatred
for England than anything else."[7]

Accompanying the baron and baroness was their black dachs-
hund, "looking for all the world like a K-9 Submarine." The dog
had traveled in the express car from San Francisco, but after arriving in Salt Lake City, it was reunited with the baron and clamored
aboard the streetcar with its owner for the three-mile ride to Fort
Douglas—"one of the first dogs to ride in a street car in Salt Lake."
The dog, however, was not permitted inside the prison camp, but
ordered returned to the baroness in the Wilson Hotel. While en
route, the dog ran away, much to the great dismay of its owners.

Perhaps the dog had been permitted on the streetcar because
the conductor was too preoccupied with haggling over who was
to pay the fares for the entourage of prisoners, followers, and guards.
A Captain McDonald declared that the army had made arrangements with the Utah Light and Traction Company for him to charge
the transportation. The conductor was, to say the least, skeptical.
He demanded that Captain McDonald pay the eighteen nickel fares
out of his own pocket and let the army reimburse him, since the
conductor had not been informed of any arrangement other than
the pay-as-you-ride practice, even for the army. The captain had
left his wallet at home that day and did not have ninety cents. The
situation was at an impasse until two policemen and a *Salt Lake
Tribune* reporter boarded the streetcar, both of whom happened
to know the conductor personally. After a brief consultation with
the two men, the conductor reluctantly agreed to deviate from the

ironclad no-free-ride rule after the policemen and reporter gave him a written promise that they would make good on the fares if the army defaulted on the dubious agreement.[8]

A final item that attracted the attention of onlookers was the sword which had belonged to Lt. Henry Bock of the German navy, but which had been surrendered to the United States. Cherished as perhaps a portent of things to come and at least a symbol of the United States "victory" in capturing the crew of the *Cormoran*, the sword was handled "as carefully and efficiently as though it were the treasured relic of Washington or Napoleon."[9]

Less dramatic was the arrival of the 365 officers and sailors of the *Geier* and *Locksun* from San Francisco on September 11, 1917. The cruiser *Geier* had been in the Chinese port of Tsingtau at the outbreak of war in August 1914. Sailing from China to avoid capture by the Japanese, the *Geier* eventually stopped at Hawaii, where its captain hoped to obtain coal. It is not clear what transpired in Hawaii. The ship was given twenty-four hours to leave the harbor, but it seems doubtful that it could secure and load the much-needed coal in such a short time. Another account notes that the ship had been followed to Hawaii by Japanese ships which were waiting just outside the harbor to attack it. In any event, the twenty-four-hour deadline passed and the *Geier* and its collier, the *Locksun*, were interned at Hawaii. While in Honolulu the crew of the *Geier* worked to foment trouble between the United States, Mexico, and Japan. Rumors were spread from the wireless on board the *Geier* that Japanese troops had landed in Mexico and with Mexico's support would launch an invasion across the United States border. The rumors were sent out from Pearl Harbor by the *Geier*'s radio while the vessel's band played afternoon concerts to cover the sound.[10]

When diplomatic relations were broken off between the United States and Germany in February 1917, the German sailors sought to put their ship out of commission by damaging the engines and setting it on fire. They were not successful. American authorities intervened to put out the fires before serious damage was done. Both ships were surrounded by Marines who arrived on a tugboat from Pearl Harbor eight miles away and army infantrymen armed with rifles and machine guns. The German sailors were then removed from the ships and transferred to Schofield Barracks where they were confined as prisoners of war even though it would be two months before war was declared between the two countries. Once in the hands of Americans, the *Geier* was renamed the *Carl Schurz*, in honor of the nineteenth-century German immigrant who became a United States senator and served as secretary of interior in the Lincoln Cabinet. The *Locksun* was renamed the *Gulf Port*.

The prisoners were transported on board the USS *Sherman* from Hawaii to San Francisco, where they boarded a train for Salt Lake City, arriving at 3:30 A.M., on September 14. At daybreak small groups of sailors under the watch of a guard were permitted to leave the train to exercise along the platform, wash themselves in the depot, and buy tobacco and newspapers at the newsstand. The German naval officers dined with American officers in the station's cafe before they were taken to Fort Douglas. Between eight and nine in the morning, the prisoners were called together and marched to the streetcars under an armed escort of police and army personnel for the ride to Fort Douglas. At the camp they were greeted by Col. George L. Byram who had taken over command of the camp two days earlier from Col. Arthur Williams.

The officers' cabins housed one or two of the officers and consisted of three rooms—a dining room, which was used as a living room; sleeping quarters; and a kitchen, which was not used for cooking since meals were provided from the mess kitchen. The mess halls could serve 100 men at a time. The barracks buildings each housed 100 men, who slept in two-tiered bunks. Care was taken to insure that the prisoners were provided with the same quality of food as that of the American soldiers. The men were divided into ten groups and each had a petty officer in charge who ordered food through the camp's general mess officer and who supervised the preparation and distribution of food.

Dr. Karl Huebecher, secretary of the Swiss Commission for the Inspection of War Prison Camps in the United States, and Charles Vuillenmier, the Swiss consul, inspected the Fort Douglas prison camp on November 20 and 21, 1917, for the commission and concluded that "the food and service is very good and the German cooks understand the preparation of the materials at hand in sufficient quantities."[11]

One sailor wrote to a friend that the prisoners had nothing to complain about. "Daily fresh meat, daily fresh bread, and very often fresh fruits, quantities as well as qualities, leave nothing to be desired. Rations are issued us and prepared in accordance with our own tastes by our own cooks."[12] The claims of fresh food were disputed by Capt. W. F. Beer, the camp doctor. In October 1917, he charged that the quality of milk coming into the camp from surrounding dairies was sour and deficient in butterfat and had a bacterial count far in excess of that allowed by city ordinances and state law. The situation portended a disease epidemic at the camp which could affect Germans and Americans alike. City health officials seemed to resent the army's interference and implication that they were not doing a good job. After nearly a month of wrangling with health officials over a proper testing of milk, Dr. Beer made his charges and concerns public, threatening to seek redress if something were not done to correct the situation.[13] His action seemed to work, for no further mention was made of the issue in the newspapers or camp inspection reports.

The prisoners were restricted to the food provided in the mess halls. There was no canteen in the camp as there would be for the World War II prisoners. Furthermore, they possessed no money with which to make purchases and were not paid in "canteen scrip" as were the World War II prisoners. The lack of tobacco among the prisoners was sorely felt, and efforts were made to have gifts of tobacco and cigars sent to the camp.[14] One exception to the tight-fisted money system was that the naval officers did receive their salaries as provided for under the POW articles adopted at the Hague Convention.

Unlike the World War II prisoners, who were clothed in regular American army uniforms marked with the letters PW, the German naval prisoners were outfitted more like civilians. They were provided with a light denim jacket, wool and corduroy trousers, a mackinaw overcoat, shoes, socks, shirts, and two suits each of summer and winter underwear.[15] The clothing was intended to be "distinctive, so that a prisoner can be distinguished easily, but will not be conspicuous so as to lay the wearer open to the curious gaze of the public." Colonel Williams was determined that the camp was not going to be "a zoo." The guiding principle for Williams, however, was that "the prisoners we have here are human beings and they shall receive the treatment due human beings." Still, according to newspaper accounts at least, Williams followed a double standard. A student of the German language, Williams was able to translate communications sent in German by the captain of the *Cormoran*, Adelbert Zuckerschwerdt, but in acknowledging his ability to translate German, he qualified the circumstances saying, "but I don't make any effort to talk it."

Newspaper reporters assured their readers that the prisoners were treated with "courtesy and consideration" and that they were adjusting well to their status as prisoners, laughing, talking, and walking about the streets of the camp with a "We-should-worry air." Capt. Adelbert Zuckerschwerdt reportedly sent a message to Colonel Williams: "We are pleased with the consideration and courtesy shown us in every way by your government and its officers."[16]

Utah seemed very agreeable to the German prisoners. On their first afternoon in the camp, the *Salt Lake Tribune* reported the prisoners to be "out of their barracks apparently enjoying the magnificent natural surroundings . . . drinking in the pure mountain air, fragrant with the odor of lilacs and lotus, with evident relish." The *Tribune* reporter concluded by comparing the Utah camp with the POW camps in Europe. Hyperbole seemed to have gotten the best of him in that he found the Fort Douglas camp by contrast "a palace in a modern garden of Eden." Still, in a more restrained but honest assessment, one prisoner concluded: "The United States insists that its prisoners be well treated, better, according to my belief, than the prisoners are treated in the camps of other countries."[17]

When the prisoners arrived in Salt Lake City, they were not in the best of health. One observer wrote: "The prisoners as a whole are not as robust and hearty as might have been expected." According to camp officials, the naval prisoners made the transition from the tropical climates of Guam and Hawaii to the Utah climate quite well. The Swiss inspectors concluded that the ailments—"cold sores and general indisposition for a few days"—were all temporary in nature.[18]

Medical care was provided in a twenty-bed hospital within the camp staffed by the German doctors and other medical personnel. Serious cases were to be transferred to the Fort Douglas hospital. Because there was no German dentist, dental work was to be done by the army dentist assigned to Fort Douglas. The army dentist, however, was overworked meeting the needs of the U.S. Army personnel, so the camp commander offered to make arrangements for a civilian dentist from Salt Lake City to serve the prisoners, "at their own expense," if there was a sufficient number of requests from the men.

Since there was no organized work program for the naval prisoners whereby they could be paid, only a few men had any money. The men were required to maintain and clean the camp, and when work was available, they could earn fifty cents a day. There were very few opportunities, however, for the men to earn even this amount. The only recorded money-making project was the construction of their own recreation hall, for which the Young Men's Christian Association paid them about $300. On another occasion a work detail of between fifteen and twenty men was allowed to work for eight days outside the camp. They were paid with "a supply of apples."[19]

American relatives of some prisoners did seek to secure their release so that the men could work on their farms. The records on these instances either are incomplete or indicate that permission was denied.[20] An effort was made under the direction of Governor Simon Bamberger by Utah's food and fuel administrator to obtain permission to employ the prisoners in the sugar beet harvest. However, the plan was disapproved because the War Department did not consider it advisable to authorize the employment of prisoners of war by the private sector.[21] Consideration was given to employing prisoners in making cement and for working on roads by the Department of the Interior in National Parks. Road building was not found to be in competition with the civilian labor force, but before any program could be implemented in Utah, the naval prisoners of war were transferred from Fort Douglas to Fort McPherson, Georgia.[22]

It was not until March 1918 that arrangements were concluded to give the prisoners—excluding officers—physical exams and classify them as fit for heavy, light, or no duty. From Fort McPherson some 600 men were sent out to work camps that were somewhat akin to the satellite or branch camp system instituted during World War II. World War I prisoners worked under close supervision as farmhands and lived in tents in government work camps in South Carolina, Ohio, Illinois, and Massachusetts. Other prisoners remained at Fort McPherson, where they "carved chair bottoms for a local firm, or worked on road crews in the company of chain gangs from the nearby Atlanta Federal Penitentiary."[23]

Recreational activities for the Fort Douglas prisoners were under the direction of the Young Men's Christian Association. As mentioned earlier, the organization built the recreation hall at a cost of $2,600, including the $300 paid to the prisoners for the construction work. The YMCA also arranged for two weekly movies, furnished writing materials, and provided educational books. The recreation hall included a combined theater for the motion pictures and a stage for vaudeville and theatrical performances. One sailor wrote, "theatrical performances, concerts, masquerades and dances are the principal form of amusement at the camp. In the absence of ladies the men dance together. . . . The activities of the YMCA go a great way toward making the prisoners more tractable and in keeping us in better health and spirits."[24]

Fifteen classes, all taught by naval officers, covered subjects in engineering, mathematics, secretarial skills, foreign languages, history, and art. The enrollment for these classes, 392, was remarkably high. The recreation building also housed a library with several hundred volumes. Many of the books were provided by local German immigrants. Textbooks for the classes were in short supply, and the men were encouraged to pay for their own books and other educational material. The YMCA did not believe that the men were to become objects of charity, but rather that activities would be "based on the principle of philanthropy *plus* self-help."[25]

An athletic club called "Vater Jahn" was organized and seems to have directed most of its work toward gymnastics. One tragic event was the death of a young sailor, Stanislaus Lewitski, who was injured while he was performing on the horizontal bar and lost his hold. Crashing to the ground, he fractured the cervical vertebra of the spine and lay paralyzed for over a month after the accident. He died on September 13, 1917, and was buried with full military honors in the Fort Douglas cemetery. During the existence of the Fort Douglas prison camp, twenty-one inmates died. With the exception of Lewitski, the rest were civilian aliens.[26]

It had been a long-held hope of the prisoners that they could organize a military band, but this depended on local citizens donating precious musical instruments—the instruments of the *Cormoran* had been lost when the ship was sunk. It was not until the crew of the *Geier* arrived that the camp had musical instruments and its desired band. A reporter for the *Salt Lake Telegram* was impressed with the repertoire of the German prisoner band. Unlike "the horrors of the 'Cherman' street bands which used to be so common several years ago," the combined musicians of the *Cormoran* and the *Geier* were "partial to ragtime," and there was an entertaining " 'Tootin' Teuton trombonist . . . [who] cavorted about in the stockade with his loosely connected horn."[27] Other recreational activities included dramatics, an eighteen-piece orchestra, a brass band, and choral groups.[28]

Religious services were conducted by the camp chaplain, Reverend Fitzgerald, who read a mass each morning in the recreation building. Protestant services were held every other Sunday by a Lutheran minister from Salt Lake City.

Discipline among the prisoners was enforced by the German officers and noncommissioned officers, who in turn were responsible to the American commandant of the camp. The system worked well. With few exceptions, discipline was maintained, morale was generally good, and the prisoners were well behaved.[29]

It was a clear-cut policy that civilians were not to have any contact with the German prisoners. A deadline, patrolled by sentries, was established around the camp, with large white signs—"War Prison Barracks. Keep Out"—placed at regular intervals. No person was permitted to cross the line without written permission from the camp commandant. Capt. Stephen Abbott, camp adjutant, appealed to the patriotism of citizens to follow the army orders.[30] Civilians who decided to make a Sunday excursion to see the newly arrived Germans at Fort Douglas were sorely disappointed when their intentions were squelched by sentries carrying out their strict orders. Civilian employees at the camp were also segregated from the prisoners. And, guards were prepared to shoot at violators. Indeed, when Robert Addison, a Salt Lake laborer, under the double jeopardy of curiosity and alcohol, crossed the sentry's line, he was shot with birdshot and incarcerated in the camp guardhouse overnight. Guards were issued a round of birdshot, loaded first as a deterrent; but this measure of mercy ended with that first shot, and the public was assured that "the others are the real steel that 'carry' and kill."[31]

Colonel Williams was not at all concerned about public relations for the prison camp: "It is none of the public's business what
the interned German prisoners are doing."[32] He declared that no
news about the prisoners would be given out while he was in command, a strict policy considering that the War Department allowed
prison camp commanders to exercise their own discretion in how
they handled the issue of publicity. At the other prison camps routine news and feature stories were given out by prison officials.

Prisoners were allowed to send two letters of four pages and
one postcard a week (officers were given an additional two pages
for their letters). Both incoming and outgoing mail, however, was
held back for ten days by the camp censor. Packages sent to the
prisoners were opened by the censor and then given to recipients
a few days later.[33] The mail activity became so extensive that it was
necessary to establish a camp post office, with appointed prisoners
handling the gathering and distribution of the mail within the
compound.

Despite the efforts of their American captors, the naval prisoners
found plenty to complain about. The enlisted prisoners were critical of the lack of clothing, shoes, socks, and underwear. They were
also upset that the original schedule of work every other day was
later changed to work two days in every three. That they received
no pay and, therefore, had no money for tobacco, stationery, or
books was a hardship. Furthermore, the men felt they were not
getting enough to eat and complained about being cheated out of
their full rations. At Fort Douglas the officer in charge had decided
to reduce the amount spent on individual rations from forty-four
cents to eleven cents per day in what he concluded was an acceptable attempt to save the government money.[34]

The list of complaints by the officers was much longer. Commander Grasshof of the *Geier* chafed at the restrictions placed on
the officers, especially in comparison with their treatment at
Schofield Barracks in Hawaii where they had been allowed many
more privileges. Other grievances that the officers had included
were the lack of a canteen in which to purchase small articles and
access to newspapers only after ten days of their publication as well
as delays in receiving their pay, items ordered from prison headquarters, and their mail. They described their barracks as roughly
constructed, cold at night, located too close to those of the

enlisted men, and too far from the showers and toilets. There was not sufficient room for exercise, and no facilities for such sports as tennis and golf, although tennis courts were constructed later. They railed at being confined too closely and wanted to make visits to Salt Lake City and take short excursions into the nearby countryside and mountains. Finally, there was "no place to receive ladies who are permitted to visit . . . except out of doors where the sailors are around."[35] A number of the officer's wives had followed their husbands to Utah—an arrangement that seems totally inexplicable given the circumstances.

There was a large number of escape attempts at Fort Douglas, indicating a high level of discontent. Writing to the adjutant general of the army in early 1918, Col. George L. Byram revealed that there had been sixteen attempts, one of them successful. Most of the attempts were credited to the naval prisoners, but interned civilians were involved as well. In one attempt, eight men—four of them interned civilians—were planning to use a tunnel discovered by American authorities and were suspected of being aided by "outsiders in Salt Lake and Los Angeles."[36]

The Fort Douglas situation was made difficult for American authorities because they had to handle two different groups—the naval prisoners of war and the civilians, which included 870 enemy aliens and 200 conscientious objectors who were held from July 1917 to May 1920. Enemy aliens were residents of the United States who had not received American citizenship and in the eyes of Americans, therefore, were still German or Austro-Hungarian citizens. The civilian enemy aliens held at Fort Douglas were brought from western states including Texas, California, Arizona, Washington, Oregon, Nebraska, and South Dakota. Most were of German or Austrian birth and were interned because of apparent pro-German sympathies, membership in the Industrial Workers of the World, socialist leanings, or other activities judged to be un-American.

There were thousands of such people throughout the United States who were labeled enemy agents by public opinion. The incarceration of most was the result of a war hysteria that branded otherwise acceptable residents as traitors. Others, as in the case of the socialists or members of the IWW, were held out of intolerance for their "radical" political views. Under such circumstances, an enraged mob could kill. In Thermopolis, Wyoming, as Congress was debating Woodrow Wilson's war resolution, a German, patronizing a local saloon, was nearly killed when he shouted, "Hoch der Kaiser!" As he lifted his drink he was knocked down by another miner, and the enraged spectators hung him from a rafter. He was cut down by the city marshal, who revived him with cold water. Before he was run out of town, he was forced to kneel and kiss the American flag.[37]

Fort Douglas was chosen—primarily for logistical reasons— as the internment camp for those enemy aliens who had been rounded up throughout the West. Salt Lake City was considered an excellent location because it was the hub for a railroad network which included the Union Pacific, Denver and Rio Grande Western, Oregon Shortline, Los Angeles and San Pedro lines. Furthermore, Salt Lake City was a central location for the area covered by Fort Douglas—all of the United States west of the Mississippi River. The enemy aliens at Fort Douglas came from a wide variety of backgrounds. Many were well-educated professional intellectuals, clergymen, and businessmen. Others were itinerant workers and some were criminals. A number came from the non-German speaking areas of the Austro-Hungarian Empire and had little sympathy for the war and the government that had made them enemies of the United States. Still others were members of the IWW. It was perhaps in the group of enemy aliens that hatred for the United States burned strongest. Opposed to the major American political parties and American capitalism, radicals and socialists had developed well-tuned methods of protest and criticism against the United States and its institutions long before war was declared against Germany.

Whereas the naval prisoners of war were all one category— military prisoners—and brought with them their own organization for discipline and control, there was a stark contrast between these prisoners and the civilian enemy aliens, and treatment of the latter was markedly different from that of the former. Initially the two groups were permitted to mingle with each other, but in August 1917 they were separated and the civilian prisoners experienced several measures of discrimination that the military prisoners did not. They were denied access to the recreation hall. They were required to provide their own clothing until late in the war, and on some occasions clothing sent by family or friends was withheld on the pretext that it did not conform with what other prisoners wore. Frequent use was made of the guardhouse, where prisoners received only bread and water. It was rumored that prisoners were whipped, and on at least two occasions prisoners were shot and wounded by guards. When a civilian prisoner died—as twenty did—they were allegedly not given respectable burials, but simply hauled from the camp to the Fort Douglas cemetery in the same wagon used to haul garbage and buried with little or no recognition. One civilian prisoner reported an incident of personal harassment by the American military guards. According to Alvo von Alvensleben, he was ordered to move from his quarters, and when he returned he found his bedding and clothing outside in the snow on the wet and dirty ground. He declared that his treatment was "worse than that accorded to the lowliest beggar."[38] Another prisoner, however, felt that von Alvensleben deserved what he got. Erich Brandeis wrote that "this man is really a dangerous enemy . . . the chief trouble maker. . . . He is a regular lodger in the guard house. Bread and water diets are nothing new to him. . . . His chief joy is to harass and torment the authorities."[39]

That many of the civilian prisoners were not model prisoners or even showed discretion in their actions is crystal clear. Fights and stabbings occurred among them, acts of sabotage were perpetrated, parades and demonstrations were staged, the leather-lunged IWW veterans shouted obscenities daily at the guards, and the songbirds of the camp mocked their captors with repeated renditions of such ditties as "Lower Old Glory to the bottom of the pole. Shit in the middle of it and bury it in the hole."[40] Disrespect was also shown by groups of prisoners who sang "Deutschland, Deutschland uber Alles" when the American army band played "The Star Spangled Banner."[41]

In the end, of the 870 enemy aliens who were interned at Fort Douglas, most chose to remain in the United States. However, 270 chose to return to Germany and left in June and September 1919. The last enemy alien was released in May 1920.

Utahns generally responded very differently to the two categories of prisoners held at Fort Douglas. On the one hand, the military prisoners were seen as professional, honorable soldiers. They were worthy of respect and humane and considerate treatment.

They had not sought to harm the United States and their only mistake was being in a situation when war began which led to the prison camp. On the other hand, the civilian aliens had rejected the hospitality and openhandedness of America by deliberate conduct to harm and discredit her. They had slandered and turned their backs on those who offered refuge and friendship. Despite the often slim and inconclusive evidence and the questionable legal procedures, the enemy aliens were considered scum. Perhaps for many contemporaries, the Germans' incarceration at Fort Douglas was further evidence of the kindness and generosity of America; there, they were protected from death threats against them.

As early as September 1917, the possibility of transferring the naval prisoners at Fort Douglas to Fort McPherson, Georgia, was investigated; but because of the expense involved, it was decided not to transfer them at that time. Rather, instructions were issued to keep the military and civilian prisoners separated, considering the difficulties experienced in having the two groups of prisoners together. The civilian aliens were less tolerant of discipline, and they were prone toward inciting the naval prisoners to acts of insubordination. When the military and civilian prisoners were treated differently, trouble resulted, and a flood of complaints deluged the Swiss Legation.[42]

After six months, it was decided to implement the earlier recommendation to transfer the naval prisoners to Georgia. The separation of the two groups had not proven effective in quelling the problems, and it was likely that at the conclusion of the war the naval prisoners would be transported east to the Atlantic for repatriation to Germany. Also, with the addition of ten to twenty civilian alien prisoners each week at Fort Douglas, the space occupied by the naval prisoners was needed to house them. Finally, it was recognized that no other country was interning both military and civilian prisoners together.[43]

The naval prisoners of war remained at Fort Douglas until late March 1918 when they were transported by train to Fort McPherson. One of the crew members of the *Cormoran*, Herman Heinrich Peters, was permitted to remain at Fort Douglas at his own request. He had contracted tuberculosis, and thought the stay at Fort Douglas would be more beneficial to him.[44] Otherwise, Fort

Douglas was the exclusive camp for some 870 civilian enemy aliens and 200 conscientious objectors.

The POW barracks at Fort McPherson were located outside the military reservation of the fort in the suburbs of Atlanta. The camp housed approximately 850 naval prisoners of war from the *Kron Prinz Wilhelm*, *Appam*, and *Etiel Fredric*. Conditions at McPherson were much more informal and lax than at Douglas, and transfer of the prisoners to McPherson did not improve their attitude toward confinement nor their treatment of those whose loyalty to Germany was suspect. If anything, the prisoners were more discontented in Georgia than they had been in Utah. Personal letters sent out by the prisoners and monitored by authorities carped about conditions, and formal complaints were registered with the Swiss Legation. Certain prisoners who were considered disloyal to Germany were assaulted, and unrest and discontentment were manifest in the number of tunnels that were dug and the escape attempts that were made. The most disruptive incident involved Capt. Adelbert Zuckerschwerdt and Lt. Otto Portwich and occurred a month after their arrival from Fort Douglas. An escape tunnel, whose entrance was located below Portwich's quarters, was discovered by American authorities. The discovery precipitated a crisis in the camp. Prisoners suspected of telling camp authorities about the tunnel were beaten at the instigation of the German naval officers. Initially, the German leaders claimed the fighting resulted when those among the prisoners who were socialists or anarchists celebrated May Day by posting around the camp extracts from President Wilson's speeches and a derogatory poem about the Kaiser. American officers acknowledged that the items had indeed been posted, but countered that the violence did not occur until after the tunnel was discovered. Captain Zuckerschwerdt was unsympathetic toward those prisoners who were assaulted, declaring, "The prisoners have worked for a long time to serve the German Government and these men have betrayed the results of their services to the American authorities and for that reason I approve of the other prisoners beating them." Some inmates reported that Zuckerschwerdt and other officers had encouraged the men to refuse to do any work for the United States and to assist in tunneling and other efforts considered supportive of the German cause. Zuckerschwerdt had threatened the men with being considered "traitors if they did not do as advised by their officers and would be punished, perhaps shot, when returned to Germany after the war."[45] Fort McPherson officials might have blamed all their trouble on the recently arrived prisoners from Utah. However, six months earlier, on October 23, 1917, ten men had escaped from the camp.[46]

Still, with the reports of low morale, the numerous escape attempts, and the nativistic tone of the camps, not all prisoners were dissatisfied with their treatment or disillusioned with America. At the conclusion of hostilities in Europe, 143 prisoners of war indicated they wished to stay in the United States. Since there were no limits on immigration, and no objection by the adjutant general of the army, the matter was turned over to the Bureau of Naturalization within the Department of Labor. Unwilling to grant blanket permission for all 143 prisoners to remain in the United States, the Bureau of Naturalization informed army officials that each case would be decided on individual merit. Accordingly, prisoners desiring to remain in the United States were instructed to complete an application which provided information on when and where they were born, the nationality of their parents, their schooling, occupation or profession, how they became a prisoner of war, why they wanted to remain in the United States, and if they wished to become United States citizens. Finally, if possible, the applicants were to give the names of United States citizens as references. Of the 143, 73 of the prisoners of war at Fort McPherson were admitted to the United States, and were not repatriated to Germany.[47] For a few of the men, discouraging news about the chances of returning to former jobs—or any job at all—back home in Germany led them to decide to stay in the United States, become American citizens, and try to make a living in their new home.[48] As for Lt. I. von Elpons (the baron), whose wife had followed him from Fort Douglas to Fort McPherson, he hoped to remain in the United States until he could return to China to work as a river pilot, a position he had held before the war. Capt. F. B. Davis, executive officer at Fort McPherson, however, was not at all sympathetic to von Elpons's request, and recommended instead he be sent to Germany with the other prisoners and not be allowed to return to the United States for any purpose. Davis found von Elpons to be "an undesirable alien, an active enemy (so far as he can be) now, and a potential enemy for the future. . . . He is a typical Prussian type of Reserve Naval Officer, is a bitter hater of the United States and all its works and . . . would never under any circumstances, become a loyal American citizen."[49] As a consequence, von Elpons was not permitted to remain in the United States.

Prisoners of war returning to Germany were allowed 350 pounds of baggage. Most prisoners returned to Germany on board the ship *Pocahontas*, which sailed from Hoboken, New Jersey, in late September 1919. Few suspected that within four decades another generation of German prisoners of war would find their way to the shores of the United States or that the next time German prisoners of war left America for their homeland, they would number in the hundreds of thousands instead of the few thousand who left as a legacy of World War I.

The World War I experience with prisoners of war offered several lessons that were not entirely lost on authorities in dealing with German prisoners of war in America during World War II. It was obvious that prisoners would remain loyal to their homeland. Security would be important since some prisoners of war would consider it their duty to escape or to sabotage the enemy war effort. Unnecessary problems could be avoided by keeping civilian and military prisoners separated. American civilians would show considerable curiosity about the prisoners. If the prisoners were well fed and housed and shown some degree of consideration, problems would be less likely to develop. Work could be an effective way of managing prisoners and maintaining morale, and it could be performed with only slightly increased security measures. Finally, among the prisoners there would be an element who would, if given the choice, elect to remain in the United States.

In Utah, the World War I legacy of German prisoners of war was remembered long after their departure. In 1929 the Utah German American community began a fund-raising campaign to construct a memorial to the twenty-one German prisoners of war buried at Fort Douglas. By the time of its construction and dedication on May 30, 1933, the monument had become a symbol that the era of anti-German sentiment was over and that Utah's German Americans could remember their German heritage with pride and honor. Contributions for the monument came from all over the country and, in Utah, from many non-German sources. Indeed, the American Legion assisted with the construction, and its contribution was recognized during the dedication ceremony and with an inscription on the back of the monument. Dedicated only four months after Adolf Hitler's ascent to power in Germany, some saw the monument as both a remembrance of the past and as a symbol of the future—that of a new, healthy, proud, and vigorous Germany. By 1946 the wounded warrior atop the Fort Douglas monument would represent not only the twenty-one dead from World War I but also an additional twenty German prisoners buried in the fort's cemetery between 1944 and 1946. On November 13, 1988, the German National Day of Mourning, the restored monument was rededicated by representatives of the German Federal Republic and the State of Utah to the memory of the forty-one German prisoners of war buried in the cemetery and in memory of all victims of war and despotism throughout the world.

TWO

From Soldiers of the Third Reich to Prisoners of the United States

As future generations look back on the significant events of the twentieth century, perhaps the greatest irony will be how the small country of Germany could rise from the devastating defeat of World War I to take on once again in only twenty years the same foes—Great Britain, France, Russia, and the United States, against whom she and the Austro-Hungarian Empire had fought between 1914 and 1918.

With the hindsight of history, the path to World War II seems almost predictable. The milestones are clear: a selfish and unjust treaty which, to most Germans, robbed them of vital parts of their homeland and saddled them with unbearable reparations for many years; inflation which destroyed the monetary system and wiped out the savings and security of millions of Germans; a democratic government which was disrespected by the rest of the world and incapable of effectively handling the country's problems; a choice between two extremes—fascism or communism—which was made in favor of the former as rabidly fomented by Adolf Hitler and his National Socialist Workers party. When the Austrian-born World War I corporal became chancellor of Germany on January 20, 1933, the milestones begin to crowd closer together, marking a steady crescendo of aggression: the occupation of the Rhineland in 1935; intervention in the Spanish Civil War in 1937; annexation of Austria in 1938; annexation of the Sudetenland after the Munich agreement with Prime Minister Neville Chamberlain of England in September 1938; the occupation of Czechoslovakia in March 1939;

and the invasion of Poland on September 1, 1939. The world had reached a point of no return in World War II.

Successful in occupying most of Europe with the 1940 blitzkrieg into France, the Netherlands, Belgium, Norway, and Denmark, followed by the occupation in early 1941 of the Balkan countries including Yugoslavia and Greece, Hitler's army climaxed Nazi aggression with the invasion of Russia on June 22, 1941. Less than six months later, Germany declared war on the United States, on December 11, 1941, five days after her Axis ally, the Japanese, bombed Pearl Harbor.

The first large-scale action by United States forces against the German army was the Anglo-American offensive in North Africa, a campaign that brought to the forefront the question of enemy prisoners of war. Thousands of German soldiers captured during the fighting in North Africa in 1942 and 1943 were sent to the United States and assigned to camps located in every state except Nevada, North Dakota, and Vermont. During May 1943, 20,000 German prisoners of war were sent to the United States; and by the end of 1943, there were 123,440 German prisoners in the country. A year later, there were 306,581; and by the end of the war with Germany in May 1945, there were 371,683.[1] In comparison, approximately 95,000 Americans were captured by the Germans and held in prison camps located throughout Germany and Austria.

The German prisoners of war who were sent to the United States can be divided into three groups. The first 140,000 were those captured in North Africa in 1942 and 1943. The second group numbered about 50,000 men, most of whom were German soldiers captured in Italy, but there were some seamen as well. Men in the third group were captured in France, Belgium, and Germany between the Allied landing at Normandy on June 6, 1944, and the German capitulation on May 8, 1945, and numbered 182,000. About 175,000 of that total had been captured by British forces, but Britain was strained beyond her ability to care for German prisoners. The official explanation for the decision to transport German prisoners of war to the United States stated that it was done "to relieve our [America's] own fighting forces of the problems of guarding, feeding and housing prisoners of war in the active theater of operations and to alleviate the critical manpower shortages which existed in the continental United States."[2] There was little extra cost in transporting the prisoners to the United States, and the undertaking was strategically sound since it freed the trained and seasoned combat forces from the burdens of guarding a large number of prisoners near the battle zone. Had the prisoners been held in Africa or Europe, it would have been difficult to supply them with the proper food, medical supplies, and treatment as called for by the Geneva Convention. Allied transportation facilities were already seriously strained in supporting troop efforts. Finally, toward the end of the war, there were those who felt that a positive experience in America could begin to dissolve the grasp of nazism upon this generation of Germans and prepare them to deal more effectively with the postwar problems that were to come. Before these reasons could be acted upon, however, the immediate decision to send German prisoners of war to the United States was made when Great Britain persuaded the Americans that she could no longer handle additional prisoners in her country. American officials agreed in August 1942 to accept 50,000 enemy prisoners on an emergency basis.[3]

For the 371,000 Germans sent to the United States and the millions of other combat personnel captured during World War II, the trauma of being taken prisoner remained forever carved in their memory. One American, captured by the Germans, described the impact on soldiers fighting on both sides: "Being taken prisoner is a terrific nervous shock, in the first place because it involves extreme personal danger during the minutes before the enemy decides to take you instead of shooting you, and in the second place because you suddenly realize that by passing from the right side of the front to the wrong you have become a non-entity in the huge business of war."[4] Eric Kososik, who was sent as a prisoner of war to Ogden and later returned to Utah with his wife and two children, recalled the fear, fatigue, and hunger that accompanied his capture during the fighting in France in 1944. His patrol of nine men had become surrounded, and recognizing the futility of their situation, the platoon leader finally surrendered. They were marched single file to a bunker, where a captain came out and stuck his revolver in Kososik's back and called him a "Nazi Schwein." Fear raced through the young German soldier as he thought, "Oh, my God, this is the end. You went through all this and now you are going to be shot." When the bullet did not come, there was

Captured German soldiers near Caiazzo, Italy, marching to a holding camp. (National Archives photo)

Captured German soldier being questioned by an American sergeant at a prisoner of war camp in Caserta, Italy, October 1943. (National Archives photo)

Wounded German soldiers await transportation to America from the port of Casablanca, French Morrocco, June 1943. (National Archives photo)

German prisoners of war disembark in Boston Harbor. (National Archives photo)

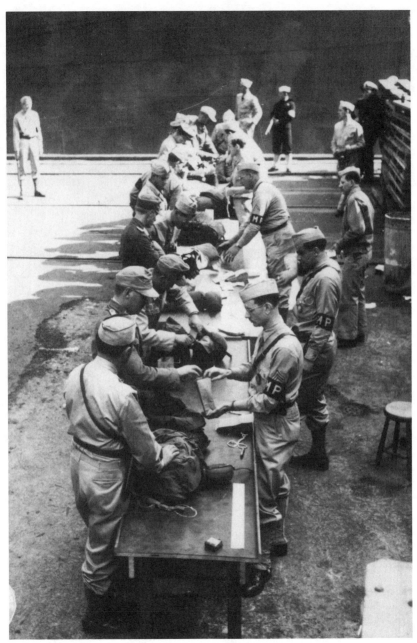

Property and clothing belonging to German prisoners were searched for weapons and propaganda. (National Archives photo)

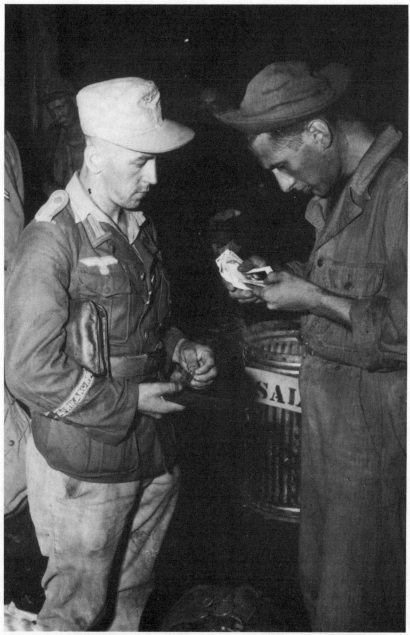

German prisoners of war being searched by American personnel at
Hampton Roads, Virginia, August 1943. (National Archives photo)

American soldier checks prisoner's identification tag during processing in Boston. (National Archives photo)

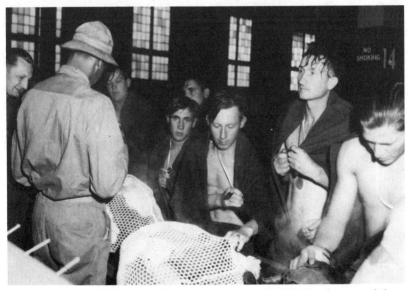

German Prisoners are given showers and sprayed with disinfectant while their clothing is fumigated upon arrival in the United States. (National Archives photo)

German prisoners board train for camps throughout the United States. (National Archives photo)

Train coaches were described by the German prisoners as luxurious and an unexpected contrast from the boxcars in which German soldiers were usually transported in Germany. (National Archives photo)

only a small sense of relief. "I was so hungry, and so exhausted. I thought I was going to die. I was in such bad physical and emotional condition. In fact, after he stuck that gun in my back, I thought maybe he would have done me a favor if he had pulled the trigger. I was so exhausted because we hadn't eaten anything for days."[5]

Like Eric Kososik, many of the German prisoners of war who were sent to Utah were captured in France shortly after the invasion of Normandy. Another of these prisoners, Richard Boettger and his comrades were sent to a cemetery the day after their capture and told to start digging graves. Fearing the worst, they assumed they were digging their own graves and their guards did not offer any word to the contrary. Their fears seemed confirmed when at noon the guards called the prisoners together and gave them K rations. Unaccustomed to cans of meat and beans, bars of chocolate, and packages of cigarettes, "We thought that it was our last meal. Then, all of a sudden, several trucks pulled up which were loaded with dead Americans. They had lain since the beginning of the invasion and so they were bloated. They were placed in the graves we had dug. But the uncertainty had worked on our nerves."[6]

German prisoners were held for a time in camps in Algeria, Italy, and France before being loaded onto troopships which otherwise would return empty to the United States. The crossing of the Atlantic was a difficult experience for many German prisoners. Some did not know that the United States was to be their final destination until they had been on the ocean for several days; most expected to go to England. Many became seasick. Often, food and water were scarce and hunger was an ever-constant companion. Cigarettes were in short supply, but the souvenir-craving American soldiers were willing to trade cigarettes for anything that reflected direct contact with the German warriors—clothes, shoulder patches, service insignia, and even German pennies. As one disdainful German observer found: "It is astonishing what dung the Americans obtain by barter for cigarettes as a 'souvenir.' [They] should be able to open up a small museum at home. In the eyes of friends and acquaintances, he [the American soldier] must have been the very wild warrior in Africa."[7]

For some prisoners the course to America was not direct. Josef Becker, who spent time in the camp at Tooele, Utah, was captured

by the English in North Africa. After spending Christmas Eve 1942
in a temporary camp in Bengazi, where the Germans dug holes
to keep warm and made the best of a diet of crackers and water,
Becker and his fellow prisoners trekked and were transported
across North Africa. They finally boarded an English ship in the
Suez Canal, which took them to the Gulf of Eden, through the Red
Sea, and south along the eastern coast of Africa to the South African port of Durban and from there to a camp near Pietermaritz-
burg. After two months in South Africa, they boarded a ship
believing they were headed for Australia. Instead, the ship sailed
northwest, stopping at Rio de Janerio for three days, then continuing north for another short stop at Port au Spain, Trinidad, before
the final leg of its voyage to New York Harbor. From there, Becker
traveled by train to Fort Hood, Texas, which he reached in August
1943. In the spring of 1944 he was transferred to Fort Lewis,
Washington. When he left Washington, he was sent to Idaho, where
he harvested sugar beets and potatoes before his final transfer to
Tooele.[8]

German prisoners who were sent to the United States entered
the country at Boston, New York City, and Norfolk, Virginia. They
were processed at these ports and, still clothed in their German
uniforms, loaded on trains destined for one of 155 base camps located in forty-three of the then forty-eight states. The attitudes of
these unwilling visitors varied widely. Some entered the New York
Harbor fully expecting to see the metropolis in ruins from German Luftwaffe bombs and believing that they would be the first
to greet the German army when it invaded America. Others looked
on the trip to America as an adventure in a world they had never
expected to see. They were on their way to the land whose streets
were paved with gold and, for some, the West of their favorite Karl
May characters, Winnetou and Old Shatterhand.

One prisoner recalled the advice of a German-speaking American soldier in Liverpool as he assisted with preparations for transporting the prisoners of war to America: "Throw everything away.
In America you will receive everything new. In America you will
get two steaks, one to eat and the other to throw away." The impact on the prisoners was "to increase our expectations and we
anxiously awaited the American wonderland."[9] Another German
prisoner described his amazement on arriving at Norfolk at night:

"The warf, the city, everything is brilliantly lighted. Hundreds of lights are reflected in the water. These people here have no idea what war means. Back home they may be sitting again in air raid shelters."[10]

At the processing center, prisoners were welcomed to the United States. More than forty years after his arrival in Boston on his eighteenth birthday, July 16, 1944, Richard Boettger recalled that they were greeted by a representative of Franklin D. Roosevelt, president of the United States, who had instructed him "to tell you that you should not consider yourselves prisoners of war, but guests of the government of the United States of America." Even an eighteen-year-old just laughed, however, unconvinced that they were to be regarded as guests of the government.[11]

As part of their processing upon arrival in America, prisoners took their first hot shower, were photographed and fingerprinted, and had their belongings disinfected and their personnel files completed. The stay was short, and soon they were marched into a Pullman coach for their journey to an unspecified camp. The train ride was an experience that surprised the German prisoners and gave them a taste of the abundant life in America. Kurt Treiter, who was captured in the North African campaign in 1943 and who spent time at the satellite camp in Orem, Utah, recalled his impressions when told to prepare to leave by train:

> It was clear to us we would be loaded in a boxcar and sent to the interior of the country somewhere. A train with Pullman coaches pulled in. I said, "My God! What kind of a train is that?" I could not imagine that the train was for us. All of a sudden the guard, an American, stood up and said, "Come on, let's go, go in." For us that was the most unlikely thing possible, that prisoners would travel in such coaches. It was not so in Germany. Everyone including German soldiers and prisoners traveled in boxcars. The first ones who were shoved into the car said, "Back, back, those are upholstered coaches. Certainly they are for the guards." So those ahead rushed back and those at the back rushed forward. The guards could not understand. It was clear to the Americans that we were to go into the train, and it was clear to us that we would go by boxcar, not in passenger coaches.

After the prisoners had accepted the fact that they were indeed to travel in great comfort, they were more surprised when the American soldiers began to pass out cups and paper plates and wooden forks, spoons, and knives. Soon, cereal, bread, coffee, tea, fruit, and other food items were distributed. Treiter reflected: "We did not need to do anything, only relax and eat. That was a wonderland for us. It was something we had not known. We had imagined it would be completely different."[12]

Other prisoners expressed wonder and amazement with the richness and wealth of the United States. But some also saw America's dark side, and that revelation was both a surprise and disappointment to them. Ernst Hinrichs noted how impressed the prisoners were when they saw the New York City skyscrapers, the extensive harbor area, and the Pullman coaches in which they were to travel. However, the American wonderland lost its shine once the prisoners reached Chicago, where they spent a half-day on the train as it moved through the stockyards and a ghettoized section of the city. Then, as they continued out of the city, on the outskirts of Chicago, "We experienced an America that none of us would have thought possible. In huts that were built into the earth, people were living!" The contrast was upsetting. "Poverty and wealth so close to each other was something none of us thought possible. The golden America lost its glow for us."[13]

Some prisoners were suspicious of the train rides, concluding that the good treatment was a well-orchestrated propaganda maneuver and that the only reason for the three- and four-day train ride was because the train reversed its route at night or was traveling in great circles to confuse the prisoners about their location and how far they were from the coast.[14]

Many of the prisoners were only a few days from the battlefield when they arrived at their first camp. The first group to arrive at Ogden early in September 1944 were "vermin-infected, filthy and starved." There were three general age groups: fifteen- to nineteen-year-old boys, young men in their twenties, and an older group of men between the ages of thirty-three and forty-eight. Some in the first group were mere children—"beardless boys with squeaky changing voices." The prisoners arrived still wearing their battle uniforms. Most were in German uniforms, but a number were clad in Russian military uniforms. These men had either changed sides voluntarily after their capture or, more likely, had been pressed into service by the Germans. Immediately upon arrival the prisoners were searched. "Knives, keys, nail files, etc. were taken, but watches, wallets, money and personal effects were left with them." Prisoners were then sent to the showers, sprayed with disinfectant for delousing, clad in blue denim fatigue uniforms, photographed, fingerprinted and interviewed and had their personnel and financial records prepared. Their clothing was fumigated, tagged, and stored.[15]

Conditions in the camps were a pleasant surprise. If from the perspective of nearly a half-century later the POW barracks seem crude, lacking sufficient insulation for winter and ventilation for summer, they were on a par with much civilian housing and were similar to the facilities for American servicemen. On seeing his POW barracks for the first time, Heinz Richter commented: "Our mouths fell open in amazement." What Richter and others found was "double deck bunks, white sheets, blankets, white pillow cases—everything new! The beds even had mattresses with springs. This was beyond belief for us. In the German army we lay on straw sacks and had a very rough blanket to cover up with."[16] Indeed, there may have been some justification for the label that some neighboring communities gave to POW camps: "The Fritz Ritz."[17]

As for the food served in the camps, nearly all prisoners experienced a significant weight gain, some to the point where larger-sized uniforms had to be issued. They "liked frankfurters, fish, cheese, cabbage, lentils, white potatoes, bread, and sauerkraut, but spurned oysters, corn meal, celery, hominy, egg plant, peppers, sweet potatoes, squash, canned fruit juice, and, above all, peanut butter."[18] One prisoner from the Afrika Korps considered the American action a very smart move in giving the German prisoners what was, in his estimation, the best food and the best barracks. He told an interpreter in dead seriousness, "When Germany wins the war that will at least be one good mark on your record."[19] Others were initially skeptical of the abundant food and concluded that the Americans "just wanted to impress us so that we would tell them what they wanted to know when they interrogated us."[20]

Where American prisoners of war in Germany were usually clothed only in what they had on when they were captured, German prisoners in the United States were given a full issue of military clothing, which included two cotton or wool shirts, two pair of wool trousers, two pair of cotton or denim trousers, four pair of drawers, four undershirts, four pair of socks, one pair of shoes, a raincoat, a field jacket or overcoat, a wool coat, a pair of gloves, a pair of work gloves, a cotton hat, and a belt. When weather conditions warranted, prisoners could be issued an extra pair of shoes, a wool knit cap, and cotton or denim coats."[21]

The uniforms were marked with the initials PW, and prisoners were instructed that they were to keep the initials in good order for easy recognition. Some Utah prisoners took pains to keep their PW's in good order, but, instead of using the usual oil-based white paint, they painted the initials with toothpaste for quick removal should an occasion warrant it.[22] The uniforms stenciled with PW on the back became the subject of a local cartoon in the *Centerville Newsette*. One of the major plant nurseries in the area, Porter Walton, apparently used POW labor, so the cartoon is a Centerville farmer watching the prisoners of war at work and saying: "I didn't know *Porter Walton* furnished uniforms for their employees."[23]

Responsibility for the location of POW camps was delegated to the respective service commands.[24] Fort Douglas was the headquarters of the Ninth Service Command, and administered POW camps in Washington, Oregon, California, Arizona, Idaho, Montana, and Utah. Camp Florence, near Phoenix, Arizona, served as a gathering point for prisoners of war destined for the Utah camps at Salina, Orem, Logan, Tremonton, Brigham City, and Clearfield. At Fort Douglas, surveys were made to determine where there was available and adequate housing for the prisoners and where their work could best be utilized.

Security was the initial factor in the establishment of prisoner of war camps in the United States. In the beginning it was recommended that camps not be located within 75 miles of the coasts or 150 miles of the Mexican or Canadian borders or near shipyards, aircraft plants, or other vital war installations. After security, such factors as climate and construction and maintenance factors were given consideration. This meant that most camps were initially located in the southern, southwestern, and midwestern states. As the emphasis shifted from security to labor, the disbursement of camps was spread more evenly across the country and the concern with their proximity to international borders, coastal areas, and war installations vanished. Although new camps were constructed, temporary branch camps consisting of tents or located in former CCC camps, state and local fairgrounds, armories, schools, and hotels were established so that prisoners could be housed near their work assignments. As the German POW population reached its zenith, and with building materials in short supply, few new camps were constructed. Military posts, vacated as troops left for the European or Pacific theaters of war, offered a solution for housing prisoners.[25]

The transition from battlefield soldier to compound prisoner entailed several phases: the initial capture; the frontline processing—often by battle-weary soldiers much like those being processed; detention in collection camps of huge fence enclosures; the march (or, if lucky, the ride) to ports of embarkation; the sea journey to North America; the arrival and processing through Boston, New York City, or Norfolk; and the train ride to the first camp. In some ways it was an intensified but broader sweeping repeat of the first transformation from civilian to soldier. In other ways the experience echoed that of European immigrants of an earlier day as they left familiar villages and cities for America, with only a dim idea of where their future lay. But where immigrants relied on a well-known, if uncertain support system of family, friends, and former neighbors, prisoners of war were at the whim of an impersonal government that sent them to Texas to pick cotton, to Oregon to cut timber, and to Utah to thin sugar beets or load and unload railway cars. But if their fate as prisoners seemed to be in the hands of others, the same had been true for them as soldiers. At a time when family and friends suffered terribly because of the turmoil and inhumanity of war, they came to accept and appreciate the clean bed, warm room, abundant food, good care, and safety from bombs and bullets that destiny had bestowed on them as German prisoners of war in America.

THREE

Utah Camps and
Enemy Prisoners

The United States had been at war with Germany for over two years before the first of more than 8,000 German prisoners of war set foot in the Beehive State. Between January 1944 and June 1946, prisoners were transferred into and out of the state as twelve different locations were used at various times to accommodate the former German soldiers.

Eight Utah POW camps were located on military installations either along or adjacent to the state's most populated area on the western slope of the Wasatch Range. These included Camp Warner at Tooele; Deseret, located in Rush Valley about twenty miles south of Tooele; Dugway; the Ogden Defense Depot; Hill Field, near Layton; Clearfield Naval Supply Depot; Bushnell Hospital, just south of Brigham City; and Fort Douglas in Salt Lake City. Four temporary agricultural camps were established in Logan, Tremonton, Orem, and Salina. In August 1945 the largest number of German prisoners in Utah, 6,151, were interned in seven camps from Salina in the south to Logan in the north. The base camp at Ogden was the largest with a high of 3,945 prisoners in September 1945. Ogden was also the longest active German POW camp in the state, having been established in September 1944 and closing as a POW facility in April 1946. It served as the base camp for the other German camps in Utah and was associated with what is now known as the Ogden Defense Depot. Construction began on the depot in December 1940 on approximately 1,700 acres of land just north of Ogden, Utah's important railroad center. At its World War II peak, 7,672 civilians were employed at the Ogden installation, making it the largest quartermaster depot in the United States. Known during the war as the Utah Army Service Forces Depot or the Utah General Depot, the facility was responsible for supplying thousands of different items including steel helmets, clothing, rations, bedding, medical supplies, cabinets, desks, and all kinds of equipment.

The first barracks built at Ogden, however, were for Italian prisoners and were a standard size: 20 by 100 feet. Guard towers surrounded the camps: six for large camps, four for medium-sized camps, and two for smaller camps like Salina. At Ogden the towers were equipped with electric heaters or stoves as well as searchlights for emergency use only. Machine guns were not mounted in the towers because housing facilities for civilian personnel and camp headquarters were located between the two POW stockades. However, at least one guard was on duty in each tower at all times. The compounds were enclosed with nongraduated hog wire fences with a three-strand barbed wire overhang.[1]

The Ogden POW compound was located at the north end of the depot and occupied a space of approximately 1,175 by 1,275 feet. Next to the compound was a recreation area approximately 500 by 1,000 feet. The only building outside the compound was a POW hospital housed in a building originally intended as a post hospital. The buildings inside the compound were covered with tar paper and insulated on the inside. The prisoners were assigned to companies of 250 men, and each company occupied five barracks with fifty men assigned to each barrack. There was one wash barrack for each company, which provided "sufficient hot water to permit the men to have as many hot baths as they wish."[2] One report listed a total of forty-five barracks, eight mess halls, eight latrines, one canteen and recreation hall, and two infirmaries. The buildings were "single story wooden buildings heated by coalburning stoves."[3] Other buildings included a chapel, a theater, a carpenter shop, and a building for day rooms. Later, in the summer of 1945, a new compound of tents was added, which provided space for approximately 800 additional prisoners. Ernst Hinrichs arrived in Ogden after a four-day train trip from New York to find his new home "a camp of barrack buildings surrounded by high barbed wire fences, no trees, only sand and dry grass."[4]

Next to Ogden in size was the first German POW camp, Camp Warner, established a few miles outside of Tooele in December 1943

and first occupied in January 1944 by prisoners from Colorado—
900 from Camp Trinidad and 100 from Camp Carson.[5] These internees stayed fewer than nine months. The camp was used again
for a four-month period from January through April 1946 when
approximately 1,000 Germans awaited final processing and their
return to Germany. Camp Warner was established as part of the
Tooele depot, situated on nearly 25,000 acres of land about four
miles south of Tooele. The mission of the depot was to store vehicles, small arms, fire-control equipment, tank and combat vehicle
tools and equipment and to overhaul and refurbish tanks and track
vehicles as well as their armaments.[6] Personnel at the Tooele depot
during World War II included approximately 2,000 civilian employees, 1,500 army servicemen, and 1,000 prisoners of war. The
experience was, in general, not a positive one in the development
of good relations between Americans and their German captives.
The hard-bitten veterans of North Africa remained faithful to the
promise of a German victory, and demonstrations of pro-Nazi sentiment marked their stay at Tooele. In June 1944 the remaining German prisoners of war at Tooele were transferred to Camp Cook,
California, and it was not until January 1946 that the Germans
returned to Tooele.

Prisoners of war were also interned at a third depot, the U.S.
Naval Supply Depot at Clearfield, located approximately fifteen
miles south of Ogden and twenty-five miles north of Salt Lake City,
for one year from May 1945 to May 1946. The 500 German
prisoners were engaged in the same kinds of work as their comrades at Tooele and Ogden and lived in Quonset huts formerly used
to house civilian workers. The Clearfield depot had opened in 1942
and at its World War II peak employed 7,624 civilians.[7]

Bushnell Military Hospital, just south of Brigham City, was completed in 1942, and had a patient capacity of 3,000.[8] Three hundred German prisoners of war arrived at Bushnell in May 1945 from
Florence, Arizona. At Bushnell they worked in the kitchens, laun-
dries, and hospital wards and maintained the buildings and grounds
at the complex. These prisoners were among the last to leave the
United States in June 1946.

Smaller groups of German prisoners were interned at other
Utah military installations—Fort Douglas in Salt Lake City, Hill Field
near Layton, and Dugway in Tooele County. These prisoners were

Friederick Poes in his German uniform before his capture by American soldiers. (Photo courtesy of his daughter, Hilda Poes Glasgow)

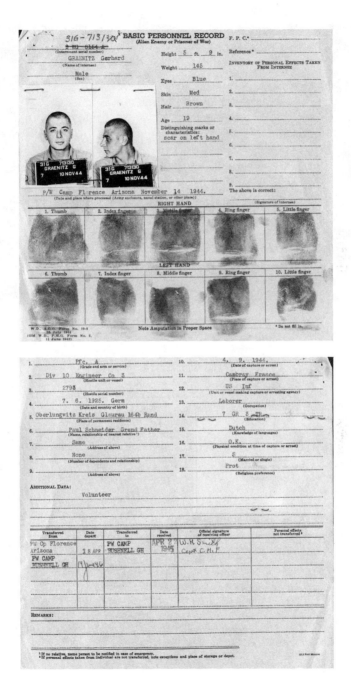

Personnel record of Gerhard Graenitz, German prisoner of war at Bushnell Hospital. (Courtesy of Gerhard Graenitz)

American singer performing at the 80th Italian Service Unit Company party at the Ogden Defense Depot. (Public Relations Office, Ogden Defense Depot)

Austrian prisoner of war company at Logan, Utah, 1945. (Photo courtesy of Rudolf Weltin)

Richard Boettger as a young German soldier, April 1944. (Photo courtesy of Richard Boettger)

held only three or four months between February and May 1946, just prior to their return to Germany. Earlier, between December 1944 and July 1945, a group of about 100 German prisoners had been interned at the Deseret Chemical Depot located in Rush Valley, twenty miles south of Tooele. This facility was used to store and ship all types of chemical warfare material including poisonous gases, chemicals, and chemically filled ammunition.[9]

At Logan the German prisoners of war were housed at the Cache County Fairgrounds from June 6 to November 30, 1945. A new building was constructed, old buildings renovated, and tent platforms made at a cost of $29,350 to provide the essential facilities to handle the peak number of 550 prisoners who were there to assist in harvesting sugar beets.

Rudolf Weltin reported that the Austrian prisoners of war at Camp Florence, Arizona, were invited to volunteer for a special all-Austrian company, which was sent to Logan in June 1945.

Weltin found Logan to be "a surprise to us; there it was more beautiful. Before we had been in the barren desert, and in Logan it was quite green." After the Austrian prisoners were through with the sugar beet harvest, they were sent to California, where they picked oranges and did other work until being sent by train to New York for their return to Europe. California made a more favorable impression on Rudolf Weltin. There, after the men picked their quota of oranges, they could lounge around the orange groves and watch automobiles pass by on the highway. Even Arizona, with its searing heat, was remembered with more fondness than Logan. In Arizona, Weltin had been assigned to work for the horse-mounted guards. One of his assignments was to clean out the horse stalls. With a truck at their disposal, he and a couple of comrades could travel alone into the desert to dump the straw, manure, and other refuse from the stables. The outing was an opportunity to be free of the direct eye of the Americans and a chance to look for precious stones, enjoy the cactus in bloom, and hunt for rattlesnakes. "It was a bit of freedom we did not have in Logan." By contrast, "things were not quite right in Logan. . . . The war was just over and people were angry about the cruelty they were learning about in Germany. That worked itself out in that we were lightning rods for everything."[10] Weltin would have liked more freedom, an opportunity to go out into the surrounding mountains, and blamed the American captain at Logan for his lack of understanding and his unnecessary strictness.

The POW camp at Tremonton was located at the Box Elder County Fairgrounds. The men were housed in buildings described as the Civilian Conservation Corps type in appearance if not origin.[11]

The table shows the months during which German prisoners were interned at these locations and their number as compiled from camp and POW work reports.

Tremonton, with its large barracks, was much better than most branch camps, where prisoners were accommodated in tents. The branch camps were judged by the prisoners to be much worse than the main camps. One Utah prisoner wrote that in the branch camps they lived in tents, slept on field cots with wool blankets, and ate from field dishes which the prisoners had to clean themselves, whereas those in the main camps ate from porcelain plates which

World War II German Prisoners of War in Utah by Camp

Month	Camp Warner/Tooele	Ogden	Deseret	Clearfield	Bushnell Hospital	Tremonton	Logan	Orem	Salina	Ft. Douglas	Dugway	Hill Field	Total For All Camps
1/15/44	1000												1000
2/1/44	1000												1000
3/1/44	1000												1000
4/1/44	995												995
5/1/44	593												593
6/1/44	599												599
7/1/44	0												0
8/1/44													0
9/1/44		0											0
10/1/44		1248											1248
11/1/44		1503											1503
12/1/44		2110	0										2110
1/1/45		2253	110										2363
2/1/45		2258	110										2368
3/1/45		2185	108										2293
4/1/45		2954	108	0									3062
5/1/45		2966	108	500	0	0							3574
6/1/45		3180	108	500	301	297	0	0	0				4386
7/1/45		3740	0	499	301	296	400	250	250				5776
8/1/45		3820		490	330	295	500	283	230				6076
9/1/45		3945		490	348	293	500	300	200				6151
10/1/45		3796		490	325	440	500	300	300				5740
11/1/45		3357		467	322	438	533	325	298				5576
12/1/45		3295		439	322	422	513	295	290	0			5526
1/1/46	0	2202		405	320	0	0	0	0	200	0	0	3127
2/1/46	1039*	2466		404	320					200	174	287	4890
3/1/46	1030*	2131		370	239					200	186	310	4460
4/1/46	1030*	1797		331	274					245	201	336	4214
5/1/46	0	0		0	220					0	0	0	220
6/1/46					220								220
7/1/46					0								0

*No longer identified as Camp Warner, but as Tooele.

were washed in the kitchen. Wind, rain, and snow made life miserable. The prisoners would return from their work dead tired and dirty, and usually there were not adequate facilities to shower. In short, a prisoner who spent several months in a branch camp felt that his situation had "all the characteristics of a front line grunt, he was filthy, indifferent, and tired."[12] With the approach of winter and shorter days, it was even more difficult for prisoners housed in tents in the branch camps to take care of their housekeeping duties. In some branch camps the prisoners left at 6:00 A.M. and often did not return before 8:00 P.M. They had no electric lights or candles. When one German spokesman was asked by inspectors "why there was indescribeable disorder in certain tents," his reply was that the men did not have a chance to be in their tents during the day and without any light in the evening or in the morning it was impossible for them to keep the tents in proper order.[13] Kurt Treiter recalled working in the damp sugar beet fields all day and then, soaked to the skin, riding back to camp in the rear of a truck, where the misery of the cold wind and wet clothes was compounded as the prisoners gazed from the truck into the homes of Utah Valley residents, "where we could see a light burning in the living room. . . . The people sat so comfortable in their living room, ate dinner. . . ." Treiter described how he and his fellow prisoners "were frozen in the open truck, . . . all nearly sick, and . . . very uncomfortable. It was as though we were a load of cattle as we traveled through the area."[14] By contrast, those who worked in Bushnell Hospital considered themselves fortunate. "It was clean, we were always clothed in clean uniforms, freshly washed clothes. We had good food, vegetables, meat, everything. We looked good. We were lucky that we came to the hospital."[15]

Similar to other camps throughout the United States, the prisoners of war in Utah were usually divided into companies of 250 to 300 men, with each company under the charge of a POW first sergeant, who was responsible to an American commanding officer and a first sergeant. In branch camps, which consisted of a single company of men (such as those at Salina, Orem, Tremonton, Dugway, Fort Douglas, and Bushnell Hospital), the first sergeant also served as spokesman for the prisoners. His other duties included holding formations—reveille, retreat, and bed check—making work assignments, seeing that prisoner details arrived at work on time, assigning prisoners to maintain and clean the company area, reporting all grievances and disturbances, and seeing that the men under his charge conducted themselves in an acceptable manner at all times. American authorities usually communicated their instructions through the camp spokesman or leader. The camp leader at Ogden, according to Eric Kososik, "was very good. He kept us in line and was always communicating with the staff. We had gatherings and he said 'now this is wrong, either you comply or your food ration or something is going to be deducted.' So we just gave in."[16]

Under the first sergeant, an office clerk, supply clerk, and utility man composed the POW company staff. The office clerk handled all POW paperwork and files, including company correspondence, time sheets and payroll, duty rosters, and records of all POW mail and fatigue details such as barrack orderlies, latrine orderlies, and kitchen police. The supply clerk, naturally, maintained records relevant to the supply room. The utility man handled a variety of duties including office porter, messenger, and company bugler. Each company was also authorized four cooks and their four helpers who prepared the prisoners' meals under the general supervision of the American mess sergeant, a latrine orderly responsible for keeping the latrine policed at all times, a barber, and a carpenter who repaired and maintained the buildings in the company area. In larger camps each company had a tailor and a shoemaker to repair their fellow inmates' clothing and shoes.

Adjustment to Utah's climate was difficult for some of the men—especially those who had left the balmy early spring temperatures of Florence, Arizona, for the raw spring weather of Utah. A number of the men suffered respiratory problems shortly after they arrived, apparently because of the change in climate. The German prisoners of war who arrived at Ogden in September 1944 were found to be in much better physical condition than the Italian prisoners who had arrived earlier. Whereas the Italians were suffering from malaria, typhus, and serious diseases of the teeth and jaw, the Germans were treated for such ailments as frozen feet, chilblains, and flesh wounds.[17]

The quality of medical service varied under individual circumstances in that German prisoners were cared for either by their own medics and doctors, American medics and doctors, or by civilian doctors. In the smaller camps, infirmaries were usually under the care of a medic who administered to both American personnel and prisoners alike. Civilian doctors were under contract to handle more serious cases; and if necessary, prisoners were transported to main camps. At Ogden, a 200-bed hospital, initially built for the Italian prisoners of war, was provided for the Germans. It was more than adequate, since the number of patients seldom reached a hundred and only three of six available wards were used. German prisoners worked in the hospital as technicians, orderlies, and ward boys. One prisoner, who had been a chemist in Germany, was trained as a pharmacist; another, a former dentist in Germany, was allowed to practice in the hospital. The American staff included a "nursing staff of five colored nurses . . . [who are] graduates of Fort Huachuca, and are rated as far superior to the civilian nurses previously serving here."[18]

Although all major camps had camp hospitals, seriously ill or injured prisoners were transported from throughout the West by airplane to Bushnell Hospital for care. At Bushnell, approximately 40 of the 3,000 beds were intended for German prisoners of war. In Idaho and Montana, prisoners were cared for at Gowen Hospital in Boise, Idaho. German doctors, who were among the prisoners, concluded that the men had nothing to complain about and that their medical treatment in the United States was much better than the German civilian population received during and immediately after the war.[19]

Prisoners in need of eye care were sent to the clinic at Bushnell General Hospital. There, between October 1944 and April 1945, over fifty prisoners received eyeglasses.[20] At Ogden, a German dental assistant provided limited treatment and instructed prisoners in dental hygiene since, as soldiers at the front, they had long neglected their teeth or not had the opportunity to care for them properly.[21] Frequent transfers, however, meant difficulties in follow-up medical and dental care. A number of prisoners who had their teeth extracted at Florence, Arizona, still had not received any dental plates three months after their arrival at Clearfield. With no way to properly chew their food, the men developed stomach problems.[22]

Despite these isolated problems, prisoners of war seemed well satisfied with their medical treatment in the United States. Josef

Becker, a prisoner at Tooele in early 1946, fell and broke both arms while working in the heating plant. More than forty years later, he was anxious to express his heartfelt thanks to Capt. John V. Steele and the other doctors and nurses at Tooele for their good care and treatment.[23]

That the prisoners were provided with good medical care is reflected in the few deaths that occurred while they were in Utah. In addition to the nine victims of the Salina shooting, there were eleven other German prisoners who died in Utah. Six of the prisoners died of natural causes, two from accidents while working at the Ogden Defense Depot, two from unstated reasons, and one by suicide.[24] The one suicide was that of Paul Karl Schaeffer, who hanged himself on May 5, 1945, in Bushnell Hospital. While stationed at the camp in Florence, Arizona, he had attempted suicide by stabbing himself with a small pocket knife. After his transfer to Bushnell Hospital, he was diagnosed as a psychotic, "manic-depressive, mixed type." Four days before he turned thirty-two, he hanged himself. His suicide was one of seventy-two recorded by American officials among German prisoners in the United States. Still, this number worked out to be a lower average than that for the German population prior to World War II.[25] All twenty German prisoners of war who died in Utah are buried in the southeast corner of the Fort Douglas cemetery. White military headstones, identical to those of American soldiers buried nearby, mark the graves of nineteen of the prisoners. The headstone for Paul Eiser, who died of cancer on June 8, 1944, was purchased by the Ogden prisoners of war and is much larger in size than the others. Made of dark granite, the monument still carries a swastika, reflective of an American tolerance for pictures of Adolf Hitler, German flags at burials, the singing of Nazi songs, and the wearing of German uniforms and insignia until the policy was reversed in 1945.

Although the focus of this study is on the German prisoners, it is essential to note that included among these men were others from many countries including France, Luxembourg, Belgium, the Netherlands, Austria, Czechoslovakia, Yugoslavia, Rumania, Poland, Lithuania, and Russia. Many of these men had been taken prisoner by the Germans and put into work gangs and later German army units. But of all, the plight of the Russians who were held as German prisoners of war by the British and Americans was the most unfortunate. Most Russians had been taken prisoner by the Germans during the fighting on the eastern front. Since Russia was not a signatory to the Geneva Convention, the Russian prisoners suffered much worse at the hands of the Germans. With very little to eat, some were told they would be given more food if they joined work battalions. Others were threatened with execution if they refused to cooperate. Many who worked on roads and fortifications in Russia were sent to France to carry out the same kind of work there when the Allied invasion threatened Germany's occupation of western Europe. Once in France, they were given German uniforms and issued rifles. Of the thousands of Russians captured by the Allied forces after the successful landing at Normandy, 4,300 were sent to the United States as German prisoners of war.[26]

Included in the initial group of German prisoners sent to Ogden were approximately 250 former Russian soldiers from all parts of the Soviet Union—White Russians, Turkestans, Uzbeks, Kirghiz, Georgians, Kazakhs, Tartars, Mongols, Letts, and Ukranians. Of these prisoners, the Mongols presented the greatest problem. No one could understand their language. "They couldn't even communicate medical needs through gestures. They seemed to be completely ignorant of civilized ways of eating, personal habits, sanitation, or use of modern conveniences—even latrines."[27]

The Russians captured by the British and Americans presented a problem for their captors, especially when Soviet authorities demanded that they be returned to Russia. Sensitive to the heavy war burden that the Soviet Union carried on the eastern front and conscious that failure to return Russian prisoners of war as requested could mean delays in the return of American and British prisoners of war liberated from German camps by Russian forces, there was little that could be done other than honor the Soviet request. Still, there was some variation between the British policy and that followed in the United States. The British simply sent all Russian nationals back to the Soviet Union—even those who "were unwilling to go home, fearing rightly they would be humiliated and ill-treated for the 'crime' of having been taken prisoner." Ten thousand prisoners left Great Britain for Murmansk on October 31, 1944. Many believed Soviet assurances that they would not be harmed once in Russia. Although some were guilty of treason by having joined the German army willingly, others had remained loyal to the Soviet Union throughout their captivity under the Germans, later under the British. However, once back in Russia, all were treated the same. From Murmansk, they departed for an unspecified number of years in Soviet forced labor camps.[28]

The Russian prisoners in America had some advantage. On December 20, 1944, American authorities explained that "all claimants to Soviet nationality will be released to the Soviet Government irrespective of whether they wish to be so released." Screening teams of Russian-speaking American officers were set up at Fort Douglas and other locations throughout the country. Unlike Great Britain, however, where all were forced to return to Russia, in the United States only those who actually declared they were Soviet citizens were required to return to Russia. Those who did not want to return could simply tell American authorities they were German, since the authorities accepted as a German citizen anyone in a German uniform unless he claimed to be a citizen of another nation. Three special camps were designated for those who claimed to be Soviet citizens—Fort Dix in New Jersey, Camp Winchester in Virginia, and Camp Rupert in Idaho.[29]

On December 29, 1944, 1,179 Russians left San Francisco for home on board the SS *Ural*. All had apparently initially declared themselves to be Soviet citizens; then about seventy of them decided they did not want to return. Either they had reconsidered, preferring to take their chances as "German citizens," or they were ignorant of the consequences in their initial claim of Soviet citizenship. It was too late, however, and all were forced to sail, including three who "attempted suicide, one by hanging, one by stabbing himself, and one by hitting his head against a beam of the barracks."[30]

Georg Hirschmann, who was transferred from Camp Rupert in Idaho with the Russian prisoners on November 11, 1945, recalled they were very reluctant about returning to Russia, where they feared being executed for joining with the Germans. After they were taken away and supposedly returned to Russia, reports circulated in camp about how many of the Russian prisoners had jumped from the ship and drowned rather than face retribution by the Communists. Evidence of the concern felt by the Russian prisoners among the Germans was found in their refusal to fill out Red Cross cards used for notifying their families of their status as prisoners of war. It was feared that their families would suffer if Soviet authorities learned of their having been captured as German soldiers. It was generally held by the German prisoners that the Russian prisoners were bent on drinking anything they could get their hands on because, as one explained, "They knew that when they returned to Russia, they would receive a bullet in the back of the neck."[31]

It may be that the Russian prisoners of war who arrived at Ogden in November 1944 from Camp Rupert were among those who denied their Soviet citizenship in order to remain in the United States as German prisoners. The Russian prisoners were kept together as a group, but were integrated with the German prisoners in the Ogden camp for a year. Conflict between the Russian and German prisoners of war eventually erupted. According to Wayne Owens, captain of one of the POW companies, "the Cossacks went berserk and beat up quite a number of Germans."[32] Such incidents led to putting the Russian prisoners into a separate compound. Isolated from the others, they still enjoyed the same privileges as the other prisoners in the camp.

In addition to Russians among the ranks of the German prisoners of war in Utah, there were others who claimed to be citizens of France and Luxembourg. Marcel This and Jacob Back, interned at Ogden, secured the support of the minister of Luxembourg in the United States in their efforts to prove that they were Luxembourg citizens. Another prisoner, Albert Gewinner, who was sent to Tremonton, declared that he was a French citizen, born January 21, 1911, in Plobsheim near Strasbourg. He explained that his wife, from the same village, was also a French citizen and that they had five children in ages from three to sixteen. He had been drafted in August 1942 for compulsory work in Karlsruhe and was then sent to the fortifications on the Atlantic coast. He worked there as a bookkeeper until his capture after the Allied invasion of Normandy.[33]

Although lumped together initially with the German prisoners of war, the Austrian prisoners, after the capitulation of Germany, sought to distance themselves by claiming that the 1936 Anschluss of Austria to Germany was in reality an act of aggression and that they had been reluctant soldiers of the Third Reich. Because of these feelings, conflicts developed between Austrian and German prisoners at Ogden, and the entire group of 300 men sent to Logan in June 1945 was made up of Austrians. This change in policy by the Americans in separating Germans and Austrians was just one of a number of policies that changed between 1943 and 1946. Utah's POW camps were typical of those in other parts of the country, and the policies which guided the control and conditions for the prisoners were the same as those in other camps.

The 8,000 German prisoners of war interned in Utah represented about 2 percent of the total German prisoners of war sent to the United States. In comparison with other states, Utah ranked near the middle in the number of German prisoners within its borders. Texas, with nearly 80,000 prisoners held ten times as many prisoners as Utah and nearly four times the number of its closest rival. Aside from Texas, the rest of the forty-four states can be divided into four general groups: those with between 20,000 and 25,000 prisoners, which included Louisiana, Mississippi, Alabama, Arkansas, Georgia, and Oklahoma; those with between 10,000 and 20,000 prisoners, which included Virginia, New Mexico, Arizona, Colorado, Nebraska, and California; those with between 5,000 and 10,000 prisoners, which included Utah, Wyoming, and Idaho; and those with fewer than 5,000 prisoners. Comparisons are difficult because most prisoners spent time in several states, and the impact of 8,000 German prisoners of war in a state like Utah, with a population of 600,000 people, was undoubtedly much greater than in other states with a few more prisoners but a much larger civilian population.

German prisoners of war at Ogden. Richard Boettger is third from the left. (Photo courtesy of Richard Boettger)

German prisoners of war at Ogden. Ernst Hinrichs is first on the left. (Photo courtesy of Ernst Hinrichs)

FOUR

American Policies and Prison Conditions

The two greatest external influences which shaped the German POW experience in the United States were the policies implemented by American authorities regarding the prisoners and the conditions inside the camps in which they lived. Policies were fair, usually humane, and sought to make captivity a winning situation for both the United States and the individual prisoners. Living conditions were better than most had found as German soldiers and even better than some had known as civilians. But fair treatment and good conditions did not erase the fact that they were confined prisoners and ultimately subject to the will of their captors.

In his study of the administration and operation of German POW camps in the United States during World War II, Edward Pluth observed that the philosophy of army administrators toward the prisoners evolved through three phases. In the first phase, the emphasis was on security, which translated into housing the prisoners in large, isolated camps where they could most effectively be guarded and controlled. Once officials realized that the prisoners posed no great threat to security and were not highly motivated toward escape, and as the obvious need for supplemental labor became more clear, policy shifted to an emphasis on engaging the prisoners in productive employment. In the second phase, the demands of security were lowered and branch camps where prisoners could effectively work in agriculture or at other essential activities were established. The third phase, that of indoctrination or "reeducation," began in late 1944, but was hampered by a continuing emphasis on work. Administrators came to realize the value of educating the prisoners in the advantages of democracy and the shortcomings of totalitarianism and militarism so that they could be an effective force in rebuilding a democratic and pro-American Germany. However, the demands for the prisoners as workers and the difficulties of implementing an indoctrination program that would not be viewed as a blatant propaganda program stopped the reeducation plan short of its goal.

In general terms, these three phases could be found in the World War I experience, especially concerns about security. However, World War I prisoners were not used as effective a labor source as were prisoners during World War II; and although World War I authorities saw some value in introducing and fostering democratic ideals, no systematic reeducation program was developed.

Throughout the three phases, several policies also governed the decisions that affected all prisoners of war in the United States. These included: fair but firm treatment; a no-work, no-eat discipline; use of a minimum number of guards; use of prisoner labor in a variety of ways, but which was not to conflict with civilian labor; and establishment of POW camps where prisoner labor was needed.

Good treatment of German prisoners of war at the hands of Americans were due to five basic factors: (1) a genuine belief by the great majority that the prisoners were entitled to humanitarian treatment; (2) a concern about how America would be viewed if it did not live up to the letter and spirit of the Geneva Convention; (3) a conviction that well-treated prisoners would be more productive workers; (4) a belief that if German prisoners were well treated, there was a greater likelihood that American prisoners in Germany would be treated better; and (5) a calculation that news of how well prisoners were treated by the Americans would find its way back to the ranks of fighting German soldiers and that as a consequence morale would decline, the will to resist would be undermined, and German soldiers would surrender more quickly.[1]

During the first years of the POW camps, contemporary and later writers criticized the quality of officers and men initially assigned to run the camps. Some complained that camp administrators were selected in a haphazard fashion with no consideration as to how well they would relate to the prisoners. Some officers were assigned to POW camps as punishment, and it was generally held that less qualified officers and enlisted men were given Stateside duty in preference to sending them overseas. Where POW camps were located on military bases, the camp commander was subordinate to the post commander, and conflicts often resulted from this relationship. Some of the American guards were described as being "of substandard intelligence." Many guard units were composed of personnel who had some disability that disqualified them from combat duty. One government official found the guards to be "hardly the soldiers to create a feeling of respect for American institutions among the German prisoners." An American soldier, assigned to a Utah prison camp, "described the quality and caliber of the guards as very poor. . . . They were of low mentality, . . . non-intellectual, and could neither understand nor see the reason for the Geneva Convention. Many drank and went AWOL. They read comic books rather than listening to news. They liked to think of themselves as heroes, their one desire being 'to shoot a Kraut.' "[2]

Beginning in 1945, the quality of guards did improve because some effort was made to use returning war veterans (especially those who had been prisoners of war in Germany) as guards for the German prisoners in the United States. Steps were taken to screen guards for potential mental problems. Part of the motivation in using former prisoners as guards was to counter charges that American officials were "coddling" the German prisoners in the United States. Former German prisoners recalled that their American guards were almost always fair-minded, usually friendly, and seldom hostile or antagonistic.

American guards had been instructed to treat the German prisoners firmly but fairly. Spelling out the relationship between prisoners and guards, one American official distilled the situation into three short and easily remembered sentences: "You are a soldier—he is a soldier. You issue orders—he obeys. You are the captor—he is the captive." The guards and other American personnel were told that they were "an advertisement for democracy [and] whether [an individual] is a good advertisement or a bad one depends on the attitudes he has toward his duties and toward the prisoners."[3] Guards also received special instructions in seven areas: fraternization with the prisoners; use of weapons in handling the

Cover of the Ogden prisoner of war newspaper *Unser Leben* (*Our Life*) for July 1945 depicting a prisoner looking toward Europe and home. (Library of Congress)

Cover of *Unser Leben* for October 1945 showing a prisoner leaving the camp under a warm and friendly sun. (Library of Congress)

prisoners; military bearing; neatness; alertness; the importance of adhering strictly to the Geneva Convention; and the importance of their job in relation to the total United States military effort.

According to Army regulations, prisoners were not to be handcuffed or tied or deprived of their rank. Collective punishment was not to be used because of misconduct by an individual, and the maximum punishment for most offenses was to be fourteen days in the guardhouse on a restricted diet of eighteen ounces of bread a day and as much water as the prisoner wished. Fourteen days had to lapse between each fourteen-day punishment, and in no case was the restricted-diet punishment to exceed eighty-four days a year. Prisoners guilty of serious infractions usually had their heads shaved, and some would-be escapees were reportedly given an oil to induce diarrhea. In Ogden an added measure of punishment recalled by the prisoners was to pour water into the cell in the morning so that the inmates would have to stand up the entire day. Although prisoners were not to be physically abused, Herbert Barkhoff wrote that some prisoners were beaten. "Certainly it was not official policy, but the blue, yellow, and green marks could be seen on our comrades after they had concluded their time in the stockade."[4]

Guard duty for American soldiers was usually routine, but tense situations did arise. One such situation occurred on a cold and snowy day in January 1945. German prisoners, who were being moved from Tremonton to Ogden, refused to begin loading the trucks. They finally cooperated, but only after the American officer in charge waved a revolver in the face of the German camp spokesman and yelled at him to get his men to work. By the time the trucks were loaded and the convoy started south for Ogden, it was dark and raining sleet. En route the brakes on one truck froze up, and it was 3:00 A.M. before the convoy could proceed. The guards were edgy that the delay and earlier difficulty might foment an escape attempt. However, the prisoners were cooperative and thankful when they finally reached the warmth of the Ogden barracks.[5]

American authorities did not hesitate to send unruly prisoners or those guilty of theft to the stockade. One prisoner of war who spent time in the Ogden stockade was Ernst Hinrichs. He and a companion were assigned to deliver by truck the noon meal for their comrades who worked with them in a uniform repair area. A friend had sewn a backpack out of spare material to carry some of his belongings when it came time to return to Germany. Because he knew the backpack would be confiscated by the guards who made daily searches of the prisoners on their return to the compound, the friend ask Hinrichs to take it with him hidden under the food cans. Hinrichs agreed, but when the truck reached the main gate, contrary to normal procedures, it was halted and thoroughly searched. When the guards found the backpack, they claimed that it was stolen and marched Hinrichs and his companion to the camp commander. They were given fourteen days in the guardhouse on the restricted diet of bread and water. Their heads were also shaved. Located in adjacent cells, the two men ingeniously crafted a chessboard and pieces from bread paper and a pencil they had smuggled into the stockade. They played chess, calling out the moves to one another, until there was a change of guards. Denying the prisoners their recreation, the new guards took away the paper and pencils. Later, more lenient guards invited both men out and taught them how to play poker. Still, conditions in the cell were sparse—with only a board to sleep on and a blanket for warmth. When prisoners had to relieve themselves, they were dependent on their guards to escort them to the stockade toilet.[6]

Another prisoner, Richard Boettger, spent fourteen days in the Ogden stockade for insubordination. In response to an admonition from an American authority to work faster, the outspoken Boettger replied in German that the American "should kiss my ass." The message was not lost on the American, who spoke enough German to send Boettger to the stockade.[7]

Discipline was strict at other camps in the West. At Camp Douglas, Wyoming, the commander declared that only the minimum requirements of the Geneva Convention would be met. When strict military discipline was enforced, prisoners complained about his lack of understanding. His conduct was in stark contrast to that of a major who served under him. The major had shown considerable goodwill toward the prisoners and had sought to make the prisoners' situation more bearable. In general, the conduct of the guards was judged to be generally positive, varying from "correct" to "exceptionally friendly." How closely the prisoners were guarded varied from camp to camp, depending on the nature of the work and the status of the war in Europe. One prisoner recalled that in Arizona, while picking cotton, the men were surrounded by a chain of guards, but as they moved north into Idaho and Montana, they were accompanied by only one armed guard, who enjoyed shooting crows with his rifle.[8]

The transfer of prisoners from camp to camp occurred for logistical and work-related reasons, but some prisoners concluded that the cause for the frequent transfer was so they would not begin to feel at home in any one place and so they could not form groups even though there was a certain core group that seemed to stay together even with the transfers. One prisoner who spent several months at Tooele reported that "every six or eight months they shipped us from one camp to another. I don't know why they did it, but it was real good. Life as a POW was not so monotonous because we saw a different part of the county, exposed to different people."[9]

Two criteria are usually employed to measure how well prisoners of war are treated—the extent of physical and mental abuse to which they are subjected and the quality and quantity of the food they are given. In the United States, the health and dietary needs of the prisoners were given close attention. Efforts were made to provide food that was more in harmony with the prisoners' national diet than standard American fare would be. Prisoners were generally pleased, if not very content, with the food. The only exception occurred right after Germany's surrender, when all prisoners commented on the decrease in the food they received.

American officials made careful observations of German eating habits and cooking practices. Their findings and recommendations were published as the *Prisoner of War Menu and Messing Guide.* For breakfast, German prisoners preferred a lighter fare of either cooked cereal, corn flakes, or coffee cake or bread and jam, jelly, or marmalade with coffee to the heavier American-style breakfasts of eggs and hot cakes or French toast. Camp authorities were discouraged from offering cocoa because, when prepared German style, it required large quantities of milk and sugar, both of which were rationed items. Soups, with the exception of lentil soup, were generally not well accepted by the German prisoners, but the heavy, greasy sauces used for stews, meat loaves, and roasts were a suitable replacement. Salads, especially large quantities of leafy greens, lettuce, and cabbages, were served frequently. Potatoes were the most popular vegetable, and it was estimated that a prisoner would consume about a pound of potatoes with a meal. Except for not getting enough potatoes, prisoners were content with the food at Brigham City. In a similar vein, Wayne Owens, commander of one of the POW companies at Ogden recalled that they had to get permission from the International Red Cross to double the potato ration and cut the meat ration in half as requested by the prisoners. Fresh fruits and vegetables in season were to be issued, but frozen fruits and vegetables were not since "prisoners are not familiar with this type of food and spoilage and waste result." When available, fish was to be served once a week. American authorities were unimpressed with the way Germans handled meat. "Beef roasts are cooked for a long period at high temperatures, causing excessive shrinkage. [Whereas] smoked bacon and ham frequently are consumed raw or partially cooked." Camp authorities were advised to teach the Germans how to cook beef and pork in order to prevent waste by overcooking the one and to prevent upset stomachs and trichinosis by undercooking the other.[10]

On February 27, 1945, there was a change in the food policy as stipulated in Article 11 of the Geneva Convention. Interpretation of the article, which had been that the food ration provided prisoners of war was to be the same in quantity and quality as that provided to soldiers, was changed to mean that only the same quantity and quality of nutrients had to be provided. This policy eliminated all the choice meat the prisoners had enjoyed and called for full use of less desirable cuts of meat and other animal parts. One former prisoner recalled that the new directive led to the German camp cooks preparing a dish called *Koenigsberg Speck*, which was made from a cow's stomach cut into fine pieces, seasoned, and served with a sauce. "Even when Koenigsberg Speck is prepared the right way, I don't care for it. . . . In the camp it was simply cooked without any seasoning or sauce, and it did not taste good at all." Another recalled that "there was no more meat, only bones. We asked where were all the bones coming from." The protests against the change in prisoner menus came not only from the prisoners themselves but also from camp authorities and the farmers for whom the prisoners worked. At Camp Beale, California, the newly appointed camp commander had just returned from

Europe, where he had been held as a prisoner of war by the Germans. While a prisoner, he had not been given enough to eat, so he was very much concerned that the Germans should get what they needed. At the camp in Clearfield, where the reduction in food was viewed as insufficient for the working prisoners, the men were allowed to plant a large vegetable garden to supplement their rations. The camp commander recognized that the imposed reductions in food meant a comparable reduction in the prisoners' work capabilities.[11] A Colorado farmer complained the prisoners sent to his farm were only given two hard-boiled eggs for their lunch. Idaho farmers groused that the prisoners were not being fed enough to perform a full day's work. In one case, a hardheaded farmer insisted on feeding the prisoners on the job, but a recalcitrant guard would not allow it, and the work detail was canceled. There were reports of prisoners "blacking out" while working in the sugar beet fields. Army officials maintained that this was caused by "the unnatural position the prisoners are forced to assume while hoeing beets rather than the lack of food." At Ogden, some prisoners elected to live on the bread and water given those who refused to work rather than continue to work when the food reductions were enforced.[12] At Salina, prisoners caught fish in the ditches and canals and took them back to camp as a supplement to their evening meal. The meager rations at Logan were supplemented when one farmer's misfortune became a windfall for the prisoners: a cold spell killed his flock of unprotected turkeys. The carcasses were delivered to the prisoners, who plucked them, cleaned them, and turned them over to their Austrian cooks, who produced a welcome delicacy.[13]

Many prisoners felt that the rations were cut because the Americans no longer needed to worry about American prisoners in the hands of the Germans and saw the cut also as a measure of revenge against the German prisoners. Actually, three reasons were given for the cut in rations in the spring of 1945. First, military officials concluded that the prisoners were getting much more food than what they needed. Most had gained weight since their arrival in the United States and some now appeared obviously well fed. Second, there was a shortage of foodstuffs in the United States, partly because of the amount of food being sent to our Allies in Europe and elsewhere. Finally, because Americans were enraged about the conditions discovered in Nazi concentration camps, the German prisoners of war in the United States suffered a measure of revenge for the atrocities committed by their government. Many Americans equated the concentration camps with American POW camps in Germany and assumed that many of the American prisoners had been subjected to the horrors of the concentration camps.[14]

The Salt Lake Telegram joined the nationwide outcry against the liberal food rations provided the German and Italian prisoners of war. Under the headline, "No More Steaks for War Prisoners," a March 19, 1945, editorial praised the change in policy by the War Department which would mean that in the future, "German and Italian prisoners are not going to be eating top quality steaks and roast beef while the average American civilian is lucky to have hamburger or veal stew." The editorial added that the prisoners were getting good quality meat not once but two and three times a day. Although not advocating that prisoners taken by Americans be subjected to the torture, enslavement, and starvation that American prisoners of war endured at the hands of the Germans, Italians, and Japanese, the editorial called for reaching a medium between "the extreme of savagery" that American prisoners had experienced "to the extreme of fatuous benevolence" that had been showered on prisoners of war in the United States. The editorial also called for an end to sending prisoners to America, "where they can fraternize with American civilians and contaminate them, where they can gorge on scarce steaks, go on sightseeing trips and make themselves into a general civil nuisance."[15]

As of April 1945, the suggested daily caloric level for sedentary prisoners was 2,500 calories, with a maximum of 3,400 calories daily for prisoners engaged in moderate activity. A month later the caloric levels for prisoners engaged in moderate activity was further reduced to 3,000 calories a day, with provisions for higher levels in some cases. Red Cross officials concluded that the rations had been cut too severely and offered as evidence the following reported reductions for a camp of 240 men:

Coffee	12-14	to	3-4 pounds
Margarine	10	to	5 pounds
Lard	12	to	1 1/2 pounds
Sugar	12-16	to	4 pounds
Condensed Milk	40	to	7 cans

One prisoner described the hunger rations at the end of World War II at Fort Lewis, Washington: some bread and coffee or soup for breakfast, two sandwiches for lunch, and in the evening a simple one-dish serving. Protests by prisoners finally led to a reassessment of the situation and in August 1945 a new and—to the prisoners— satisfactory menu guide was issued. The food crisis was over. Prisoners were given enough to eat and, for the most part, the quality of the food returned to what it had been prior to the end of the war.[16]

Closely related to the issue of food were the compound canteens in which the prisoners could make purchases from the money they earned. Article 12 of the Geneva Convention provided for the establishment in all camps of a shop or room in which the prisoners could purchase food and necessities at prices comparable to those for civilians in the surrounding area. Prisoners were paid with coupon books, and used the coupons, generally worth one, five, and ten cents, to make their purchases. Loose coupons were not accepted in order to discourage the use of the coupons as an inter-camp currency or for gambling. It was American military policy that prisoners be required to purchase soap and other toiletries in the belief that they would not waste them since they had paid for them. For items such as tobacco and beer, prisoners had to present a ration card on which their purchases were recorded. Cigarettes were rationed at the rate of one pack per day for each prisoner. Prices at the canteens were considered reasonable. A pack of cigarettes cost thirteen cents, a bottle of beer ten cents, a bar of soap was ten cents, and a piece of apple pie or a bottle of milk was also ten cents. The canteens were usually well stocked with such items as combs, towels, soap, thread, underwear, and other personal items.[17]

At the same time that restrictions were placed on the amount of food prisoners received, the plentiful supply of American cigarettes was also curtailed. In some camps no tobacco was available at all; whereas in others, the men had to be content with making their own cigarettes from tobacco available in small sacks of Bull Durham, called "Arizona Dust" by the Ogden prisoners.[18]

By May 5, 1945, the quart of 3.2 beer that was rationed to the prisoners was no longer available, and strict orders were issued from Fort Douglas that beer, candy, cigarettes, cookies, crackers, and all cola soft drinks were to be removed from the German POW canteens in the Ninth Service Command. After September 1945, restrictions were lifted.[19]

A small fee, added to the price of each item purchased in the canteen, went into the camp fund. Money from the camp fund was used to purchase radios, record players and records, musical instruments for the camp orchestra, an organ for the chapel, sports equipment and trophies, educational supplies, books for the camp library, and magazine and newspaper subscriptions. The canteen was important to the community life of the camp in a material sense, and it was important to the prisoners in another sense. They could attend to some of their personal needs themselves and were not solely dependent on the Red Cross or the YMCA for things they desired.[20]

If sufficient food was critical to the physical well-being of the prisoners of war, contact with home through letters and packages was paramount to their psychological welfare. For the month of April 1944, the 589 prisoners at Tooele sent a total of 1,896 letters, or 3.2 letters per prisoner, and 1,478 cards, or 2.5 cards per prisoner. On the receiving end, the prisoners got 1,618 letters and 681 packages for an average of 2.8 letters and 1.15 packages for each prisoner.[21] Rules governing prisoner mail were explicit and it was monitored carefully. Letters were restricted to twenty-four lines on a special form provided to the prisoners. The letters had to be written in dark ink and could not be sealed. Prisoners were instructed to write in a clear and understandable manner. Quotes from books, codes, musical notes, signs, and shorthand were prohibited. Letters could be addressed only to family members or close friends, but could not be sent to other prisoners of war. The letters could not disclose any information about military affairs, the guard strength at the camps, or anything critical of conditions in the camp or of other prisoners. A censorship office reviewed the prisoner mail, and its function was strictly maintained until after VE day. Letters usually took about two months between America and Germany, making it an average of four months from the time a letter was written until a response could be expected. Distance was a major factor, but others were the disruption of transportation facilities in Germany; civilian deaths from the Allied bombing raids;

dislocations from homes, especially as the Russians pushed into eastern Germany; postal restrictions in Germany as the Allied occupation began; incomplete and illegible addresses; the review by American censors; and transfers of prisoners from one camp to another.

Immediately after Germany's surrender, prisoners in America were forbidden for several months to send letters abroad. In Ogden at the conclusion of the war, the prisoners were no longer permitted to write any letters, and they could receive only a few letters.[22] When the army prohibited prisoners of war from writing to their families in Germany because of the disruption in the German mail service, one prisoner was able to maintain contact with his mother through letters written by her to an American friend with whom he worked at the Ogden depot. The friend also wrote letters to the prisoner's mother telling her of their work and how things were with her son.[23] One Red Cross delegate reported from Bushnell Hospital in June 1945, that the prisoners could not send letters to Germany because of the closed borders and the great backlog of letters already clogging the system. He went on to note that it was a particular hardship at Bushnell since most of the prisoners had been captured in France and had not yet received any mail from abroad. Another Red Cross delegate wrote in August 1945 that in a branch camp of Camp Rupert, a few letters had arrived from Germany, but most of them were dated from the beginning of 1945 and brought only bad news.[24]

In Germany, however, the letters from husbands and sons in the United States brought comfort as the men reported on their well-being and urged their families not to be worried about them. Even children recognized the letters from their POW fathers in America. When the five-year-old son of Willi Klebe would bring the mail to his mother, he would hold it in his hands behind his back and ask, "Mama, which hand do you want?" When she replied that it didn't matter, he would give her the mail from one hand and say, "Here are the letters without stamps, they are from father."[25]

Packages could not be sent from America to Germany, although an exception was made as the prisoners prepared to depart for Germany; and, initially, packages could not be sent from Germany to the United States, although this restriction was modified to permit one package a month from a close relative. Prisoners who received packages signed a statement acknowledging receipt of the package and authorizing American military authorities to open and inspect it. Items which did not pass inspection were either returned to the sender or destroyed. Some families did not believe the reports that prisoners of war in America were provided with more than adequate food. The parents of Herbert Barkhoff sent cans of meat and locally made sausage. Of seven packages sent, however, Barkhoff reported receiving only three.[26] Another prisoner of war asked in a letter written on June 30, 1944, to his wife in Germany that she not send any more packages. He had already received thirty packages.[27] The German Red Cross also sent packages. When prisoners in Tooele received a large number of canned sardines from the German Red Cross, the Tooele camp commander tried to reduce the daily rations provided by the American army. Other camps received cans of split pea soup in packages known as "Fuhrer packages."[28]

In November and December 1945 every prisoner of war was permitted to send a card to try to locate his parents or wife. The prisoner checked off on the card whether he was being held by the Americans, British, or Russians and whether he was healthy or in a hospital. It contained blanks for the date the card was sent, his signature, his birthdate and birthplace, and his current address as a prisoner of war. There was also space for a message of no more than twenty-five words to the recipient. Many prisoners refused to send the card because of a printed statement on it: "A member of the defeated army seeks his next of kin." They felt humiliated and disgraced by the "defeated army" reference. Others sent the card, but never received an answer due to the mail problems and chaos in Germany. For some, such as one prisoner in Tooele, a reply arrived with the comforting news that his parents were alive and had not suffered any significant damage to their property.[29]

Although American authorities were conscientiously attentive to humane physical care of their prisoners and adhered to the provisions of the Geneva Convention—all of which insured a variety of opportunities that no other prisoners of war had known—few understood the real mental state of the prisoners and to what extent the close confinement and years of imprisonment affected the men. Indeed, it was difficult for the prisoners to analyze their own situation and state of mind during the years of captivity. One former prisoner of war at Tooele offered several interesting perceptions about the common experience.

> Everything is temporary, nothing is of lasting value. He is indifferent to his fate and is seized by mistrust and lack of feeling toward others. He loses respect of himself and for others. He avoids all work that is not interesting to him, the will and joy of accomplishment and responsibility dies. Innerly he is dull, heartless and never satisfied. He hardly knows the name of the man in the adjoining bunk and he forgets both yesterday and tomorrow. He lives for the moment and repells true feelings of happiness. He no longer sees a purpose to his life accept the quick and inappreciable passing of the day. . . . He is shut out from the life of nature and can only suffer under its hardship.[30]

Herbert Barkhoff, a prisoner of war in both Salina and Ogden, wrote of the problems in living with a large group in a confined space. Walks along the compound fence gave only temporary breathing room. The close contact in the barracks and the constant conversation meant that "everyone knew, in time, all the most private things that one normally would not learn. The time came when you did not have anything more to say. Voices were raised. We got on each others nerves. Private concerns that were reported in letters that arrived from family members in Germany did not help the situation." On the frustration of the situation, Barkhoff concluded: "Sometimes isolation for a time would have been a gift."[31] For Fritz Noack, the open conversation described by Barkhoff was difficult. He lamented that after three years behind barbed wires, "you get ideas you never can tell to somebody else. You know what you want to do in your youth. . . . If you think it over once or twice, your situation starts to become rough."[32]

The German historian Kurt W. Boehme found that German prisoners of war responded in a variety of ways to their situation. The indifferent were concerned only with getting enough to eat; those who were fed up with politics cursed it and chased anyone from the barracks who brought up the topic; those who deceived themselves "acted as though there were no unresolveable questions, tomorrow everything would be better even if they did nothing about it"; the fatalists were silent; those who discussed the political situation and their future carried on their debates without end and offered more confusion than clarity; the intractable were unwilling to acknowledge the destruction of the fatherland; the "eternal soldiers" considered politics foreign to their profession, while holding their oath of loyalty to the German flag as inviolable. These prisoners asked themselves why be involved in political or educational activities when there was nothing they could do about events outside and no practical use for what they might learn through educational programs. They were assigned work in the military installations or on farms and could not pursue professional interests, except for those attracted to agriculture. But another group considered themselves responsible, personally, for the defeat of their comrades and Germany. These were serious, educated, experienced men who did not impose anything on themselves or allow others to do so. They understood that each German had to answer personally the questions of why they and Germany were in such dire circumstances and how had it happened.[33] It was this last group that authorities hoped to most effectively influence toward favorable views of America and democracy through a carefully structured but subtle reeducation program. Encouragement for such a program came from German exiles and immigrants in the United States.

One careful student of the American policy toward German prisoners of war in the United States was the outspoken critic of nazism, Gerhart H. Seger. A native of Leipzig and a journalist, Seger was a member of the German Reichstag. He was reelected to the Reichstag in March 1933, two months after Adolf Hitler became chancellor of Germany. Shortly after his election he was imprisoned by the Nazis and spent three months in jail and six months in the Oranienburg concentration camp near Berlin. He escaped from the camp on December 4, 1933, and made his way to the United States via Czechoslovakia and England. Writing against the Nazi regime, Seger authored the book *A Nation Terrorized*, which sold over 300,000 copies in seven languages. In the United States he lectured on such topics as "That Man Hitler," "Why I Became an American," "Democracy Versus Dictatorship," and "Cooperation in the Post-War World." On March 14, 1944, he spoke in Salt Lake City at the Rotary Club luncheon at the Hotel Utah. In his speech, he maintained that Nazi groups were active in American POW camps "primarily to stem any movement among German prisoners to show any interest in democracy or America." He also warned that the American camps for German prisoners were nurturing conditions "which may defeat the democratic forces in postwar Germany." Three months after his visit to Salt Lake City, Seger wrote Utah's Senator Elbert D. Thomas seeking his support in furthering the activities of a committee established by Seger for the reeducation of German prisoners of war in the United States. He maintained that such a committee was necessary since the War Department was unlikely to undertake a reeducation program which would "drive a wedge between the Germans and the Nazis." Seger's reeducation proposal called for voluntary, not compulsory, participation by German prisoners. He estimated that the German prisoners in the United States fell into three categories: 25 percent who were "rabid Nazis, in the extreme sense, capable of anything including murdering their fellow prisoners"; 15 percent who were anti-Nazis; and 60 percent who ranged "from Nazi sympathizers to those who begin to doubt already what they have been taught." Seger proposed that the die-hard Nazis be treated like the Japanese American internees considered incorrigible who were assembled at one camp—Tule Lake in California. Under this arrangement the anti-Nazis could work on the middle group free from the pro-Nazis' influences. Once the pro-Nazi prisoners were segregated, voluntary lecture programs, books, and other reading material would be made available to the prisoners. The lectures would focus on historical topics with a strong emphasis on the participation of German immigrants in building American democracy in the fight against the persecution of minorities, in the defense and exercise of freedom of religious worship, and in the establishment of a free press. A final element of the program would be to rescind a recent directive against prisoners of war corresponding with Americans of German descent who were not relatives. The more liberal policy, Seger maintained, would stimulate the exchange of ideas and would, in the long run, prove to be a useful weapon against the hold of nazism. Not all of his ideas were incorporated into the War Department's reeducation program, but Seger helped keep attention focused on such an effort, and his encouragement made such an undertaking a logical extension of the nation's fight against nazism.[34]

A local advocate of a vigorous reeducation program for German prisoners of war was Kaspar J. Fetzer, a native of Germany, a Salt Lake City businessman, and a religious leader. Fetzer contacted Utah's Governor Herbert B. Maw and Senator Elbert D. Thomas and found both men sympathetic to his concerns. In his letter to Senator Thomas, Fetzer noted that he had talked with some of the German prisoners and was astonished at how little they knew about America. The prisoners were surprised to learn that Fetzer had attended a German military school and as a young man had served in the German army. His conversations with the prisoners led him to conclude that "the education of the land in which I was born had radically changed in the last forty years, since I left it. . . . It means reeducation. . . . If we can give it to the persons here I think most of them will take it right."[35]

The reeducation program implemented by the War Department included several elements: publication of a national bimonthly newspaper in German, *Der Ruf* (*The Call*), for distribution in all the camps; publication of local camp newspapers; relocation of incorrigible Nazis to special camps so they could not hinder the work among the other prisoners; special training for those prisoners who, on the recommendation of their camp commanders, seemed to be pro-American and prodemocratic and, hence, potential leaders in rebuilding Germany; classes, films, lectures, and discussions among the prisoners; assignment of a German-speaking American officer to each of the main camps as an assistant executive officer responsible for the reeducation programs; and some testing of prisoners to measure the effectiveness of the denazification effort.

The purposes of the reeducation program were several. Two immediate objectives were (1) to eliminate or at least weaken the control of the German prisoners by the Fascist/Nazi leadership which prevailed in many camps and (2) to present a positive image of America. This second objective served a long-range purpose of having the returning prisoners act as "a democratic yeast" in postwar Germany and as emissaries in promoting friendship between the two countries. The reeducation program did not stress the errors of nazism, but rather focused on democratic principles so that the prisoners could make their own comparison between democracy and fascism. The program did not always meet with success. At Camp Rupert, Idaho, one former prisoner recalled that after the war, professors came every Sunday to convince the prisoners of "the Glory of America, and the unquestionable material worth of Democracy." Since a number of intelligent and articulate prisoners participated in the discussions, they challenged the professors (or American propagandists in the prisoners' opinion) and their theories of democracy by countering with the reality of American discrimination of Blacks, the failure to pursue Franklin D. Roosevelt's Four Freedoms, and the fact that since the end of the war they had lived in constant fear of beatings and other severe punishments. Prisoners familiar with the treatment of Blacks in America were often prone to compare it with Germany's treatment of the Jews. Another complaint was that at the same time Americans were trying to educate the Germans against militarism, there was still a great deal of standing at attention in rank. Some prisoners, although conceding that they were not required to attend the reeducation programs, said they elected to do so in order to avoid trouble. Others found the programs very interesting, but felt that they would not be very effective "bridge builders" between Germany and America since they had experienced only a superficial glimpse of America.[36]

One of the most important elements of the reeducation program was the bimonthly publication of *Der Ruf*, which was printed on high-grade paper and profusely illustrated. The prisoners were required to pay five cents a copy for the newspaper in an effort to arouse less suspicion about the intent of the paper since they had to buy it rather than getting it free. Edited by two prisoners, Dr. Gustav Rene Hoche, a German novelist, and Curt Vinz, a former publisher in Germany, the publication was a project of a Prisoner of War Special Projects Division located in Fort Philip Kearney, Rhode Island. The newspaper was intended to give "the German prisoner . . . realistic news of all important military and political events, a true picture of the German homefront, . . . entertainment and a true understanding of the American way of life." There was a conscious effort to appeal to the more literate prisoners in the hope that they would influence other prisoners. The name of the paper—*Der Ruf*—symbolized a call from the homeland to the prisoners to prepare for the future by building their "mental and physical strength." Prisoners were admonished "to answer the call with a strong echo . . . [so] they will know at home that we . . . have used the time during our imprisonment to become self-thinking ripe men."[37]

In Ogden *Der Ruf* was not successful initially, being considered "a political mouthpiece." Subsequently, however, it received a more favorable response from the prisoners. Seventy-five prisoners at Bushnell hospital "subscribed" to it regularly.[38] In other camps the reception was much different. In Camp Trinidad, Colorado, POW officers burned copies of it. In Camp Hulen, Texas, it was characterized as "Jewish propaganda" and "not fit for the men." Some prisoners expressed skepticism about its intent or irritation at its pedantic style.[39] Nevertheless, considering that the press run of *Der Ruf* grew from 11,000 copies for the first issue in March 1945 to more than 73,000 copies by October 1945, it was a success.

At the local level, the Ogden POW publication, *Unser Leben* (*Our Life*), served much the same purpose that *Der Ruf* did at the national level. Publication of *Unser Leben* began in April 1945, one month after the first issue of *Der Ruf* made its appearance. The camp spokesman introduced the first issue of *Unser Leben* by noting that its purpose was to chronicle all aspects of life in the camp and to keep the prisoners informed about camp activities, such as education courses, movies, sports, musical events, and painting classes. He urged his fellow prisoners to "think back to six months ago. What was in the camp at that time? Practically nothing. I do not need to count what we have accomplished in that time, you can see it everywhere." In a subsequent issue the editor succinctly described the purpose of the paper to be "a bridge to the homeland, an intellectual reflection of our camp community and an untiring voice to stimulate."[40] Ernst Hinrichs recalled that "everyone got a copy of the newspaper, or else it was available in all the barracks. We read it with great interest."[41]

In order for the reeducation efforts to succeed, it was generally agreed that ardent Nazis had to be separated from other prisoners and held in special camps. These special camps included Camp Alva in Oklahoma, Camp Pima in Arizona, and Camp Huntsville in Texas. Ardent anti-Nazis were also singled out and were sent to Camp Campbell in Kentucky, Fort Devens in Massachusetts, Camp McCain in Mississippi, and Camp Ruston in Louisiana. A select few, including 100 prisoners from Camp Rupert, Idaho, were transported by train to Fort Wetheril and Fort Getty, Rhode Island, for a two-month police course in which they studied English,

American, and German history; political science; first aid; military government; and criminal and police law. On completion of the course, they received a diploma and were sent back to Germany.[42] Others, including Herbert Barkhoff, were sent to Fort Eustis, Virginia, for a special two-week course in democracy, American history, and other topics before they returned to Europe.

Those selected for either the Nazi camps or the special training, such as the Fort Eustis course, were screened by the assistant executive officers, who spoke German and were in charge of the reeducation programs in the individual camps. Calvin Bartholomew was the assistant executive officer in Ogden. He had attended Brigham Young University in Provo, Utah, for three years before leaving in 1937 for a Mormon proselyting mission to Germany. He had been in Germany for two years when World War II broke out. Evacuated from Germany along with other missionaries, he returned home and had time to finish his final year of college before he was drafted for military service. Proficient in German by virtue of his schooling and two years in Germany, he volunteered for training as an interrogator. He took part in the landing at Casablanca in the North African campaign, and was an interrogator of German prisoners until he was ordered back to the United States in June 1943 to train other soldiers as interrogators. Then, after the Normandy invasion, a new assignment for working in POW camps came along. Authorities were concerned that many of the camps were controlled by efficient Nazi noncommissioned officers who manipulated the prisoners through fear and violence. The reeducation program was launched to return control of the camps to American personnel and provide the German prisoners with a clear view of the differences between a dictatorship and the democratic way of life. A serious problem for initiating the program was the lack of American personnel who could speak German well enough to carry out the reeducation objectives. Bartholomew was an obvious candidate for the program. He attended a course on Governor's Island, New York, scored the highest on a proficiency test, and was allowed to pick the POW camp of his choice. Anxious to return with his wife to Utah, he selected Ogden.[43] Bartholomew was highly praised for his work at Ogden. When necessary he saw that Nazi troublemakers were sent away.

But most of his efforts were directed toward education programs and other activities to broaden the prisoners' perspectives and better prepare them to return home with a positive outlook and commitment to rebuild a democratic Germany.

Compared to Bartholomew's success at the Ogden camp, implementation of the reorientation program did not run as smoothly in other camps. Administrative problems and distrust of the program's methods and intentions hamstrung its operation. At the camp in Clearfield, the assistant executive officer, 1st Lt. Denzel S. Curtis, failed to inform the camp commander about the reorientation program since "his mission was secret and it was therefore impossible for him to converse with anyone else on the aspects of the Intellectual Diversion program." Seeking as much latitude as possible, the young lieutenant informed the camp commander that he was not to be assigned any duties beyond those for the reeducation program. And, in a breach of military protocol, he sent out official correspondence over his own signature without acknowledging he was acting for the commanding officer. At Douglas, Wyoming, the camp commander resisted the reorientation program. Convinced that it would not succeed, he told his assistant executive officer that he was not wanted there and the less he did the better.[44]

Success of the denazification program was tested by a questionnaire which the prisoners filled out in private, protected from threats or influence by others. One of the questions asked the prisoners to indicate their political preference from three choices: communism, democracy, or nazism. One prisoner from the village of Inzlingen on the Swiss-German border, indicated that, like Switzerland, he was neutral. For other prisoners, the three choices presented a serious dilemma. As Georg Hirschmann recalled: "The war was not over. We did not know anything about democrats. From school we had only heard about the Communists and the Nazis. The people were so brainwashed that they did not believe Germany could lose the war and they voted as Nazis. . . . They were afraid when they went back to Germany and had chosen either democracy or communism they would be hanged."[45] Hirschmann sensed that the American authorities understood their predicament since nothing happened to those who voted as Nazis. Still, the actions of enough prisoners were cause for concern among American authorities about the depth to which nazism continued as an active force. They were skeptical of the chances for eliminating it from among the prisoners in their charge and, as the last prisoners left their camps, many wondered if they had effected a permanent change in the thinking of the former Nazi soldiers.

From the perspective of nearly a half-century later, American treatment of the German prisoners of war in the United States was humane, and usually, with a few temporary exceptions, reflected a liberal and magnanimous interpretation of the captors' obligations under the Geneva Convention. This treatment stands in sharp contrast to that of Japanese American civilians who were forced to leave their homes and businesses for internment in camps like Topaz, Utah, located seven miles northwest of Delta in Millard County. According to former German prisoners and other sources, the military prisoners were well clothed, housed, and fed. Certain luxuries could be purchased in the canteen. Work requirements, although imposed, were generally not excessive, and prisoners could usually pursue recreational and educational activities in their free time.

Concern for their families at home was paramount among the German prisoners once they reached America and relative safety. Although there was nothing they could do about the situation at home, at least they could correspond with family members on a regular basis or to the degree that bombings, disrupted mail service, evacuation, and death allowed.

Whereas American treatment of its prisoners can be described as humane, it was affected and shaped by sometimes seemingly conflicting values and priorities. Security, work, and reeducation would have been difficult ingredients to combine in the right proportions under normal circumstances. Given the shortages of basic staples that hit America just as Hitler's Third Reich collapsed, the thousands of American soldiers and civilians involved in the POW program, and the differing public attitudes toward prisoners of war which demanded attention, it was too much to expect that the management of 371,000 enemy prisoners would be flawless or serene. Still, given the lack of experience in dealing with large numbers of prisoners of war; the American perception of the Nazi soldier; and the thousands of American farmers, workers, guards, and officers who were a part of the prisoner's experience, it may be unreasonable to expect a more logical, humane, or effective course for the POW program in the United States than the one followed between 1943 and 1946.

FIVE

American Prisoners of War in Germany

America's care for its German prisoners of war was grounded in a tradition of humane consideration for the individual and in the hope that her captured soldiers would be properly treated by the Germans. To be sure, conditions in Germany were much different from those in the United States. Bombing raids by the Americans and English left significant numbers of civilians dead and thousands of dwellings and businesses destroyed. Rationing and food shortages were much more severe, and the German population was subject to fanatical propaganda and the suicidal declaration of "total war" and no surrender. In short, the German population was by and large on the battlefront, whereas for the American population the fury of war was far away. But what of Americans held prisoner by the Germans? Here, a brief diversion to glimpse the POW experience for those Americans in Germany can add perspective to a closer examination of the German experience in America and Utah. If part of the strategy was to let Americans grumble about how well German prisoners of war were treated in the United States and not have the American government publicly admit to its golden-rule philosophy that the better German prisoners of war were treated the better Germans would treat American prisoners of war, it worked. As historian Arnold P. Krammer observed, "While Russian prisoners in Germany drank melted snow and ate rodents and French prisoners were humiliated and kept on short rations, American POWs—while uncomfortable to say the least—received adequate if not decent, treatment."[1]

One of the major initial differences for American prisoners was that they were often airplane crew members who had to bail out over Germany during a bombing mission. As might be expected, relations between German civilians and American prisoners were sometimes hostile. David A. Foy concluded that if American cities had been the target of German bombs, Americans would probably have reacted much as German civilians did. "It is difficult to be cordial or even humane toward an individual who, with or without malice, has destroyed your home, eliminated your job, or killed your family." There are accounts of shootings and lynchings of Americans by German civilians.[2] This practice was confirmed by Lt. William F. Higgins in an interview with a reporter for Utah's *Hillfielder* newspaper. Higgins noted that crew members picked up by German soldiers were protected from the civilians and taken to a prisoner camp. However, if civilians were the first to find the downed men after a nearby target had been bombed, they were lucky to escape alive.[3]

Perhaps more typical of the treatment by civilians of downed crewmen was that of Ray Matheny, today a professor of anthropology at Brigham Young University in Provo, Utah, but in January 1944 an eighteen-year-old flight engineer and gunner. His B-17 was struck on its way home from a bombing mission over Kiel, Germany. Matheny managed to get out of the damaged aircraft, but went unconscious at the altitude of 25,000 feet and fell about 10,000 feet before he came to. Opening his parachute, he landed in a canal in rural northern Germany. He was assisted from the canal by a sixty-year-old farmer, was asked in English by the village schoolteacher if he was hurt and needed help, and was taken to a farmhouse, where a German family gave him a woolen blanket to wrap up in and a cloth to stop the bleeding from a cut on his forehead and invited him to eat with them. He remained with the family about twelve hours, at which time an infantry captain came to pick him up.[4]

Matheny and other captured American Air Force personnel were processed through an interrogation center at Oberursel, eight miles from Frankfurt am Main. For Matheny, the train he took to Frankfurt was comparable to what German prisoners in America rode in. He traveled, under guard, on a regular passenger train with German civilians. In Frankfurt the prisoners were loaded onto a crowded streetcar and required to stand in deference to the women passengers. The Americans were transported to Dulag Luft, a processing camp for American and Allied airmen, but not before an incident took place reminiscent of one in Salt Lake City over a quarter of a century earlier when German prisoners were being transported to Fort Douglas. As before, the streetcar conductor refused to honor the red tickets issued by the German government to cover the fares of prisoners and their guards on public transportation. Ultimately, the German soldiers paid the fares out of their own pockets, but did get a receipt from the unbending conductor.[5]

The interrogation of downed American flyers has been described as intense. Matheny went through several interrogations. In Hamburg, a non-English-speaking German officer asked him questions through an enlisted interpreter of limited translation abilities. Matheny offered off-the-wall answers and the German corporal translated them into answers he thought the German officer wanted to hear. Later, at Dulag Luft, Matheny was confined for a week in a four-by-eight-foot cell, where the window was boarded up, a bell chimed every fifteen minutes, and the room temperature alternated between freezing cold and unbearably hot. German soldiers marched through the prison corridors with their hobnailed boots and staged mock executions to intimidate the prisoners locked in their cells. An interrogator, posing as a Red Cross representative, tried to get Matheny to reveal where he had been stationed, the name of his squadron leader, and other military information. At one point, he was threatened with being turned over to the Gestapo as a spy.[6]

Authentic Red Cross personnel were important in the process by which Americans became prisoners of war. Once the men arrived at an interrogation center, they were each given a Red Cross form to fill out, which was sent to the International Red Cross in Geneva, which in turn informed the United States government that the individual had been captured.[7]

One of those Red Cross forms was filled out by Benjamin Gabaldon, who was captured near Bologna, Italy. Gabaldon, a native Utahn, had landed in Naples, fought northward and supported the landing at Anzio, and then had continued north to Rome, where his company spent a few days in the suburbs before resuming the

march north. In a small village near Bologna, his company was surrounded by Germans and forced to surrender after a day and a half
of fighting when the Germans brought in their Tiger tanks and
began a systematic demolition of the village. Gabaldon's company
of 300 men suffered nearly 90 percent casualties, including the
company commander and second in command, both badly
wounded. American soldiers captured in Italy were taken to Germany for internment. The trip to Germany was often demoraliz-
ing, exhausting, difficult, and dangerous. Gabaldon was marched
through Genoa, Italy, where "the civilians started throwing rocks
at us, hitting us with clubs, spitting on us. Some of the German
guards had to fight them off to keep them away from us." He was
taken to a small holding camp outside Genoa to await transportation. The camp was attacked by Allied airplanes and a number of
American prisoners were killed by their own planes. The tragedy
was repeated ten days later when Gabaldon and his group were
loaded into boxcars and sent north into Germany. Their train was
attacked by American fighter planes and twelve of the sixty American prisoners in Gabaldon's boxcar were killed.[8]

Among those captured during the Battle of the Bulge was another Utahn, Wallace Butterfield. He was twenty years old and had
arrived by troop transport in England in October 1944. In December his unit was sent to Le Havre, France, and after a few days transported to the front line to relieve another unit. Arriving in the midst
of a snowstorm, the unit was put in dugouts outfitted with stoves,
the men unaware of what the next few days would bring. On December 18 they left the comfort of their warm dugouts in retreat.
The next morning the Germans opened with a barrage of artillery
fire. At 10:00 A.M., the men were told that because of their hopeless situation, they would surrender. Butterfield recalled: "At that
time I had not even seen a German. . . . It was an hour or two hours
before the Germans came in and surrounded us. We had our rifles
bent around pine trees by that time." After his capture, Butterfield
was marched back through the battle zone to trains for transport
to Germany. As he walked he saw "frozen bodies, frozen at the place
they had died in the battle. All of the shoes were taken off and some
of the clothing had been stripped off. They were both German and
American."[9]

Harvey Sundstrom was also captured during the Battle of the Bulge. From Utah and Idaho, Sundstrom was twenty-three years old at the time of his capture; he spent four months as a prisoner of war. The events leading to his capture on December 17, 1944, were still a vivid memory in 1987. With night falling, his unit was told to dig foxholes in a fruit orchard. With German tracer bullets flying over their heads, the men slept very little during the night. The next morning Sundstrom abandoned his shallow foxhole for a farmhouse two hundred yards away just before a mortar round took out a huge boulder in the bottom of his recently abandoned foxhole. The farmhouse was occupied by a mother and two teen-age girls, who had chosen the basement as the safest refuge. Nearly a dozen other soldiers had found their way to the farmhouse and had moved upstairs where they could observe the surrounding terrain. In short order, the farmhouse was surrounded and Sundstrom and the others surrendered. When the German soldiers rounded up the Americans, "the first thing they asked, and we knew by their actions that was what they were asking, they wanted to know if we had molested the women. We shook our heads and said no, we had not molested them. I know that I would not have been here if that had been the case."[10]

The first few hours of capture were always tense and humiliating. Butterfield described his captors as "a bunch of cocky young kids. It is quite frustrating to have a sixteen-year-old kid come over and start ripping your clothing and going through your pockets." He managed to keep his wristwatch, but all his other personal possessions were taken. Gabaldon was happy to lose only his watch and money because his captors "took us outside and lined us all up in the courtyard. We thought maybe they were going to shoot us because they had machine guns." After the prisoners were searched, they were interrogated. Stanley Blackhurst, who had been captured near Bastogne, was totally amazed at the response he got from his interrogator after stating his name, rank, and serial number: "Oh yes, we've got that. You were born in American Fork [Utah] and you went to school at South High. Your daddy is Hyrum Mitchell and your mother is Amy. You have a sister Janet and three other brothers. That's all we need to know. Thank you very much." The information on Blackhurst may have come from American newspapers which were scrutinized by Germans in America for articles on American servicemen and sent to Berlin where information was kept for use should they be taken prisoner. Gabaldon's captors knew very little about him. He too offered only his name, rank, and serial number, but when his captors pushed him to find out if he were Jewish, his buddies urged him to explain that his parents were from New Mexico and that he was Mexican, not Jewish. The disclosure kept Gabaldon with his group, whereas a couple of Jewish members of the unit were taken away.[11]

After his capture, Blackhurst was marched for four days to Gerolstein, Germany, where he spent six weeks before being transported to Stalag XIIA near Limburg an der Lahn. His train ride was an unforgettable experience. He and fifty or more prisoners were packed in a boxcar, with very little food for the journey. The train was strafed by American fighter planes and several prisoners were killed. More lives were spared when the train found refuge in a tunnel, but because of the constant pressure from the American fliers, the train had to remain in the tunnel for several days. The cramped boxcars, lack of daylight, no food, and bombing was nearly unbearable. "It was like going bugs. It really plays on you. . . . You didn't know if the tunnel was blown closed or caved in on you or what because you could feel the vibrations when the bombs would hit."[12]

Conditions in the German POW camps led one Utahn to describe imprisonment as "the shits, something I wouldn't wish on my worst enemy." Little food, dysentery, an abundance of lice, no clean clothes or opportunities to shower, cold and poorly equipped barracks, dangerous work, and uncertainty of the future all took their toll. American prisoners in Germany were usually housed in wooden huts with windows on each side and two long stoves in the middle of the floor. The prisoners slept on three-tiered wooden bunks with flimsy mattresses. Outside latrines brought an unwelcome and sometimes all-permeating stench to the camps. The poor sanitary conditions and infrequent opportunities to bathe drove one American prisoner to describe his POW camp as "a compound of unwashed bodies, dirt, grease, smoke, filthy bedding and damp masonry."[13]

Food was paramount in the minds of the prisoners. Their diet was based on potatoes and black bread (*Kriegsbrot*), which was presumably laced with a filler of sawdust and which, by the time it reached the Americans, was moldy on the outside but edible on the inside. One American prisoner listed the individual POW diet as follows: 8 1/3 ounces of bread per day, 16 ounces of potatoes per day, 4 ounces of horsemeat per week, 1/2 ounce of ersatz margarine per day, 1 1/3 ounces of barley per week, 5 ounces of dried rutabaga per week, 4 ounces of sugar per week, 2 to 3 ounces of cheese per week, and 2 to 3 ounces of ersatz coffee per week.[14]

All American soldiers lost weight as prisoners. A loss of 60 to 70 pounds was typical. Harvey Sundstrom dropped from 225 to 110 pounds from the time of his capture to his liberation. For him, a typical day at his Luckenwalde POW camp started with a tea made from aspen leaves or a hot barley drink and nothing else. On Sundays they were given a wheat or oat cereal with a little strawberry or peach jam to sweeten it. The second and last meal of the day was a thin soup with a few sugar beets or potatoes. The daily ration of bread was usually three slices of *Kriegsbrot*. The men were sure the bread contained a good portion of sawdust because when it got a little dry, "you could light it with a match and it would burn just like pine." Ray Matheny, at Stalag XVIIB in Krems, Austria, encountered nails and pieces of wood in the bread. On occasion they would get some meat. Stanley Blackhurst, imprisoned at Stalag XIIA near Limburg, said that the prisoners were served small pieces of horsemeat that tasted very good. At Luckenwalde, Sundstrom was served horsehead soup. "They would take horses' heads and throw them into the soup and they would cook. Then they would take their ladles and skim as much of the hair off the top as they could." On one occasion, he was fortunate enough to get a horse's eye in his portion. Envious of this prize, other prisoners offered to trade anything for the eye. He didn't trade, "but chewing that thing was just like chewing rubber."[15]

The sparse rations were supplemented by American Red Cross food packages. The Red Cross packages contained cans of spam or corned beef, liver paste, concentrated orange paste, fruit jelly, powdered milk, sugar, raisins or prunes, coffee, chocolate, sticks of gum, a small package of cigarettes, toilet paper, and matches. Toward the end of the war, one Red Cross issue consisted of cans of corned beef tinned in Argentina in 1918 that had been in storage in Switzerland since World War I. Some cans were poorly sealed and contained only dust. In others, the meat was only partly spoiled and the protein-starved prisoners cut away that portion and ate what was left. Some lucky prisoners got full cans of meat in perfect condition.[16] Understandably, some American prisoners were critical of the American treatment of German prisoners. One asked why German prisoners were fed meat, potatoes, and butter, whereas the Americans "got so weak we couldn't get out of our bunks on the liter-a-day of watery soup we received."[17]

One of the prisoners' favorite pastimes was talking about what would be their first meal when they returned to the United States. One group planned to get together in New York and go to a restaurant where each one would order what he really liked. "We were going to have that piled on the table and each one of us would have a chance to taste everyone's delight." Blackhurst, whose father and grandfather were in the poultry business, dreamed of a roast turkey dinner with all the trimmings.[18]

Most prisoners saved some of their bread ration each day so that they would not be completely without food. Theft of food from fellow prisoners was met with swift and extreme retribution in some camps. Sundstrom recalled the time a prisoner was convicted by a kangaroo court of taking food from another prisoner. The man was shoved up to his neck into a trench of sewage. When he was finally allowed to crawl out, he was not given clean clothes and had to wrap himself in a blanket with a rope for a belt. Ostracized by the other prisoners, the man died of dysentery.[19]

Dysentery was a common malady in the German POW camps, but there was little treatment available. At Gabaldon's camp, they were given "some black stuff like charcoal," which helped. Russian prisoners at Luckenwalde advised the Americans to burn potatoes until they were black like charcoal and then eat them without any water. "You never had anything so dry in your mouth. It was just like chalk . . . but it seemed like it worked."[20]

Other ailments plagued the prisoners. Some of the men suffered from frostbite, others from scabies. No one escaped the lice that infested clothes, beds, and hair. Clothing was in short supply and most prisoners were liberated wearing the same clothes in which they had been captured. Showers were infrequent and then only with cold water. Prisoners were encouraged to shave each day, and camp barbershops were set up—although the long lines and quick, slipshod haircuts were a trial.

Next to the lack of food, the cold was the most constant physical reminder to captured soldiers of their miserable conditions as prisoners of war. When stoves were provided in the barracks, there was usually little or no fuel to burn in them. Prisoners were issued a blanket or two, which helped, but was certainly inadequate in shutting out the biting cold of the German winter of 1944-45. Sundstrom, who was quartered in an old unheated cavalry stable, recalled that they were given two blankets—they slept on one and under the other. The men soon learned to sleep huddled together in threes for warmth. "One would be in the center and those on the end would sleep with their backs toward the center. Every so often we would change places so that the one on the outside could be in the middle to get warm." By drawing straws, the men in Blackhurst's camp determined the positions for an entire night. Those unlucky enough to draw outside positions could only look forward to a new chance the next night, whereas those lucky enough to secure center positions were assured of them even if they had to get up to relieve themselves in the night. Unwritten rules prevented anyone from taking another prisoner's place.[21]

Like their German counterparts in America, prisoners in Germany were permitted to send two letters and four postcards a month. For incoming mail and packages, however, delivery ranged from five weeks for airmail letters to three months for surface mail and packages. Prisoners could send one parcel every sixty days and they could receive one five-pound package of books every thirty days. Letters were important to the families of American prisoners of war. They brought comfort and reassurance that all was well with their husbands, sons, and brothers. Letters written in August 1944 by T.Sgt. Rondo Edler to his parents in Grantsville, Utah, are representative of American POW mail. The letters, which took just under four months to reach Utah, reported that he and all of his crew got out safely when their plane went down, that none of them were injured, and that he was well. He reassured his parents that prisoners were provided with three meals a day and that they received Red Cross packages. "We have some athletic equipment and play football and baseball and cards. . . . I go to church on Sundays and I pray that you are well and don't worry."[22] Christmas was an especially depressing time. Ray Matheny recalled the terrible effect of hearing Christmas music played by the Germans over the camp loudspeaker. Many of the homesick prisoners cried openly when they heard Bing Crosby sing, "I'll Be Home for Christmas."

American prisoners were permitted to perform theatricals, see movies, establish libraries, attend classes, do handicrafts, undertake gardening projects, and engage in such sports as baseball, softball, football, basketball, tennis, soccer, and badminton. At one camp, American prisoners laid out a six-hole golf course and played with one set of clubs, four balls, and other balls made out of salvaged leather and rubber.[23] Prisoners generally devised their own form of recreation and took advantage of group activities. At Stalag XVIIB, Matheny and a friend manufactured a cribbage board and made a point of playing at least one game every day. They also reproduced a Monopoly game. Matheny and his comrades attended a camp-produced musical comedy, *He Wears a Pair of Broken Wings*, which included, among other acts, a slender prisoner in a turban impersonating Lena Horne singing "Saint Louis Woman." On another occasion a Red Cross representative brought to camp an American movie about John L. Sullivan, which was a great boost to morale. The Red Cross also provided old books, which were read with great interest. The Germans provided books as well, but most of them were Nazi propaganda. For example, American airmen were given English translations of *Der Adler* (*The Eagle*), a magazine about the German air force. Intended to demoralize the American prisoners by demonstrating the superiority of the German air force, the articles on German aircraft and battle techniques were instead read with interest by the Americans. Copies of *Mein Kampf*, in English, were provided and read by some, including Matheny, who was amazed that Adolf Hitler had put in print in 1925 what they were experiencing twenty years later.[24]

Although camp newspapers were not permitted by the Germans, underground publications flourished in some camps with news supplied through BBC broadcasts that were picked up on radios hidden in the prison compounds. The clandestine publications were reputed to be such an accurate source of information that some Germans asked trusted American prisoners for news. One paper, the *POWWOW*, boasted that it had in print the story of the Normandy invasion before the *New York Times* hit the streets with

its extra edition with the news.[25] The Germans had their own publication for the Americans, known as *O.K.* for *The Overseas Kid.*
The publication was a propaganda effort, roughly comparable to
Der Ruf, which the American government produced for German
prisoners in the United States.

Medical treatment and sanitation varied greatly from camp to
camp. Some returning American prisoners had great praise for their
treatment by German physicians, but others were extremely critical. Prisoners could keep reasonably clean with the soap provided
by the Red Cross, but in some camps cold-water showers were permitted only once a month, and bedbugs, fleas, and lice were a continual plague.

Fear of violence at the hands of their captors was an ever-
present reality for the American prisoners. Stanley Blackhurst was
once hit with a rifle butt by a sixteen- or seventeen-year-old guard
who was angry when he did not move fast enough to suit him.
As the Russian advance pushed into eastern Germany, the Americans feared that any who fell behind during the forced evacuation
march were being executed; rifle shots could be heard and some
prisoners were never seen again. In Stalag IXB at Bad Orb, Wallace Butterfield and other prisoners were rousted out of bed at 3:00
A.M. by German guards who were tracking a couple of prisoners
who had broken into the mess hall to steal some food. A German
guard had found the mess hall door ajar, and was killed with an
ax by one of the prisoners when he went in to investigate. When
German authorities discovered the crime, they used bloodhounds
to track the men, the trail leading to the barracks where Butterfield was sleeping. Nearly paralyzed by fear, the American prisoners
were hustled out of their barracks and lined up in a field surrounded
by heavily armed guards. German authorities were yelling and
shouting as they searched for the murderer. Butterfield recalled
that "if it hadn't been for our camp commandant, there would have
been an atrocity there that day. . . . When Germans start talking
under heated circumstances, it sounds like everything is going to
break loose." Butterfield and his fellow prisoners were not harmed,
but they were told they would be given no food until the guilty
men were identified. Rumor had it that the American leader found
blood on two men's jackets and directed them to surrender to the

Germans or he would turn them in the next day. What became of the two men is not known.[26]

Not all confrontations between guards and prisoners threatened violence. Harassing the Germans, or "goonbaiting" as it was called, was a pastime pursued in a variety of ways by the American prisoners. When a German, posing as a Red Cross inspector, entered Stalag XVIIB at Krems, Austria, the men went along with him long enough to steal his bicycle and throw it into the camp cesspool. On another occasion, when a local brickmason was sent into camp to repair a chimney on one of the barracks, the prisoners started a fire in the stove, using a greasy army cap to make it smoke. The brickmason yelled for them to put out the fire; and in the confusion the prisoners stole his ladder and burned it in the stove, leaving him stranded on the roof for a couple of hours until German guards could locate another ladder to get him down. Another time the prisoners built a snowman with coal-black eyes and a mustache, making it look like Adolf Hitler. When the German camp commander saw the snowman, he sent his aide to knock it down. Much to the delight of the Americans, the man fell in the snow when he slipped trying to kick the head off the snowman. An order to refrain from throwing rocks at airplanes was met with howls of laughter after prisoners had nearly downed a low-flying German aircraft that was performing stunts over the camp. The laughter was more circumspect when they taught a slow-moving, sloppily dressed, overweight guard to say such English phrases as "I am a dumb son of a bitch" and then offered fanciful and erroneous German translations of the phrases.[27]

Because prisoners who were officers or noncommissioned officers were not required to work (as per the Geneva Convention), most of the harassment of Germans occurred in their camps. The imprisoned enlisted men, conversely, had much less time for playing games with their captors. They were assigned to work details and were required to work fifty-six to sixty hours a week—the same as required of German male civilians. Hence, American prisoners worked an average of sixteen to twenty hours a week more than their German counterparts in the United States. Working conditions for American prisoners were also different from those for Germans in America. First of all, the extensive Allied bombing of German cities, factories, and rail lines had disrupted normal activities. Some prisoners cleaned up the damage from air raids in the cities. Others mined coal or potash; quarried stone; repaired roads; constructed power plants; unloaded railroad cars; and worked in factories, sawmills, breweries, coal storage plants, and railroad yards. Still others cut trees or worked on farms.[28] Individual circumstances determined how much and what kind of work the prisoners were required to perform. At his camp, Wallace Butterfield volunteered to cut wood and clean latrines for a little extra food. William Blackhurst repaired railroad tracks damaged by Allied bombing until he complained of being sick and was able to escape the work details. Later, when he was transferred to Stalag XIIA, he worked in the camp hospital and on burial details for those Americans who died in the camp. Benjamin Gabaldon was transported from Italy to a camp at Moosberg, Germany. From there, he and other prisoners were transported by train about twenty-five miles to Munich to assist in cleaning up the bomb-ravaged city. With temperatures below zero, the prisoners were loaded into the cold boxcars at 5:00 A.M. and left there for an hour or two before the train made its way into Munich. The prisoners were returned to camp around 5:00 P.M. A few months later, about four hundred prisoners were transferred to a camp in Munich so they could be sent to work without the long and sometimes dangerous train ride. During the last months of the war, Munich was subject to almost continual bombing. Gabaldon and his fellow prisoners had more than enough work in searching for victims who had been buried alive from the bombing and in cleaning up the tons of rubble. When their work was interrupted by air raids, the American prisoners joined the citizens of Munich in the bomb shelters. The bomb shelters were a sanctuary, but they did not necessarily mean security. On a few occasions, dud bombs crashed through the shelter roof, and there was always the possibility of being buried alive should only one bomb not be a dud. Gabaldon was nearly killed when the steps of a bomb-damaged building collapsed under his weight, burying him in the rubble. With an injured back, he lay undetected for a couple of hours until he was discovered by his German guard, who quickly called on other prisoners to carry him on a stretcher back to their barracks. Forty-two years later, the injured back had become a lifelong reminder of his sojourn as a prisoner of war, as had the memories of cries from women and children huddled in the bomb shelters, the rush to pull victims buried in the rubble, the details of men in striped uniforms from concentration camps working near the American prisoners of war, the continual bombing, and the resignation that came with knowing it was more than likely he would not survive to the end of the war.[29]

Liberation was a day long dreamed of by Americans in German POW camps. For some, the day was filled with drama as American soldiers in Sherman tanks rolled into the camps to the cheers of the prisoners. For many, however, the transition from captivity to freedom did not occur in one bold stroke, but was drawn out over a couple of days and even weeks. At Bad Orb, Wallace Butterfield knew American forces were near when the Germans put a red cross out in the field and most of the guards disappeared. Butterfield and the others remained in camp until American troops arrived a few days later on April 2, 1945. At the Limburg camp, Stanley Blackhurst and a group of prisoners were marched into the city to move them away from the advancing armies. Their guards herded them into an icehouse the first night, but when they awoke, the guards had vanished. Unsure of what to do, they milled around until Blackhurst and three fellow prisoners stumbled into a little bar. "The innkeeper was real friendly toward us. He said, 'Anything you want that I have you can have.' So we all had a jug of beer and got sick. We lay on the floor and went to sleep." The next morning, with still no sign of German guards or American soldiers, Blackhurst and his three companions were walking down a road when they smelled bread baking in a small house on a hill. As they walked toward the house, a German woman greeted them with "Come on in. I just baked some bread for you." Later, they were met by American soldiers and taken to a recovery area. Ray Matheny and other American prisoners were taken out of Stalag XVIIB as the Russians advanced on Vienna. They were forced to march across most of Austria to the German border near Hitler's birthplace at Braunau-am-Inn. The seventeen-day march took then across the Danube River at Linz and past the concentration camp at Mauthausen, where they could look down from the road into the camp and see men and women carrying rocks in slings on their backs. The march was a terrible hardship for the Americans, who were ill-fed and in poor condition. Once they reached Braunau, they were sent into a forest and kept under guard by a few armed Germans. Since they had no tents, the prisoners set about erecting shelters from saplings and fir boughs and tried to coax some warmth from fires they built with rain-soaked wood. Seven days later an American army captain drove into the woods and announced that the prisoners were now free. Since the American captain was without any support forces, he instructed the German guards to stay on duty with their weapons one more night until he returned the next day. Compared with the fantasies that had filled the thoughts of the prisoners during their stay at Stalag XVIIB, the circumstances of their liberation in a Bavarian forest outside Braunau was bitterly anticlimatic. Perhaps it was their disappointment that sparked a frenzy of looting and vandalism as they broke into museums, raided houses, and demolished equipment and machinery, including airplanes, locomotives, and steam shovels.[30]

Food was undoubtedly the greatest immediate danger facing the newly freed men. Half-starved and their bodies accustomed to thin soup, tea, and sawdust in bread, the former prisoners were not able to assimilate the rich food or the generous helpings that were lavished on them. Most got sick and a few died as their bodies reacted to the sudden change. Illustrative of what could happen is an account by Harvey Sundstrom. When he and a buddy went scrounging for food in a nearby U.S. Army field kitchen, an accommodating cook gave them peanut butter, strawberry jam, freshly baked bread, and a mess cup filled with hot chocolate. At that moment, a mess sergeant came in and, realizing the consequences, chased Sundstrom and his friend from the mess tent and accused the over-indulgent cook of trying to kill them with kindness and too much food. Only a few feet from the mess tent, Sundstrom and his friend doubled over with terrible stomach pains. They were rushed to the hospital, where hoses were shoved down their throats to pump their stomachs.[31]

The freed American prisoners of war returned as heroes to the United States as soon as they were fit to travel. Sundstrom recalled that his group was met at the New York pier by Sammy Kaye's Orchestra, which played from the time the men left the ship until they boarded the train for Camp Kilmer. At Camp Kilmer another orchestra played music during their meals. After a sixty-day leave to go home, Sundstrom reported to West Palm Beach, Florida, where he spent ten days in the Sands Hotel and "learned how a millionaire lives."[32]

It has been forty years since men like Harvey Sundstrom, Benjamin Gabaldon, Ray Matheny, Wallace Butterfield, and Stanley Blackhurst returned from war-torn Europe as survivors of Nazi POW camps, and much of the bitterness they felt toward their former captors has vanished. When questioned about relations with Germans during their captivity, most of these men recalled some act of kindness shown them by civilians or their guards. The German guard on a detail to which Gabaldon had been assigned went out of his way to find extra food and "good German beer" for the Americans. At Stalag XIIA, a German guard shared his lunch with Blackhurst and others when they were out on burial details. Sundstrom and another prisoner were sent by passenger train to Salzgitter on a tree-planting detail, and they were instructed to change trains in Magdeburg. The crowded station and wait between trains gave the two American prisoners a unique opportunity to talk with several German citizens. Recognizing the war was lost, the Germans expressed their concerns to the two men. "How will the Americans treat us?" "Will they torture us?" "Our leaders tell us that we will be tortured and that we will be raped." Sundstrom tried to ease their anxiety by reassuring them that they would not be harmed but that they should obey the Americans and do what they were asked. On reaching the forestry camp near Salzgitter, Sundstrom found the detachment of guards under the command of a lieutenant who was crippled from a wound suffered on the Russian front. The lieutenant would secure extra food from government warehouses and invite two or three prisoners at a time into his office, where they could eat and listen to news of the war from the BBC. When German authorities came to inspect the camp, the lieutenant told the American prisoners, "I am going to change my way of doing things and my guards are going to follow every command that I give and you are going to think that all hell is breaking loose, but I am doing it to protect you. . . . Just act like you are so scared of me that you would eat dirt if I told you to." The charade went as planned, and after the inspectors left, the camp functioned as before until the Americans in their tanks arrived. When the American soldiers began to abuse the German lieutenant and his guards, the former prisoners quickly came to their defense, insisting they had been well treated and requesting that their former guards be permitted to ride with them on the tanks. Their good treatment was reported to the American colonel in charge, and when he and the German lieutenant spoke, the lieutenant asked "that he be allowed to bid us all goodbye. We all lined up at attention and the lieutenant came to each one of us, shook hands, and pulled us close to him and wished us good luck in our lives."[33] Some American prisoners demonstrated a like measure of humanitarianism when, during the retreat west from the advancing Russian army, they "came to the aid of a collapsing aged guard and shouldered his pack and rifle, a scene that would be often repeated."[34]

Other Germans, who had mistreated American prisoners, paid the ultimate price. The officers and guards responsible for killing escapees at Stalag XVIIB were tried and shot by former prisoners during the anarchy of liberation. German soldiers captured by the recently freed inmates of the Krems camp were forced to give their boots to Russian prisoners.[35] One tragic event for which there was never a specific punishment was the execution of approximately seventy American prisoners by their young German guards at Baugnez, Belgium, on December 17, 1944. The machine-gunning of the American prisoners was an isolated act, yet one which brought fear to other prisoners that such happenings were within the realm of possibility for every American prisoner.

How each American prisoner of war in Germany viewed his treatment depended on the circumstances and his outlook on life. One prisoner said there was not "one act of mercy or compassion all the time while I was a prisoner of war on the part of the Germans." Another conceded that "the Germans had been far from humane or generous, but usually at least minimally correct." Another found that in spite of Hitler, the Germans were Christians and did adhere to the Geneva Convention. "I can in all honesty say that our treatment was not 'horrible,' in any sense of the word. It could have been better, and it certainly could have been worse." Then, with the perspective of how other American prisoners of war fared by comparison, he concluded, "We had it far, far better than our buddies who were prisoners of the Japs, and we were in Paradise compared to what American prisoners went through during the Korean war and the Vietnamese war."[36]

Clock crafted by Italian Service Unit members at Ogden Defense Depot.
(Public Relations Office, Ogden Defense Depot)

SIX

Italian Prisoners of War in Utah

American ships brought Italian as well as German prisoners of war to the states for incarceration. The Italian prisoners had been captured in North Africa, Sicily, and southern Italy prior to the capitulation of Italy to the Allies in early September 1943, and numbered 51,071, or about 12 percent of the total number of German and Italian prisoners in the United States.[1] Utah was an early and an important location for the Italians, whose numbers in the state nearly equalled that of the German prisoners.

Some Italian prisoners came directly from North Africa, others spent months in Egypt and South Africa before ending up in the United States. The Ogden Defense Depot, designated as a POW camp on October 11, 1942, was one of the first ten camps in the country and one of eight locations in Utah where the estimated 7,000 Italian prisoners were sent. The following list, compiled from incomplete records, provides the names of the camps, dates of operations, and an approximate average of the number of Italians in each camp.

Deseret Chemical Warfare Depot	30/11/44 to	5/9/45	100
Fort Douglas	30/11/44 to	5/9/45	207
Dugway	31/5/45 to	15/9/45	94
Hill Air Force Base	15/6/44 to	16/1/46	762
Tooele	30/6/44 to	9/1/46	981
Ogden Depot	9/4/43 to	1/3/45	4,657
Bushnell Hospital	15/1/45 to	22/4/45	280
Salina	30/6/44 to	22/11/44	195

The first Italian prisoners of war arrived at the Ogden Defense Depot from New York on April 9, 1943. The 1,030 men had been captured during recent fighting in North Africa. Other prisoners sent later to Ogden had been captured in 1940 by the British.[2]

Upon arrival at Ogden, the Italian prisoners were processed and assigned to companies of 250 men. The physical condition of the men was of paramount concern. During the first year at Ogden, 2,067 prisoners were admitted to the POW hospital. Respiratory problems and malaria accounted for 886 and 167 cases, respectively, with injuries at 113 cases. Other ailments included Vincent's angina, scabies, gonorrhea, diarrhea, pneumonia, tuberculosis, dysentery, diptheria, impetigo, rheumatic fever, measles, mumps, and nineteen mental cases that were sent from Ogden to Bushnell General Hospital. There were over 17,000 dental cases, with an average of nearly four visits to the dentist for each prisoner, during the first year and a half at Ogden. The number of cases is perhaps representative of the status of dental hygiene at the time. "Many of them had serious mouth conditions including osteomyelitis and necrosis of the jawbones. . . . Most of the men still have teeth missing and about everyone on post has had teeth pulled."[3]

Food was plentiful and weight gains of fifteen to fifty-four pounds were reported among the Italians at Ogden. Italian bakers baked bread and cooks made egg noodles until they were forced, because of sanitary concerns, to use commercially produced noodles. Pasta, rice, soups, and stews were the primary fare. Elaborate menus were provided on such holidays as Thanksgiving, Christmas, and New Year's. Chaplain Raphael Monteleone, a native of Italy who immigrated to the United States in 1933, bragged that the Italian prisoners ate "better than the American soldiers because the Italians have better cooks." Still, the meals were not quite the same as back in Italy: the customary wine was unavailable except at Christmas, vegetable oil was substituted for olive oil, and raw bacon proved an unacceptable substitute for prosciutto.[4]

At Ogden the Italians loaded and unloaded material at the huge warehouses and did road and railroad maintenance around the depot. They also operated a dyeing plant for POW uniforms for use throughout the country, staffed tailor and shoe repair shops, and did some office work. In fifty acres of ground surrounding their camp, the prisoners grew an impressive variety of crops in 1944.[5]

For a time after Italy's surrender to the Allies, the status of the Italian prisoners in the United States remained essentially the same as that of the Germans. After six months, however, Italian service units were set up to better utilize the services of the Italian prisoners who were loyal to the newly organized pro-Allied Italian government under Pietro Bagdolio. However, the process of getting the program started was difficult. Orientation sessions were held for the Italian prisoners to explain the options and to encourage them to give their allegiance to the new Italian government. The men were urged to follow Bagdolio's December 14, 1943, declaration that their duty as Italians was now "to help the Allies in every way possible, excepting actual combat." Those who took up the cause would be joining "the fight for our redemption from the century-old enemy as the very populace in Italy is now doing alongside the Anglo-American forces for the liberation of the homeland."[6] In March 1944 the first Italian prisoners were enrolled, and eventually about 33,000, or 65 percent of the 51,071 Italian prisoners, joined the service units. Those who refused to join remained in camps under the same restrictions as for the German prisoners. Members of the Italian service units were quartered in separate facilities. There were incentives offered the Italian prisoners to join the ISU. Each enlisted man received a standard khaki military uniform with a green shoulder patch with the word "Italy" on it. They were no longer obligated to wear the army fatigues with PW painted on the front and back. They were paid twenty-four dollars a month, with eight dollars in cash and sixteen dollars in post-exchange coupons. They were given the same access as American personnel to most of the camp facilities and were permitted to leave the camp for nearby towns and cities. Some who were reluctant to join were threatened with being thrown in with large numbers of German prisoners of war. Most Italians weighed carefully the prospective advantages against both real and perceived disadvantages. The twenty-four dollars a month represented no actual pay increase over the eighty cents a day they earned as prisoners of war, although payment of one-third in American currency did offer an advantage. The American uniforms would be of little value unless the

Italian Service Unit members at work in warehouse 8D at the Ogden Defense Depot. (Public Relations Office, Ogden Defense Depot)

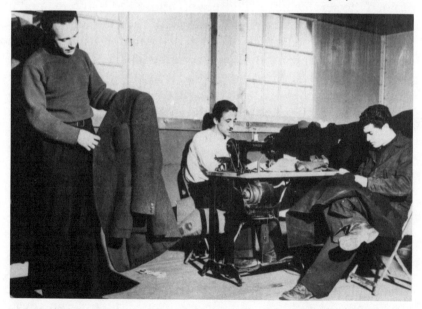

Italian Service Unit members at Ogden relax in their barracks. (Public Relations Office, Ogden Defense Depot)

Italian Service Unit bakers at the Ogden Defense Depot. (Public Relations Office, Ogden Defense Depot).

Delicacies for the 81st Italian Service Unit Company party at the Ogden Defense Depot. (Public Relations Office, Ogden Defense Depot)

vague promises of greater freedom outside the camp became a reality. Many Italians were from areas still held by the Germans, and they feared reprisals against their families if it became known that they were collaborating with the Americans. Some believed that Allied success was only temporary and that their lives and those of their families could be in jeopardy from the vengeful Nazis. Others felt that the applications and signatures were completely unnecessary; if the Americans wanted them to do something, they only had to issue the order and it would be followed. This was especially true for those who had been drafted and were skeptical of volunteering for anything.

One of the primary reasons for creating the Italian service units was to help meet the manpower needs on the West Coast as the Allied offensive against Japan gained momentum. The Italians did well with on-the-job training and made excellent workers in supply depots such as at Ogden. That Americans seemed more anxious to accommodate the Italian prisoners than they did the Germans is reflected in the Italian classes that were held at Hill Field for those personnel who worked directly with the Italians.[7]

In Ogden, the Italian service unit concept was launched on August 29, 1944. After more than four years fighting against the Allies, it was hard to switch sides. With only a limited view of the situation, the Italian prisoners were naturally suspicious and were susceptible to the arguments of those prisoners who claimed that their families in Italy would be persecuted and that they would be sent back as Allied soldiers to fight against the Germans. When it came time to make a choice, approximately 2,300 of the 4,000 Italians at the Ogden depot cast their lot with the new service organization. Efforts to persuade the others were largely unsuccessful. Some men were content to remain prisoners of war, assured that they would have good food, proper care, adequate shelter, and sufficient clothing. When two Italian officers were sent to Ogden to try to change the minds of those who did not join, they were met with boos and rocks. Although some men indicated they might sign, when the time came to meet with one of the officers, none of the prisoners showed up. Capt. S. T. Viviano reported that the effort was unsuccessful: "The non-signers have developed a strong resistance against signing. All that was accomplished by these officers was the conformation of this resistance."[8] Those who refused to join the Italian service units were separated from the others and many were sent to Camp Rupert, Idaho, and Tulare Lake, California. In February 1944, Ogden officials had submitted a list of nearly 100 Italian prisoners to Washington, D.C., urging that the men be transferred because they were either pro-Fascists likely to commit sabotage at the military installation or were incorrigibles and misfits, creating disturbances and refusing to work outside the compounds, and were "setting a bad example to other prisoners of war."[9]

Both Italian service unit camps and regular Italian POW camps existed in Utah. The service units were located at Ogden and Tooele. The Italian prisoners at Hill Field, who did not join the service units, were described as being "mostly all pro-Fascists." They were "very suspicious and yell 'propaganda' at almost anything that seems tainted or contrary to their beliefs." They resented those who had joined the Italian service units, and when some from the service units were returned to Hill Field, they had to be segregated from the other Italian prisoners.[10]

But the service units could foment trouble as well. The Ogden camp executive officer "considered the Italian service units a great 'pain in the neck.'" Even after the end of the war, many of the Italians who joined the service units demonstrated "strong fascist sympathies" and "egged on" German prisoners of war to cause as much trouble for the Americans as they could. At Ogden, an American typing instructor complained that her Italian students "insisted on rest periods every hour, would sometimes talk for twenty minutes to get out of two minutes' work, were hard to discipline, and completely disinterested in achievement."[11]

Theft was a major concern of American authorities: "The change from prisoner of war status to Italian service units did not seem to make any change for the better in the epidemic of stealing among these men." Indeed, the new freedoms seemed to intensify the theft of everything from "metal washers to use in slot machines to radios, flashlights, and innumerable articles discovered in the periodic 'shakedowns.'" When fifteen Italians were arrested and confined awaiting trial for sneaking out of the depot and going into Ogden, the entire Italian service unit camp staged a sit-down strike in protest on May 30, 1944.[12] There were other incidents, some of a more serious nature. On May 30, 1945, twenty

Italian prisoners at Fort Douglas were confined to the post guard-house for "administrative punishment" because they had quit their shift in the post laundry at 4:00 P.M. instead of a half-hour later, the scheduled time. The Italians argued that since the civilian employees in the laundry were permitted to quit at 4:00 P.M., they should be treated accordingly. The next day, the 164 Italians, nearly their entire number at the fort, joined in a sympathy strike. All of the Italian prisoners were placed in wire enclosures out of doors and given only bread and water until they called off the strike nearly four and a half days later.[13]

Italian newspapers published at the Ogden depot and Hill Field were *Domani* (*The Italy of Tomorrow*) at the former and *Il Mine* (short for minestrone) at the latter. Prizes of twenty-five dollars for the best article and fifteen dollars for the second best were offered. As far as recreational and educational opportunities were concerned, Hill Field was considered one of the best Italian camps. There were three English language classes, an artistic drawing class, a thirteen-piece orchestra, and a theater group. Prisoners made a variety of handicraft items, perhaps the most popular being the reworking of American silver coins as jewelry. They made scale models of submarines and battleships, and one prisoner "made a clock out of parts of a hardwood chair, a talcum can and nails bent for the pendulum."[14]

As for sports, they were well organized with a variety of activities. ISU soccer teams were permitted to join a local Utah soccer league, and a team from Ogden that played Salt Lake City teams composed mostly of German and other European-born immigrants won the league championship two years in a row.[15]

Perhaps the most attractive opportunity for the ISU men was the chance to leave their camp to enjoy a weekend with an Italian American family. Filippo Notarianni, an employee at the Tooele Army Depot, made a regular practice of having ISU soldiers from Tooele join his family at their Magna, Utah, home for a meal, conversation, and music.[16]

For others, the opportunity to associate with women whom they met on the job or through social activities was a significant change from their POW status when American officials consciously sought to prevent contact by Italian and German prisoners with American civilians—especially women. Interaction among the

Italians and American women was encouraged with dances arranged in the camps. When Italians were allowed to go into town in groups of four or five, they were escorted by an American soldier. The result was predictable: "These good-natured, often good-looking young men pursued and at times were pursued by young girls, wives whose spouses were overseas, middle-aged widows, and, in the second instance, by angry husbands and irate fathers."[17] At the Ogden Depot, "some of the female employees encourage familiarity, not realizing the different social standards of the Italians, who in turn fail to discriminate between the common and the true woman." As a consequence, some women did not appreciate "the boisterous shouting, whistling, insolent glances, remarks, and advances from the prisoners."[18] In Salina, unconfirmed reports had three local girls running off with three Italian prisoners; when they were apprehended, the three Italians were returned to the prison camp and the three young girls to their parents.[19]

Perhaps advocates of the Italian service units overstated the freedom and rights the Italians could expect. Difficulties arose "because the Italians assumed that since they had signed up with the Italian service units they would be able to have the same liberties as American soldiers such as free passes to go into Ogden without guard." Disappointed with what many considered a broken promise, the Italians were indignant with American authorities who claimed to understand their position but were fearful of public repercussions since Utahns still considered the Italian prisoners enemies. Attempting to meet the commitment for greater freedom, authorities provided government trucks and gas for Sunday trips and picnics for one company each weekend. A further concession allowed those companies not scheduled for the motorized outings to go into the mountains on foot "provided no town or village is entered, nor ranks broken in the vicinity of farm houses." Where German POW companies would have gladly accepted the offer of a hike in Utah's mountains, the Italians were unenthusiastic. Even the supervised group tours "met with an indifferent, if not sullen reception." Unable to appease the Italians, who saw the tours as much less than the expected trips into Ogden on their own, and sensitive to public criticism that the army was squandering much-needed gas on enemy prisoners, depot officials decided to discontinue the organized outings. A compromise of sorts was reached as the ISU members were allowed to go into Ogden if escorted by an American soldier.[20]

In Ogden, St. Joseph's Hospitality House became the center of attraction for the Italians. Located in the basement of St. Joseph's Catholic Church, the Hospitality House was open four nights a week—one night for officers and three nights for enlisted men. A jukebox and games were provided by Catholic groups in Ogden and Salt Lake City. The greatest attraction, however, was the American girls. Initially, the ratio was approximately one girl for every four men, but in time the ratio of girls to men improved considerably." A "clubhouse" was also established in Ogden, with Lila Petersen of the personnel relations office at the Ogden depot appointed the official hostess. The clubhouse had a stage large enough for the twenty-five piece band, and the weekly entertainment schedule included bingo and other games, company parties, birthday celebrations, concerts, and other social activities.[21]

Many Americans resented what they considered special treatment for the prisoners of war. American Legion posts sent scores of angry resolutions and hundreds of letters to congressmen protesting the soft treatment of the enemies who were on American soil. One protester asked, "If these Italians are prisoners of war, why are they given such special treatment? If they are our allies, why don't they go home and fight?" Bill Cunningham, columnist for the *Boston Herald*, echoed the sentiments of thousands when he wrote that to reward men who were in America "only by virtue of having shot it out on the battlefield with American kids and lost" by allowing them to wear American uniforms; inviting them as houseguests; arranging dances; providing them "with so many hundreds of pounds of Italian pastry, bocci balls and operatic recordings"; and taking them on sightseeing tours, outings, picnics, and to special church services "on our almost priceless tires and rationed gas . . . is a queer way of adding up the score." The American public, putting German prisoners in the same category as the Italians, "thought all prisoners of war were dancing with American girls, touring American cities, smoking countless packages of cigarettes, and squandering the items civilians had to purchase with ration stamps and hard-earned money."[22] Congressman Charles B. Hoeven of Iowa spoke about the way prisoners were "coddled" in his region. He made no distinction between German and Italian prisoners in his exaggeration of conditions in one camp with which he was familiar by charging that "[it] is supplied with every luxury—innerspring beds, the newest type of Frigidaire, and the finest food." He condemned this situation by claiming to know of a hospital that had been unable to get a new refrigerator despite a long-standing request.[23]

The freedoms granted the ISU members, especially the contact they were allowed with American women, led to resentment among American personnel against the Italians. Although fraternization between any group of prisoners and women civilians would have undoubtedly created difficulties, some Americans maintained that the Italians were especially troublesome and that transfers of prisoners from such places as Brigham City and Hill Field were because of indiscretions with American women. American authorities, in an official history of the prisoners of war in the United States, recognized the problem: "There were incidents of which the War Department cannot well be proud, but which were inevitable in view of all the circumstances. Prisoners' friendships with American young women resulted in not a few illegitimate pregnancies." These situations often led to requests by the young women and some family members for exceptions to the restrictions against marriage. However, the War Department stood firm, maintaining, "To have granted an exception to the anti-marriage rule in pregnancy cases would have placed a premium on immoral relationships."[24]

The story of Gene Miconi, who was in Ogden from April 1943 until the summer of 1946, offers an interesting, though perhaps not typical, glimpse of life in an Italian service unit. Born March 27, 1919, in Rome, Miconi was drafted into the Italian army in 1939. After spending two years near the Italian-French border, Miconi's regiment was sent to North Africa. Following his capture by Australian soldiers at Tobruck, he was transferred first to English then later to American custody. He spent nine months as a prisoner of war in Egypt and another nine months in South Africa before reaching the United States. He was sent directly to Ogden, arriving in November 1943, and signed up for the ISU when the opportunity arose. At the Ogden depot, Miconi was treated just like any other worker and was able to make the acquaintance of American women with whom he worked. A romance developed between Miconi and

one of the American women, and they took advantage of opportunities to meet at the camp recreation center or in town when
he had a pass and could find an American soldier to escort him.
The Italians used bribery, paying a dollar each, to get the soldiers
to take them into the city; and, if all else failed, there were places
where they could slip undetected under the three strands of barbed
wire that enclosed the camp to meet their women friends. If arrangements were made to have another prisoner answer the roll
call, the excursions could last for an entire weekend.

With the end of the war, Miconi tried to stay in Ogden, but was
required to return to Italy. Following the birth of their son, Miconi's
American sweetheart flew to Rome, where she and Miconi were
married on September 30, 1946. With the legal obstacles out of
the way, Miconi was able to return to America as the spouse of a
United States citizen. Moving into the economic life of Ogden, he
established a tile-laying business which, since his retirement, has
passed to his sons.[25]

Miconi was one of at least five former Italian prisoners of war
who made their way back to Utah as spouses of women who undertook the long journey to Italy to marry them. Ruggerio Purin
was captured in Tunisia, North Africa, early in June 1943 and, after
a couple of transfers between camps in the United States, was sent
west to Hill Field. He met his future wife just seventeen days before he was returned to Italy after the war was over. She eventually joined him in Italy, where they were married. Although he
deeply loved Italy, he consented to return to America at the insis-
tence of his bride. Twenty years later, he compared his treatment
as an Italian soldier with that as an Italian prisoner of war in the
United States: "I was treated better by the American Army than by
my own Italian Army. I suffered while in the Italian Army. There
were various times when I even had to beg for food from civilians
in order to stay alive." He recalled "how humane my treatment was
here as a prisoner of war. Otherwise, I would never have returned
to live in this country. I think the treatment is a credit to the United
States."[26]

Although the treatment of the Italian prisoners may have appeared generous, they nonetheless occupied a second-class status that was unrelated to their status as prisoners of war. To expect
more at a time when other minority and ethnic groups, including

the Italian Americans in some parts of the country, were viewed as second-class citizens would have been unrealistic. Italian immigrants had entered Utah in large numbers at the turn of the century to work in the coalfields and the Bingham Copper Mine and on the railroads. Non-Mormon, foreign, viewed as radical and un-American in their attraction to and support of labor unions and liberal policies, and often considered racially inferior, Utah's Italian community was not looked on with great favor by the dominant, Mormon American-born population. That members of the service units did not meet with greater prejudice in a state with a tradition of antiforeign/nativistic tendencies was due to their location in the camps around Ogden—a city that since the nineteenth century had been a more liberal and progressive city than others in the state—the tremendous social impact caused by the arrival of military personnel and civilian workers from all over the country; the acceptance of the ISU men by Utah's Italian community, which was gaining acceptance, and in some quarters, respect; and the realization that the Italian prisoners were one small manifestation of the tremendous and irreversible change from a traditional agricultural economy to one dependent on the defense industry.

That the Italian POW experience in the United States was in significant contrast to that of the German prisoners of war cannot be denied. However, for those German prisoners who looked with optimism to the future, the treatment by the Americans of their one-time Italian enemies suggested that perhaps their own treatment at the hands of the Americans would improve once the war was over.

SEVEN

Loyalty and Resistance

When Americans learned that German prisoners of war were being sent to the United States, their first question was how would the arrogant and fanatical Nazis conduct themselves once in the country. Between the rise of Adolf Hitler to power in 1933 and the arrival of the first German prisoners in 1943, a strong resentment of Germans and dislike for Germany had emerged in America. Germany, defeated in World War I only a few years before, was now the ungrateful, ill-mannered, headstrong bully of the Western world. Americans, with their propensity for fair play and for judging situations as either good or evil—and sensing that they were viewed as inferior by Europeans in general and by Germans in particular—felt little initial compassion for the prisoners. Americans, anticipating conflict and struggle when face to face with the attitudes and behavior of fascism, looked with apprehension toward the coming deluge of prisoners from abroad.

German soldiers had been instructed on how to conduct themselves if captured. They were to be wary of listening devices, to keep secret any special skills, and to do as little as possible if assigned to a work detail. They were to study the Geneva Convention so they could insist on their rights, keep physically fit and strong, and take advantage of every opportunity to escape. Finally, prisoners were warned that after the war they would have to account for anything which went against regulations.[1]

German prisoners who arrived in 1944 were lectured by Afrika Korps prisoners, who had arrived earlier, that there was strength in unity, which would prevent the Americans from getting the better of them. The German prisoners claimed that their discipline and training was much admired by the Americans. According to a former prisoner: "When our company came marching in, goosestepping, halting in unison and then clicking our heels, then the American officers just watched and said my soldiers will do that tomorrow."[2]

Although many of the one thousand men who arrived at Camp Warner in Tooele, Utah, in January 1944 were still loyal to the Nazi cause, there were some who were not. Lt. Col. Frank E. Meek, the camp commander, found it necessary to request the transfer of three prisoners, August Allabauer, Harald Koberne, and Franz Schneider because of the threats of violence made against them for their anti-Nazi statements to other prisoners. The three men had also cooperated with the camp's intelligence officer, providing "much valuable information concerning saboteurs and agitators among the other prisoners." One of the apparent agitators fingered by the three men was the camp spokesman, whose ardent nazism landed him a transfer from Camp Warner to the special camp at Alva, Oklahoma, where he would be with other incorrigible Nazis.[3] A group of 450 prisoners, who arrived in Ogden on December 29, 1944, from Scottsbluff, Nebraska, were described as "insolent, arrogant, pro-Nazi" veterans of the Afrika Korps who wore "the German uniform conspiciously in the compound in order to intimidate those prisoners of war who have been cooperative and who may not share the political beliefs of the pro-Nazis."[4]

In 1944 there was probably no "safe" camp for those who spoke against Hitler. Edwin Pelz recalled that one of the men in his group concluded that since America was an ally of Soviet Russia there was no danger in declaring himself a Communist. When he did so, "hundreds of other prisoners chased him around the camp, throwing stones at him and trying to lynch him." The near riot was quelled by the American guards. Pelz explained, "In our eyes at that time he was a traitor and everyone tried to spit in his face when he was taken away by the guards."[5] A former German prisoner, writing of his sojourn in Camp Lordsburg, New Mexico, declared that the worst thing was the political terror waged by the fanatical Nazis in the camp, most of whom had been captured in Africa. It was unwise to express anything against Hitler or the Third Reich. The men simply would not admit that the war was lost.[6]

Herbert Barkhoff described his first camp in America as "a true reflection of Nazi Germany." A handful of zealous Nazis and supermilitarists held the rest of the prisoners in check through terrorism. A camp gestapo compiled a list of those whom it considered candidates for military tribunals and concentration camps. Barkhoff found that in some camps both the ardent Nazis and the dedicated Communists kept their own lists of prisoners from whom they would demand an accounting after the war. Not surprising, some individuals' names could be found on both lists.[7] An American reporter concluded that, even if fanatical nazism were excluded from consideration, "German militarism is buried so deep in their minds . . . that . . . this militarism may never wear off, at least not in this generation."[8] Prisoners who spent time in a serious study of English were apt to be viewed as traitors, since, according to the fanatics, "After the war's over, everybody is going to speak German here. The whole world is going to speak German."[9]

In order to protect prisoners from violence, a notice, written in German and signed by the commanding officer, was posted in each compound. A prisoner who believed "that his life is in danger or that he may suffer physical injury at the hands of other prisoners . . . will immediately report that fact personally to any American officer . . . without consulting his spokesman." Any prisoner who followed these instructions was assured of adequate protection "by the camp commander by segregation, transfer or other means." The notice concluded with the warning that "prisoners who mistreat fellow prisoners will be severely punished."[10]

Pro-Nazi prisoners circulated false reports about German military successes to maintain a stronghold on the other prisoners. At Ogden, the camp spokesman, an Austrian with "very definite anti-Nazi sympathies," had quite a bit of trouble with "the strong-arm boys in the compound" until they were separated from the others. Slowly the situation improved as those considered incorrigible Nazis were removed from the camps and placed in special camps with other hard-core Nazis. However, it was not until after Germany's surrender that it was possible "to express openly another political opinion without endangering your life."[11]

Although most camps housed prisoners whose attitudes toward nazism varied, special camps were established to house the hard-core Nazis at Camp Alva, Oklahoma; Camp Pima, Arizona; and

Camp Huntsville, Texas. Ardent anti-Nazis were sent to Camp Campbell, Kentucky; Fort Devens, Massachusetts; and Camp Rushton, Louisiana.

Nazism died hard in some prisoners. In Ogden there were manifestations of continued Nazi sentiment even after the end of the war. When camp commander Arthur J. Ericsson made a public announcement to the prisoners that hostilities had ended in Europe, many did not believe him; and clandestine newspapers, typed and mimeographed sheets, circulated among the prisoners urging them not to lose faith because Germany would be victorious. Nearly a year after Germany's defeat, Sture Persson talked in private with some of the German prisoners in Rupert, Idaho. "It gave me a rather discouraging feeling as they seemed to hold on at heart to their old ideas and ideals very much. The occupying powers in Germany were given much blame and the only guilt they seemed to feel was that Germany had lost the war and not won it."[12]

When he and his comrades arrived in Florence, Arizona, in 1944 prior to his transfer to Bushnell Hospital, Paul Hupfner found a group of German prisoners screaming that they should sign nothing and agree not to work for the Americans. The new arrivals were separated from the others, who screamed "Sieg heil!" whenever an American officer came into their compound and who threatened those who did work with hanging as traitors to the fatherland when they returned to Germany.[13]

The agreement that men like Paul Hupfner and others were expected to sign read: "I herewith promise on the honor of a German soldier, that, during the tenure of this parole, I will not escape and will not undertake anything which could make easy an escape for myself or another prisoner, or encourage same." The agreement called for the prisoners to do their work assignments to the best of their ability, return promptly to camp from their assigned tasks, and do nothing that would in any way be injurious to the interests of the United States. It concluded with the provision that promises made to honor the agreement could be withdrawn by a written notice to the company commander.[14]

Prisoners who signed the agreement—and most regular soldiers did—adhered to the promises made, but the agreement did not alter their loyalty to Germany. Camp commanders were instructed to assess the strength of Nazi sentiment in their camps by considering five activities as indications of Nazi influence: "Nazi indoctrinated pamphlets and newspapers, fake rumors created by 'fluster propaganda,' unwillingness of prisoners to cooperate with camp authorities, mass demonstrations and sit-down strikes, and kangaroo courts."[15]

One indication of the prisoners' ties to Nazi Germany was their enthusiastic response to the Ardennes offensive, or the Battle of the Bulge as Americans called it. At Fort Robinson, Nebraska, the prisoners celebrated the Ardennes offensive by flying a large swastika flag in the top of a tree. Frederick Weber described the attitudes of many German prisoners at Ogden on learning about the Ardennes offensive as, "Here is the breakthrough we had been waiting for. Now we would be saved." Another prisoner in Ogden noted that prior to the news of the offensive, "the prisoners had been very tame and timid, or intimidated." But afterward, their timidity turned to defiance. "Hey, Germany is going to win the war anyway. We knew it all the time. . . . You are going to be in our camp. We are going to trade places."[16]

Eric Kososik recalled that there were some at Ogden as late as March 1945 who thought Germany would still win the war with the long-promised secret weapon. However, most prisoners recognized that they had to be very discreet in expressing their political views. "We didn't dare say anything. If I had said something and Germany did win the war, then they could come back on me. They knew my name, they knew my face, and they would have remembered me."[17]

To reduce tensions among the prisoners, Commander Ericsson ordered that German uniforms could no longer be worn in the Ogden compound. The uniforms were locked in a special room and returned to the prisoners when they left Utah. Prior to this order, a number of the prisoners "made sure that they had their swastika insignias and displayed them. If someone had lost his uniform, he went to the tailor and had a new one made."[18] Shortly after the ban on German uniforms was announced, two officers, German medical doctors, arrived in the camp. Unaware of the political tensions in the camp and the ban on uniforms, they accepted an invitation to the compound canteen, where "they appeared in uniform with their decorations and gave the Nazi salute." Other prisoners in the canteen, believing their action was a provocation, attacked and severely beat the two unfortunate officers, leaving one with a broken nose. There was also a short-lived boycott of the compound hospital because of the supposedly Nazi doctors who had been sent to Ogden. In time, confidence was restored and patients returned when they realized that the physicians "did not dream of stirring up politics, for they are doctors above everything and nothing else . . . [and] are not trying to do anything except carry on their profession."[19]

Some prisoners not only demonstrated their loyalty to Germany and its leader but also exhibited definite evidence that Nazi doctrine, such as anti-Semitism, had accompanied them to the United States. On one occasion, hundreds of crudely printed leaflets were thrown from a POW train warning Americans that they were being used by Jews. One read: "Americans, who is sitting behind the front line? The Jews. Who gets killed in action? The American Soldier! . . . Jews are the Americans' ruin and Jews need the American people for their personal interest."[20]

The Pro-Nazi sentiment did provide for humorous situations. According to one story, an American solder was marching a group of prisoners down a road in Texas. He needed to stop the group, but either forgetting or not knowing that the world "halt" means the same in English and German, he threw up his arm hoping the gesture would bring the Germans to a stop. It worked: "The entire platoon came to attention, shot their arms upward, and chorused, 'Heil Hitler!' " In Chandler, Arizona, German prisoners unfurled a swastika flag from the back of the truck as it took them to and from the cotton fields.[21]

During the Christmas season of 1944, some ornaments sent to the prisoners through the International Red Cross arrived in Utah with hidden messages from Germany. The messages were inside artificial walnuts and were intended to remind the men of home and to encourage them to remain loyal to their oaths as German soldiers. Bookmarks with bright drawings of German and Austrian cities and national landmarks that were sent to the prisoners were considered instruments of propaganda. Some also carried words of encouragement, such as "I remain faithful," "By the lamplight we want to stand as before, Lili Marleen," and "Your heart will be my anchor." Intelligence officers in camps of the Ninth Service Command were informed by Fort Douglas officers to examine all

Christmas tree ornaments received from the International Red Cross and send to Utah any examples of secret messages or Nazi trinkets that were found.[22] In Tooele, Col. Frank E. Meek was in a quandary as to how to dispose of 5,000 packages of cigarette papers that had been received from the German Red Cross because of the possibility that messages were included in them.

The German prisoners were a trial for their American guards, especially before the war ended. The prisoners hurled insults at them, and under the circumstances, it was easy to understand why a guard might "bust them in the nose or shoot in the air" if pushed too far.[23] On one occasion, the guard of a Tooele work detail fired his rifle at the prisoners because they defied his orders against smoking. Luckily, he did not hit any of them.[24]

A more widespread act of defiance occurred on April 20, 1944, when the entire camp refused to work in honor of Adolf Hitler's birthday. The prisoners not only refused to work but also made elaborate plans to celebrate Hitler's birthday with "cakes, pastries, and several different kinds of meat plus other dainties which the prisoners had obviously been saving for the occasion." The prisoners were permitted to enjoy the food only because the camp commander concluded that the waste of food would otherwise be too great. This was the limit of his concession, however, and when the prisoners refused to work, he forced them all out of the compound area and into the unprotected recreation area, where rain—then snow—dampened the auspicious celebration.[25] In other camps Hitler's birthday was celebrated in a more dramatic fashion. Karl Altkruger participated in one such event in which Hitler was honored with songs and a torchlight parade complete with swastika flags. Altkruger and the others were punished with confinement and no food for three days. Fortunately, prisoners from other compounds threw food to them.[26] There were other kinds of demonstrations of loyalty to Adolf Hitler. When German prisoners in Aliceville, Alabama, learned of the attempt to assassinate Hitler in his headquarters on July 20, 1944, they marched from their morning roll call to the camp chapel and held a prayer service to thank God for saving their leader.[27]

Ideology was not at the root of all disturbances. In Camp Rupert, Idaho, prisoners called a strike because of what they considered very strenuous work requirements. During the strike three prisoners attacked and beat an American officer, for which they were arrested and sent to Fort Douglas, Utah, for trial. As a result, there was a great deal of bitterness between the German prisoners and their captors. The camp spokesman was replaced, and instead of allowing the prisoners to elect a new spokesman and other company leaders, the Americans appointed them.[28] Such actions did not necessarily occur because prisoners were responding out of pro-Nazi sentiments. In his study of the administration of German POW camps, Edward J. Pluth was concerned with the dividing line between the soldier as a Nazi and the soldier as a patriot. "Did an expression of hope for German victory in the war mirror Nazi sentiments or only pride in the German military forces?" Pluth concluded that it was extremely difficult to determine to what extent certain actions were grounded in Nazi influence. He argued that "although German camp leaders might urge work slowdowns and censor reading material, such actions were not *ipso facto* evidence of Nazi influence."[29] Many of the German prisoners were Nazis when in a group and had to be, "but when you got [them] by themselves they didn't have any morale underneath. Inside they seemed naked and defenseless."[30]

Theft, pilfering, and minor acts of sabotage were perpetrated by German prisoners in almost every camp—just as they were by American prisoners of war in German camps—and seemed to have little to do with ideology. The defense depots were a prime target. Josef Becker, who worked in Fort Lewis unloading boxcars of material sent back from Alaska, admitted that prisoners did steal from their American captors. Sometimes the prisoners were lucky and the guards allowed them to pass without an inspection. Other times, the guards searched the prisoners for stolen goods, which meant that those in the front ranks were out of luck. Those further back had time to dispose of the items through what was called "the emergency drop. We did not have the items secured very tightly. . . . So when 3,000 men marched into camp, you can imagine what it looked like after they passed."[31]

Strict measures were taken in Ogden to prevent pilfering. Richard Boettger admitted that "in Ogden, the German prisoners of war, generally speaking, stole whatever they could steal. . . . Nowhere else were we so thoroughly searched as at Ogden. Not one week passed that they did not thoroughly search our barracks. They

even looked in our toothpaste to see if they could find anything
. . . and resorted to putting powder on items so that they could
trace who had stolen them." When the Americans searched the
prison barracks to look for unauthorized items, they were usually
accompanied by German prisoners. On the one occasion that this
did not happen at Clearfield, prisoners complained that a number of private items were missing. Although the American officials
admitted their mistake, they denied that any items had been taken
since the Americans who conducted the inspections were
thoroughly searched after they left the barracks and no stolen items
were uncovered. Stories circulated among the prisoners about comrades who stole American goods and sold them to civilians for cash.
In April 19, 1945, there were thirty-seven prisoners of war in the
guardhouse, most of whom were there for stealing. The tempta-
tion was great. With such extensive operations and large quantities of material, there was plenty of opportunity to "requisition"
goods and material for personal use. Still, "if they caught someone, they took him away, cut his hair and locked him up for four
weeks."[32]

In addition to theft, there were petty acts of sabotage and
general mischief. Prisoners would request trousers thirty-five inches
in length regardless of their measurements. The men would then
cut the legs off and use the pants for shorts and in the process
"waste more material than would be possible were they to draw
their correct sizes." The prisoners also stole combat infantry merit
badges made out of sterling silver and melted them down for rings.
Ernst Luders, who was sent to Utah in late 1944, admitted that while
at work in an Illinois cannery he made a practice of throwing away
good corn and filling the cans with bad corn, not sealing the cans
properly, or putting pieces of paper with a swastika in the can just
before the lid was sealed. Reflecting on such deeds, Luders said,
"It was all quite childish, but of the thousands of cans that we filled,
to ruin a few hundred cans, that did not make much difference."
The general goal was to make "every effort . . . to sabotage the
American war effort without running the risk of being detected."[33]
Even camp pets were pressed into service. A number of dogs that
were adopted by the prisoners accompanied the men outside the
compound on their work details. Oblivious to camp rules, the dogs
would bound past the guards into the camp as the prisoners were

returning from their work and being searched by guards looking for stolen goods and excessive quantities of cigarettes. Since the dogs were never searched, some innovative prisoners "fastened packs of cigarettes under the bellies of the dogs with a band. Many cigarettes were smuggled into the camp, but one day an MP discovered what we were doing and that was the end to a full supply of cigarettes. The dogs in our camp were caught and hauled away. We could no longer keep any dogs in the camp." In recounting the same story, Leonhard Mombar declared the dogs were not only removed from camp because of the smuggling but were also shot by one of the guards for "committing an act of sabotage."[34]

Accompanying the animosity of the prisoners that was directed toward the Americans was the tension between German natives and those from lands annexed or occupied by Germany. Defeat, the revealed horrors of the Nazis, and the selective memory of a "forced" annexation brought a churlish response to German prisoners from their former Austrian comrades at camps throughout the country. Although both groups had fought on the side of the Third Reich of Austrian-born Adolf Hitler, the Austrians, at least as the war came to a close, held the Germans responsible for the war and considered themselves the victims of German militarism. Georg Hirschmann recalled that the clash between Austrians and Germans was most apparent on the soccer field when the two groups played against each other. Although camp police were present at games, fights often broke out "not because of soccer, but because of politics." Eric Kososik also described the high feelings especially evident during soccer games. "Sometimes an Austrian would kick a German in the shin, or a German would kick an Austrian during a soccer game and a fight would start." When the news reported the Russian occupation of Vienna, Austrian prisoners at Ogden proclaimed that "Vienna has been liberated from the Nazis. But it did not take long before the reports came of what the Russians were doing, and the Austrian prisoners did not say anything else." Later, Hirschmann had an encounter with the Austrians when, through a misunderstanding, he was transferred to an Austrian group. In spite of his request for assistance, the Austrians refused to help him move his footlocker and other possessions into the barracks. He spent only one night with the Austrians. They charged him with being a Nazi and vowed not to work with him. The next day he was returned to his own group. He recalled: "Although I was no Nazi, for the Austrians if you were a German you were a Nazi." Political discussions about the war also increased tensions. "There were a few arguments about politics among those who thought Germany was going to win. They would start talking politics about the war and get red faced." The camp leader, who was Austrian, separated those who did not get along, so "the Austrians tended to group together in the barracks."[35] Ernst Luders described the effect the hostility had on individual relationships. An older Austrian in his group, ten or fifteen years senior to the younger prisoners, had come to be considered something of a father figure. "Just as the war was over, he was no longer a German; he was now an Austrian." What bothered the men was not his desire to be identified as an Austrian, but "that he no longer wanted to have anything to do with us."[36]

Further evidence of the Austrian/German conflict is found in the pages of *Unser Leben*. Austrians were incensed when an article on the writing of "Silent Night, Holy Night" appeared in the Christmas 1945 issue under the title "The History of a German Christmas Carol." The next issue carried a correction which pointed out that the world's most beloved Christmas song had been written and composed by two Austrians. Anticipating an argument that since the song was composed in the German language it was therefore a German song, the writer maintained that just as you could not regard Englishmen as Americans or Americans as Englishmen because they spoke the same language, it was an error to call Austrians Germans. "Silent Night, Holy Night" was held to reflect an Austrian, not German, mentality. The correction asked that Germans honor and treasure the accomplishments of their neighbors.[37]

Even among the Austrians there were divisions and some tensions. In Logan, where the entire camp was made up of Austrians, the camp spokesman and other movers and shakers were all from Vienna. "It was so that the Viennese had everything in the hand, there were so many of them that they did not let anyone else in." Still there were no serious problems under such circumstances; Rudolf Weltin compared the groups to those that undoubtedly existed among Americans from the North and South, East and West.[38]

Both Austrian and German prisoners in Ogden were required during the summer of 1945 to view a film, with photography by the American press and entitled *German Atrocities,* of the horror and inhumanity of the Nazi concentration camps in Europe. Response to the film was varied. Some were convinced the film was the work of American propagandists. Georg Hirschmann recalled that every prisoner had to sign a statement that he had seen the film. "We did not believe it. We simply could not believe that there were such people that could do something like that. We said it was propaganda."[39] Other prisoners claimed that guards armed with blackjacks stood behind the last row and threatened to hit them "in case we did not believe what was shown on the screen." Another prisoner held that the Americans were very disappointed when the Germans watching the film were photographed and the pictures disclosed that only part of the prisoners were interested in the film, whereas the others were fed up with what they considered excessive American propaganda.[40] After seeing the film, one Ogden prisoner concluded that "Hollywood had been working overtime" to produce the film and simply did not believe what had been depicted on the screen.[41] But most were affected by the film and even those who charged the Americans with a gross propaganda effort must have wondered if it did not contain some truth. Heinz Siegel recalled that after seeing the film the prisoners took up a collection and "nearly everyone donated all their money for the survivors." In other camps, money was sent to the German Red Cross for use in assisting those who had "suffered the most during the years of the German government." One camp spokesman for the prisoners reported that the film had convinced the whole company that "the German government . . . has mistreated and tortured to death citizens, foreigners, and prisoners of war in concentration camps and POW camps. . . . We hope that all those criminals, regardless of class, religion, party, organization or military unit, will suffer just punishment."[42] A contemporary account, written by Joachim Oertel and published in the August issue of *Unser Leben* noted that many prisoners were deeply moved by the film, yet there were perhaps those who shared Georg Hirschmann's mistrust. Oertel recorded that the prisoners "stand evenly shaken by the fact that in a Germany that calls itself civilized, there were these kinds of crimes. . . . Shamed, humbled, and deeply angered, we learned of the inhumanity that no one had held to be possible. . . . That sadists . . . were allowed free reign." Oertel went on to indict anyone who would still honor the name of Hitler and who "still has a spark of Nazism in him." Such men he judged as criminals since "by their loyalty they endorsed the atrocities depicted in the film. . . . The film we saw has left deep marks in our hearts. Never should we forget the stain which burns in us like a hot iron, and in the future we must prove to the world that we are worthy to be recognized as members of the society of mankind."[43]

The response from other camps reflected a willingness among the prisoners to accept the truth about the concentration camps, but they claimed to be unaware of the atrocities. The rationale of one prisoner was that the soldiers had fought with their lives for Germany but that neither the soldiers at the front nor their families at home had known about the heinous crimes being committed in the concentration camps. He concluded that it was incumbent upon them as soldiers to declare that they had no knowledge of or part in the disgraceful crimes that had been committed.[44] Some of the prisoners captured late in the war realized that the situation in Germany had deteriorated to the point where, as one reported, "I personally did not want Germany to win the war because I saw there was too much inhumane treatment toward the Jewish and Polish people." He had witnessed Russian prisoners walking around with rags on their feet who were beaten with rifle butts for taking potato peels. "When I saw the way they were treated, I was very deeply disturbed. . . . I had the feeling then, and I was only 16, that something was deeply wrong."[45]

Despite the film, articles in *Unser Leben*, and lively debates, the flame of nazism still flickered in the Ogden camp. Six months after the capitulation of Germany, charges continued to be made that Hitler and nazism were not dead for some Germans. One prisoner wrote that he had worked, eaten, played, and lived in a confined space with fellow prisoners for months. "I am a witness of what you say to one another, and what has been said to me. . . . We cannot hide anything from one another. I know, because you have given me the proof, that the Hitler Youth is not dead, not yet." He went on to explain that he made no accusations, did not intend to scold or convert his comrades. He reasoned that they continued to hold such views because of their training during the past twelve years, which had not fostered free and harmonic development of personality or independent thinking, but instead had sought to develop blind faith and unquestioning obedience through a fanatical hate-filled upbringing. But, he continued, their trainers had not been completely successful. A spark of individuality still glimmered and could ignite to help bring forth a new, beautiful Germany. He concluded with the recognition that lies and treachery were all around and would continue to exist as long as the soldiers were bound, like slaves, to the teachings of the past years—teachings which had promised them "a thousand year Reich, but instead had left a field of rubble."[46]

EIGHT

Escape

Every soldier knew that it was his duty to try and escape if he were captured. But with some notable exceptions, when individual prisoners sized up their chances to successfully return to friendly hands and weighed the consequences if they were caught, few American prisoners in Germany or German prisoners in the United States considered escape a real possibility. Most German prisoners would have responded to the opportunity to escape the same way Frederick Weber and his comrades did on a work detail outside Ogden. They were working next to a group of Mexican nationals who were to be transported back to Mexico in large trucks. Two of the Mexicans approached the Germans announcing that they had four empty seats on their truck and invited a like number to go with them. There were no takers. "What could we expect in Mexico. We had it so good. . . . Here the Americans would take care of us and see that we got home. So there was no interest to do such a foolish thing."[1]

But there were exceptions. Of the 2,222 Germans who attempted to escape from American POW camps between 1942 and 1946, more than half, 1,149, succeeded between February 1945 and June 1946. Of the 1,073 Germans who attempted escape between November 1942 and February 1945, 60 percent were captured within one day or less of their escape and 85 percent were captured within three days. Upon their return to camp, escapees usually faced thirty days in the guardhouse and during the first fourteen days were on a restricted diet of bread and water. Most of the prisoners who escaped simply walked away from work details while guards were not watching. Others cut their way through wire fences, dug tunnels, or hid in drainage tunnels and crawled out after dark. Some slipped into civilian delivery trucks, secured U.S. Army uniforms, and left the POW compound as American soldiers. Others forced open hospital and guardhouse windows, dropped from roofs over compound fences, or jumped off trucks or trains while being transferred. Usually they were assisted by fellow prisoners who covered for them as long as they could.[2]

Boredom with camp life was the primary reason most escapees gave for leaving the camp. They hoped for a few days' vacation before returning to the all-too-familiar prison camp routine. Others were anxious to return to their homeland and to their families. Some felt bound by their duty to escape and made repeated attempts to carry out this obligation. A few wanted to see more of America than was possible because of their confinement. One prisoner wanted to put to the test the novel idea that if a German "was able to experience life in America for two weeks, he would never wish to leave."[3]

American authorities took precautions to make escapes more difficult and to secure a quick apprehension of escapees by paying civilians a $15 reward and up to $10 in expenses for capturing escaped prisoners.[4] Prisoners in Tooele were upset at a policy that prohibited them from keeping civilian shirts and pajamas they had received in packages from Germany. Since such clothing might be used in escape attempts, the camp commander was instructed to store the clothing, identify it as the property of the prisoner of war, and return it to him when he was repatriated.[5]

A mass escape of twenty-five German prisoners from Camp Papago Park, Arizona, on December 23, 1944, drew a lot of attention—particularly from military leaders of the Ninth Army Service Command at Fort Douglas, Utah. Located only 130 miles north of the Mexican border, Papago Park was considered the ideal camp for would-be escapees who hoped to cross the border and establish contact with anti-American, if not pro-German, civilians. Ten months before the mass escape, five former U-boat captains escaped from the camp hidden under a truckload of plywood. Two were captured after taking a train to Tucson the night of their escape. The other three avoided all contact with Americans, and by hiding out during the day and walking at night with the North Star to their backs, they made their way into Mexico. After ten days they stopped at an isolated ranch seeking food and shelter. The Mexican family informed authorities, and with the assistance of American army guards, who had crossed the border without official permission, the three were taken into custody. After spending three or four days in a Nogales jail, they were returned to Papago Park. Alarmed at the success of the men in crossing the border into Mexico, Ninth Army officials proposed sending undercover men into Mexico to identify potential escape routes, but the FBI claimed that runaway prisoners of war were their responsibility, not the army's. Papago Park became the problem POW camp for Gen. William H. Shedd, commander of the Ninth Army Service Command. On March 13, 1944, less than two weeks after the three escapees had been returned from Mexico, prisoner Werner Dreschler was murdered by fellow inmates. Dreschler was a known informant who had actively collected information from other German prisoners for the Americans. Sent to Papago Park, he was recognized and executed. Seven prisoners were tried in August 1944 in Arizona, found guilty, and given death penalties. When General Shedd received their cases in Fort Douglas, he recommended that they not be executed, but given life imprisonment instead. President Harry S. Truman did not agree, and the seven men were hanged in Fort Leavenworth, Kansas, on August 25, 1945.

In an attempt to deal with the volatile situation in Papago Park, General Shedd sent Col. William A. Holden from Fort Douglas. Holden proposed that Papago Park's guardhouse stockade be expanded into a small, independent facility to house the fifty or sixty most ardent Nazi troublemakers in the camp. General Shedd approved the plan and transmitted the proposal to the War Department in Washington. Even with the War Deparment's approval, the plan was not carried out because neither General Shedd nor Colonel Holden could get the necessary construction materials. While plans were being formulated and reviewed for handling the troublemakers, Colonel Holden consolidated them in compound 1A of the facility. Here, the prisoners set to work digging a 178-foot tunnel from the compound, under the fence and patrol road, to the edge of the Arizona Cross Cut Canal. A coal box eight by ten feet wide and four to five feet high was used to conceal the tunnel entrance, and there was a blind spot that kept the guards from discovering the nightly activity as the prisoners worked in three ninety-minute shifts to complete the work. In mid-November, when a group of high-ranking officers came down from Fort Douglas to tour the compound, one of the colonels allegedly "planted both feet firmly on top of the tunnel entrance and proclaimed in a confident voice that Papago Park need never be concerned with tunnels. It simply was impossible to dig in this soil, it was hard as a rock."[6] The digging was difficult, but not impossible, and the tunnel and other preparations were completed on schedule for the planned break at Christmas time 1944. The men expected that the holiday weekend would delay the discovery of their escape.

The escape was preceded by loud disturbances from adjacent compounds 1B and 2B. The first occurred when beer was ordered removed from the canteen and fifty cases of stockpiled beer and twenty-two gallons of fermenting homemade alcohol were confiscated from within the compound. As one American officer described the scene in following orders: "About a hundred or so men were . . . yelling, shouting, calling me all kinds of vile names. . . . Two men came toward me, pushed me aside, and the prisoners grabbed all of the beer." Later, the second occurred when inmates of compounds 1B and 2B congregated along the intervening wire fence and then unfurled a large German flag and started singing Nazi marching songs—to the accompaniment of an accordian. When the American officer of the day tried to quiet the disturbance, he "was greeted with hoots of derision, laughter, and clownish shrugs . . . [while] the singing continued, even grew louder." The officer ended the disturbance by picking up a grenade and pretending to pull the pin. When he dropped his arm back as if to throw it, "the singing stopped abruptly. There was almost complete silence." Then, according to the *Salt Lake Tribune*, army guards were forced to use clubs to disperse the demonstration.[7]

With tensions in the camp at a high, American authorities remained alert to quell any further demonstrations. However, the December escape went off without any problems except that it took longer to get through the tunnel than had been anticipated. That twenty-five prisoners were missing was not discovered until late afternoon on December 24th. By 7:30 P.M. a list of the escapees had been compiled just as the first reports were coming in on those who had been captured or had voluntarily turned themselves in. The escaped men had divided into several groups, intending to reach Mexico by different routes. Perhaps the most ingenious, if not ill-conceived, was the attempt by three of the men to float west down the Gila River to its junction with the Colorado River and to continue south into Mexico. They had constructed a canvas boat in camp, which they disassembled to take through the tunnel and the river. With luck on their side, the three reached the river the morning of December 28. As one of them recalled nearly thirty years later, "The Gila wasn't much of a river. . . . There simply was not enough water in the mighty Gila to float our tiny craft."[8] They tried to launch the boat, but once the three men with all their gear were aboard, it would not budge from the bottom of the river. The men trudged on, following the river for another eleven days until they were spotted on January 8, 1945, and brought into custody.

All twenty-five escapees were captured, the last on January 27. He was arrested in downtown Phoenix without food or money. The escape caused a certain amount of fallout: Officers of the Ninth Service Command, despite the November inspection report that no tunnel could be dug at Papago Park, saw the escape as one more piece of evidence of a poorly administered camp. And the Fort Douglas officers came under fire from their superiors at the War Department who were dismayed at the delay in sending reports about the escape to Washington. As one War Department officer put it: "It is a little embarrassing for us to get such news through the papers," instead of proper army channels.[9]

Most of the twenty-five escapees were sent to an isolation camp a short distance outside Papago Park. No more tunnels were dug, and the men occupied their time with the recreational and educational activities available to them. In February 1946, fourteen months after their escape, they were sent east to Camp Shenks and from there by ship back to Europe.

Although the Arizona escape is chronicled in *The Faustball Tunnel*, by John Hammond Moore, it is a relatively unknown event from World War II. Better known is the March 1944 escape of seventy-six English, American, and other allied prisoners of war through a tunnel out of Stalag Luft III at Sagan, Germany—sixty miles southeast of Berlin. That dramatic escape was recounted in *The Great Escape*, by Paul Brickhill, a former inmate of Stalag Luft

III. These two mass escapes were exceptions, with most escapes on both sides involving an individual or small groups of two or three. The latter escapes may not have had the epic sweep of those at Sagan and Papago Park, but they had their own sense of drama. One prisoner sent to Utah in 1945 to work as a library assistant at Dugway was known as Ralph by his American acquaintances. He had undertaken two nerve-shattering escapes before he reached Dugway. He had studied in Paris and Rome, intending a career in the German foreign service. Drafted into the German Army, he was captured in Egypt by British Indian troops. He and a companion escaped, clad in British officers' uniforms. Posing as free-French officers, they boarded a train bound for Cairo and even persuaded British officers to lend them money for train fare. From Cairo they headed west and successfully recrossed the German lines, only to be captured by the British a few days later when Montgomery launched his offensive against the Germans. Sent as a prisoner of war to the United States, he escaped and made his way to San Francisco, where he passed as a Frenchman and found work in a print shop. Unhappy in San Francisco and wanting to find a way to return to Germany, he planned on making his way south through Arizona and from there to cross into Mexico. After reading about the escape and hunt for the twenty-five Papago Park escapees, he altered his plan and headed straight for Tijuana. At the border he was detained on suspicion of being a Frenchman who had entered the country illegally. Three days later, a check of fingerprints revealed him to be an escaped German prisoner. Within a few months of his recapture, he was sent to Dugway, Utah.[10]

The first known escape attempt by German prisoners in Utah was made at Camp Warner. On a cold, foggy, January 1944 morning, just a few days after his arrival from Colorado, a prisoner cut his way through the double fence and walked approximately five hundred feet through the snow. Reassessing his chances of survival outside the compound, he turned around, retraced his steps, crawled back through the fence, and rejoined his comrades. His short journey was a well-guarded secret from camp authorities.[11] Later, in March of 1944, another attempt was made by three German prisoners in Camp Warner who cut a hole through the fence at about 2:00 A.M. When the escape was discovered, American soldiers were called out to cover all roads and railroads the fugitives might try to use in their flight. By early afternoon the escapees were spotted by railroad workers, who contacted authorities; the prisoners were back in camp by dark. The men had covered nearly forty miles in their brief excursion.[12]

There were many other attempts at escape, the men usually captured and returned after a brief adventure. In Ogden, one prisoner escaped on May 29, 1945, and was recaptured the following day. His motive appeared to be depression caused by not receiving any news from home. A German prisoner working on a truck farm near the Ogden camp became friendly with the farmer's son who had been a Mormon missionary in Germany from 1936 through 1938. The prisoner thought that the young man would help him escape, so he hid in the family's granary overnight. The young man refused to help and called camp authorities, who sent guards down to pick up the escaped prisoner. On another occasion, two young prisoners escaped from the Clearfield camp. They were described as "mere kids" who "apparently wanted to see the world and turned themselves in at the prisoner-of-war camp in Greeley two days later."[13]

American authorities treated as escape attempts those occasions when prisoners slipped away from camp with the intention of returning after a few hours. F. D. Lietz, an American guard in Ogden, recalled one occasion when he took 200 prisoners to the movies and returned one man short. None of the prisoners would disclose who was missing. Lietz and the others spent an hour and a half trying to find out who was missing. The missing prisoner had put a blanket and pillow under his bedcovers to make it look occupied. While the guards were searching for him, he walked back through the main gate. He had spent the evening with a girl he had met in a depot warehouse.[14]

In Salt Lake City, two German prisoners slipped out of the Fort Douglas compound in civilian clothes on a Friday evening in April 1946 and made their way to a downtown bar, where they were picked up by FBI agents and returned to the camp. As a consequence, the next morning American personnel made a thorough search of the POW barracks looking for money, civilian clothes, and other items the prisoners were forbidden to have in their possession. Perhaps anticipating the search, one prisoner hid his money, clothes, dye, and letters from an American civilian under the barracks, and they were not discovered.[15]

Ernst Luders and Richard Boettger planned an escape after Luders read in the newspaper that the transport ship they were to take from Stockton, California, to Germany was going to France instead. "It was a dumb thing to do, but we simply did not want to go to France." With another prisoner, the three made their escape by walking away from the California camp while they were supposed to be attending a movie. Ill-prepared for a successful escape, they were recaptured a short time after they left. "We had no goal, we did not have any equipment. We had no map. We had nothing, not even a warm coat." Justice was swift for the men. "The first thing they did was to shave our heads. Then we went to our hearing." Although at least two of the prisoners could speak good English, they told court authorities that they wanted a translator because they did not know enough English. This strategy had a purpose: the prisoner could understand the question asked in English by the judge and formulate an answer while the question was being translated into German. In any case, the men were sentenced to four weeks in the stockade. The stay was cut short, however, when military police escorted them to their ship and locked them in the ship's brig, where they remained until after the ship sailed through the Panama Canal and past Puerto Rico. Luders recalled, "We were separated from the others. There was a toilet and shower and three beds. The food was always brought to us. . . . I found that quite nice. The Blacks were very sympathetic to us and they always brought us something. Perhaps it was because they themselves were not so well treated in those days."[16]

Thus, although German soldiers were instructed that they had a duty to try to escape, relatively few did. The 2,222 escapees among more than 371,000 German prisoners in the United States amounted to about .6 percent, or one escapee for every 167 prisoners. Most prisoners simply saw no advantage or purpose in escaping when the disadvantages were considered. Of the 2,222 escapees only 17 remained at large by November 1947. By 1953 only 6 were still at large. Two were arrested that year, then one in each of the years 1954, 1959, and 1964. Only one German prisoner, Georg Gaertner, remained at large. Gaertner was a sergeant in Rommel's Afrika Korps when he was captured and sent to the

United States. On September 21, 1945, he escaped from Camp Lordsburg, New Mexico, and jumped a freight train bound for California. There, he changed his name, became a ski instructor at Lake Tahoe, and in the early 1950s made trips with a good friend to ski at Alta, Utah. Later, he became a tennis pro for several California clubs. He married an American and moved to Hawaii, where he became involved in construction. In 1979 he was named director of marketing for Morrison-Knudsen's Hawaii region. For thirty-seven years, Gaertner never disclosed his POW background; he had fabricated a story of growing up an orphan in Connecticut. Finally, in March 1982, with his marriage on the brink of divorce, he told his wife the amazing story. He later contacted Arnold Krammer, and the two men collaborated in recording Gaertner's adventure in the book, *Hitler's Last Soldier in America.*[17]

Georg Gaertner found the vastness of America an aid in his escape on a California-bound freight train that carried him quickly from his New Mexico prison camp, but other prisoners saw the dry, vast and unpopulated expanse of western America as a deterrent to escape. Slipping away from camp was the easy part, and tunnels served only for mass escape attempts from well-guarded camps. But there was only a remote hope that a prisoner could avoid identification while on the loose, to say nothing of negotiating the tremendous obstacles to return to Germany. Considering the hundreds of miles between Germany and England that Allied prisoners faced compared with the thousands of miles between Utah and Germany that German prisoners faced, the chances were many times greater for American or English prisoners to escape successfully than it was for their counterparts in America. The Allied prisoners also had organized undergrounds in Europe to help them. Still, firm beliefs, desperation, and a sense of adventure drove some men to try, and their stories add color to the German POW saga in America.

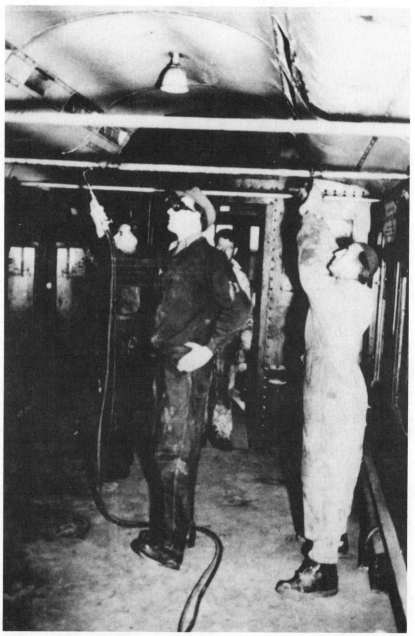

German prisoners remodel rail coaches at the Ogden Defense Depot.
(Public Relations Office, Ogden Defense Depot)

NINE

Work

The *Geneva Convention provided that prisoners* of war, with the exception of officers, could be put to work as long as they were healthy. Noncommissioned officers could only be used to supervise other prisoners. However, prisoners could not be assigned work that was considered dangerous or beyond their capability to carry out, and they could not be assigned work that involved handling munitions or weapons.

Throughout the United States, the German prisoners engaged in a variety of work assignments that were generally divided into two categories: post labor—which included work in warehouses, shops, and kitchens as well as maintenance work—and contract labor—which usually involved agricultural details such as working in the fields, picking fruit, cutting timber, or harvesting and processing commercial truck-garden produce.[1] Other prisoners toiled for state and municipal agencies constructing and repairing buildings, doing maintenance jobs, working on flood-control projects, cleaning ditches, planting trees and shrubs, tending the greens and fairways of municipal golf courses, and working in state-operated fish hatcheries.[2] A group of twenty-five German prisoners were assigned to construct a ski run and lift at Snow Basin in Ogden Canyon for use in the rehabilitation of convalescing soldiers, including amputees, from Bushnell Hospital.

Initially, the German prisoners were not to be considered a work force for immediate assignment. With security a major concern of many authorities, the idea of extensive use of large numbers of prisoners was considered a risk because of the enhanced possibility for escape, the opportunities to carry out acts of sabotage, and the myriad of problems that contact with the civilian population was likely to bring. Despite the concern over security, the severe labor shortage throughout the country, which frustrated government and business leaders, and the complaints by civilians about the seeming inefficiency and high cost of simply feeding and watching prisoners made it clear that a more extensive POW employment program was in order. Launched in 1943, the employment program developed slowly. In January 1944 the majority of the 123,000 German prisoners in the United States were still not employed; and of those who were, only a small percentage were engaged in what could be considered necessary or useful work. However, early in 1944 the plan to relocate many of the prisoners from the large camps to smaller branch camps close to work opportunities was adopted. By the end of May 1944, approximately 73 percent of all eligible prisoners were at work, and by April 1945, 91 percent were employed.[3]

The Ogden Army Depot was a leader in the utilization of POW labor. It was the first to use prisoners of war in technical service operations. This was in late 1942. Although most army officials were reluctant to use prisoners for such assignments because of a fear of sabotage, Ogden officials successfully organized Italian prisoners to carry out both skilled and unskilled work assignments. In time, the Italian prisoners were joined by German prisoners. Gradually, other technical service depots throughout the United States followed Ogden's lead and used POW labor.[4]

In Ogden, German prisoners were assigned to a wide variety of jobs, including such activities as clerical and office work, loading and unloading freight cars, and working as field hands for local farmers and in the canneries. They were especially appreciated for their skills in carpentry and locksmith work and in repairing used and damaged equipment that ranged from shoes to field kitchens.[5] In the repair shops, prisoners worked in two shifts—early morning until noon and then afternoons from three until midnight. The men were on the early shift one week and the late shift the next. One of the most favored jobs for some prisoners was cleaning up the barracks recently evacuated by American soldiers headed overseas. The newspapers, magazines, and pinups left behind were a welcome find.[6] Inspectors from the Department of State's Division of Special War Problems found that there was excellent morale among the Ogden prisoners and that a model training program had been established for forklift operators, repairmen, typists, and clerks. Typists and clerks were given an hour of English instruction each day so they could better understand the documents with which they worked.[7] All who completed the training were given a certificate of proficiency. Authorities were "well satisfied with the work performances of the prisoners . . . although they were hesitant in the beginning about using them on . . . the skilled jobs."[8]

Ogden prisoners of war who were unable to do regular work undertook a unique unpaid work program. A local farmer invited the POW camp commander to harvest all the fallen apricots from his orchard near the camp. The prisoners gathered the fruit and took it to camp, where it was washed and then sun-dried on racks constructed by the prisoners. The dried apricots were then treated with sulphur, packaged, and given to the quartermaster for local military use.[9]

But if Ogden officials were in the forefront in utilizing POW labor, others were more cautious. In Clearfield, as late as June 1945, highly skilled prisoners were given only manual labor; and the outlook was for a continuation of that policy "until responsible Navy officers are convinced that the prisoners of war can be trusted not to sabotage the work of this vital depot."[10]

In order to determine what work by prisoners would adhere to the Geneva Convention provisions, the War Department established the Prisoner of War Employment Reviewing Board to make a final decision on questions relating to acceptable work assignments. The board found that maintenance and repair work on any vehicle which carried cargo or personnel and not combat weapons was acceptable. Scrapping and salvage operations were permissible as was work on gas masks and the shipment of hydrogen-filled cylinders. Prohibited, however, was work on the preparation of motor vehicles or transportation equipment of a unit alerted for shipment overseas and work connected with rifle ranges, bayonet courses, guns, or anything needed to train personnel in the use of combat weapons. An example from Tooele of the hair-splitting decisions that were sometimes required was whether prisoners could handle brass shells. Col. Clifford S. Urwiller, assistant director of the Prisoner of War Division, held that prisoners could handle brass shell cases if the casings were to be melted down as scrap.

German prisoners pruning trees in a North Ogden fruit orchard. (Public Relations Office, Ogden Defense Depot)

German prisoners from the Salina camp with a load of sugar beets in Sevier County, fall of 1945. (Photo courtesy of Shirley Probert)

German prisoner harrowing with a team of horses near Ogden. (Public Relations Office, Ogden Defense Depot)

Sketch by E. Scholz depicting German prisoners harvesting sugar beets near Rupert, Idaho. (Courtesy of Hilda Poes Glasgow)

Processing apricots at the Ogden Defense Depot. (Public Relations Office, Ogden Defense Depot)

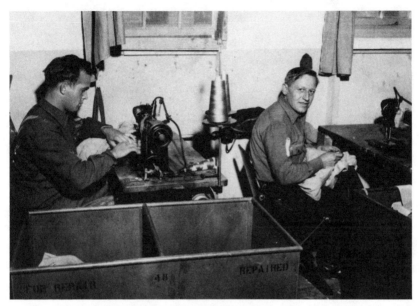

German prisoners at work in a clothing repair shop at the Ogden Defense Depot. (Public Relations Office, Ogden Defense Depot)

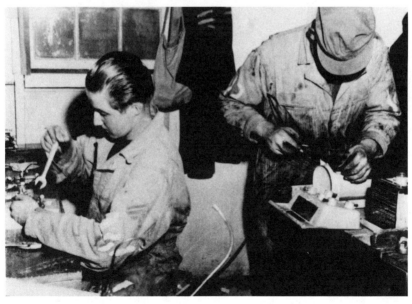

German prisoner refurbishing used equipment. (Public Relations Office, Ogden Defense Depot)

German prisoners working in a Utah cannery. (Public Relations Office, Ogden Defense Depot)

German prisoner operating a forklift under the supervision of an American civilian at an Ogden Defense Depot warehouse. (Public Relations Office, Ogden Defense Depot)

German prisoners at a Utah Poultry Producers Cooperative Association plant in Tremonton, Utah. (Public Relations Office, Ogden Defense Depot)

Turkeys processed by prisoners at Tremonton were sold to the army quartermaster. (Public Relations Office, Ogden Defense Depot)

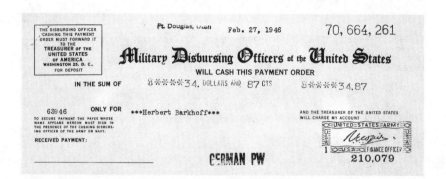

Check paid to Herbert Barkhoff for his work as a German prisoner of war at Ogden. (Courtesy of Herbert Barkhoff)

If the casings were to be reloaded as ammunition, it would be a violation of the Geneva Convention for the prisoners to handle them.[11] Adherence to the provisions of the Geneva Convention brought frustration for many administrators. An American general, Wilhelm D. Styer, argued, "We must overcome the psychology that you cannot do this or that. I want to see these prisoners work like piss ants."[12]

A prisoner was paid eighty cents a day for his work. The amount was determined by what a typical American soldier received—$21 a month. The pay was credited to his account, with the provision that one-half of what he earned could be issued in canteen coupons. Payment for work was an effective tool in managing those prisoners who seemed to appreciate recognition for their labors and who enjoyed the sense of freedom that came with the choice of when and how to spend their coupons. Still, the coupons did not seem adequate compensation; so to provide additional incentives, the army introduced a task or quota system in which prisoners had to attain a certain level of productivity or have their pay reduced. If a prisoner persistently failed to meet the established quota, he could be confined in the stockade on a reduced diet. Under the quota system, highly productive prisoners could earn as much as $1.20 a day for exceeding the quota. And once the set quota was met by the work detail, the men could return to their barracks or tents.

The incentive program proved less than successful, however. The establishment of quotas that were either too low or too high and different working circumstances and conditions proved to be a serious problem. Indicative of the difficulties was the situation in Idaho, where it was reported that during the potato and grain harvests prisoners could meet their quota by 10 or 11 A.M. and then go swimming in the Snake River; during the fruit harvest they seldom made more than half the set quota after a full day's work.[13]

Once prisoners were employed, they found their days taken up with a full but not overly demanding schedule. An eight-hour work day, six days a week, with an hour off for lunch and four hours free time in the evening was typical. With some variations from camp to camp in the usual routine, prisoners rose at 6:15 A.M., ate breakfast at 6:45 A.M., fell in for morning roll call at 7:30 A.M., began work at 8:00 A.M., ate lunch from 12:00 to 1:00 P.M., worked another four hours from 1:00 to 5:00 P.M., attended evening roll call at 5:30 P.M., ate dinner at 5:45 P.M., then had the rest of the evening free until lights out at 10:00 P.M. Prisoners usually worked Monday through Saturday with Sunday free, but in some camps the men worked shifts which included nights and weekends.

In order for prisoners of war to become an effective work force in the United States, four policy changes were necessary: (1) prisoners had to be moved into the areas of greatest labor shortage, (2) smaller branch camps were needed, (3) a "calculated risk" policy, which eased and modified security measures, had to be implemented, and (4) the War Department needed to establish a good working relationship with the War Manpower Commission through a Memorandum of Agreement outlining the POW employment process. Officials recognized that the situation for prisoners was not conducive to the highest possible levels of productivity. Their earnings could be used to purchase only the few limited items available in the POW canteen. There was no long-term incentive for saving money—no house, property, or other signs of stability could be acquired. The men were confined under guard, and when work was done there was no home or family to return to—only a barracks shared with fifty others or a tent with no light and few comforts. Their primary incentive to work was to avoid punishment at the hands of their captors.[14]

Despite these circumstances, one former prisoner of war reflected that work was a welcome relief to the monotony of imprisonment. "We looked forward to the time when we could go out, even backbreaking work like thinning beets. . . . We were really delighted that we could work and not just stay in the barracks and look at the walls."[15] Heinz Richter recalled that his stay at Camp Grant during the summer of 1944, mowing lawns with a tractor, was "a very happy time. High up on the tractor, a canopy over my head, I drove over acres and acres of grass. All alone, no guards, a free man. . . . My boss was an elderly American who was like a father to me."[16]

Prisoners were generally content with the eighty cents a day they received for their work. One prisoner recalled that the four dollars he was paid each week stood far above the one mark a week he had received as a first-year apprentice in Germany and even the seven and a half marks he earned during his fourth year of apprenticeship. He noted that cigarettes, chocolate, underwear, and other items available at the camp canteen were incredibly cheap. "I got everything I needed or wanted and was still able to save $125 during my imprisonment from 1943-1946."[17]

Although American officials viewed the POW employment program as a great success, there were some problems in using prisoners, and at times the tasks assigned to them seemed unimportant and unnecessary. One officer at Tooele complained that the United States was getting considerably less than the usual eight hours of work that the prisoners were expected to perform. The prisoners could not be picked up to begin their work until after the civilian employees had begun theirs and had to be returned to the prison compound before the civilians left for the day. Then there was time lost for breaks and visits to the latrines, which were often some distance from the work site. The same officer criticized the inadequacy of civilian supervision of the prisoners and grumbled that work details were overstaffed. He felt that both factors gave "a WPA complex to the type of work turned out by the prisoners." As an example of this, he described the scene at a scrap lumber project to which prisoners had been assigned: They sat "with a few pieces of wood in front of them. This work consisted of pulling nails out of these pieces of wood. The lack of speed with which they performed this operation was amazing."[18] (There was another perspective to this sort of make-work—that of the prisoners. One prisoner in a group in Ogden assigned to removing nails from a pile of wood remarked, "After we took out the nails, they burned the wood and threw the nails in the garbage. Under those circumstances, you can imagine just how hard we worked."[19]) The uninspired work effort at Camp Warner in Tooele may have been one reason for the decision to transfer the German prisoners of war. An American soldier concluded that the Germans "did not cooperate any more than they had to, they objected to doing anything that aided the war effort, which is what we would have done if we had been the prisoners."[20] The Germans at Camp Warner not only were uncooperative in the eyes of their captors but also were suspected of having committed acts of sabotage such as pouring sand in the crankshafts of trucks and tanks.

One prisoner in Ogden found the night shift to be peaceful, with considerable freedom and no pressure. "The American guards did not have any desire to force us to work. They said 'take care,' then lay down to sleep . . . so hardly nothing was done during the night shift." The lax circumstances permitted German and Italian prisoners to interact in the large depot halls. "We had concerts. All those who were working in the area got together in one hall. . . . Two or three or maybe four Italians would sing arias from Verdi, Rossini. . . . There were a couple who had voices for the opera."[21]

If supervision was often easygoing, there were occasions when discipline was required. Wesley Andersen, a civilian employee in Ogden, recalled that a detail of German prisoners who should have been unloading a boxcar were simply doing nothing. Andersen told them, "Now suit yourselves, either go to work, or I'll call your military commander out at the camp and you'll be confined." Faced with a choice, "They got right to work."[22]

Work in Utah compared favorably with most parts of the country. For those who came to Utah after stints in the cotton fields of Texas and Arizona, their new situation was a tremendous improvement. Experienced field hands were expected to pick 300 to 400 pounds of cotton a day; the German prisoners were expected to harvest 200 pounds, and they thought this amount excessive. They grumbled about the work, complained of the intense summer heat, and many supplemented the weight with dirt, rocks, or water and found other ways to fight back against the perceived oppression. Kurt Treiter admitted that many prisoners had no second thoughts about questionable means to insure they met their quota. One practice was to throw a bag of cotton off the truck to a comrade after it had been weighed. The man would return later with the same bag to have it weighed and counted to his credit as well. Another was to wet the cotton with water or urine. Others were aware of these practices but could not bring themselves to cheat. As Paul Hupfner recalled, "We had a farm at home and I knew what work was. I could not cheat the farmers."[23] To a few cotton planters, the POW help was better than nothing, but it was much worse than any labor they had used before, so "there was no comparison." Others were more generous, conceding that the cotton crop would have been lost and would have rotted in the fields had it not been for the Germans. The same was said of the POW contribution in saving crops in Minnesota and in Louisiana. One Louisiana rice planter was so grateful to have the German prisoners' help that he treated a platoon of them and their American guards to a seafood dinner in a Lake Arthur restaurant.[24]

Using prisoners of war in agriculture was part of a much larger labor shortage issue which the Farm Labor Act of 1943 sought to alleviate by establishing local fair-wage scales and maximizing the supply of farm labor. In Utah this was done by mobilizing local citizens and schoolchildren, recruiting Navajo Indians and inmates of the Topaz War Relocation Camp as well as workers from Mexico, and looking at the prisoners of war as a measure of last resort.[25]

During World War II, Utah's sugar beet industry gained importance in the national and worldwide economy, since the Japanese conquest and occupation of the Philippines and Indonesia practically eliminated sugarcane production in these two major areas. Also, the war in Europe had severely disrupted the cultivation of sugar beet fields there. In 1945 Utah ranked eighth in the nation in the number of acres—36,000—planted in sugar beets.[26]

Indicative of the Utah situation was the severe labor shortage in Salina. The extension-service county agent reported that some 1,200 men from the area were in the armed services and that most of these men were farmers, sons of farmers, or day laborers who had worked on local farms at least part of the year. To ease the labor shortage, a temporary work force of 206 Indians, 67 Mexican nationals, 50 Filipinos, and 936 students from local junior and senior high schools joined with the 300 German prisoners of war in Salina "to assist the farmers of Sevier County in carrying out the greatest agricultural production program the county has ever achieved."[27] In Davis and Weber counties, 551 prisoners worked in eleven different canneries during the summer and fall of 1945.[28]

Government officials concerned about food production met in Salt Lake City in January 1945. The primary issue was the availability of prisoners of war for farm work in the intermountain area and how their labor could be obtained. Maj. Robert Taylor, chief of the Works Product Branch, Prisoner of War Division with the Ninth Service Command in Fort Douglas, instructed the representatives of western state extension offices, the War Food Administration Office, and farm organizations on the requirements for establishing a branch camp for POW farm labor. First was the need for 250 men within a twenty-five mile radius of the proposed camp, and second was the need for adequate housing for the prisoners. Finally, farmers would have to put up an advance deposit of at least $4,000 or 10 percent of the minimum total value of the contract.[29] Under these conditions, four satellite camps were established in Tremonton, Logan, Orem, and Salina, where between 300 and 500 prisoners worked in agricultural activities between the months of May 1945 and January 1946. In Tremonton, farmers were obligated to pay as a deposit the equivalent of two months of man-days for 300 men before the army agreed to provide the requested POW labor. Beyond this investment, $7,000 was spent to renovate an old CCC camp in Tremonton to house the prisoners and provide quarters for the American guards. Donations from the Utah-Idaho Sugar Company, Box Elder County Canning Crops Growers' Association, Rocky Mountain Packing Corporation, South Box Elder Beet Growers Association, Garland Beet Association, and the Box Elder County Commission provided the necessary money for the temporary camp, which was rented from the state for a minimal amount of money. The initial contract was for 300 men to work from May 15 to July 10, 1945, to thin and hoe sugar beets, pick berries and cherries, and perform other farm labor. Box Elder County farmers were well pleased with the prisoner labor and extended the contract from July 15 to October 1, 1945, with a third extension from October 1 to December 10, 1945. The third extension increased the number of prisoners from 300 to 450. Most of the men worked in the sugar beet fields. Because of the abundant crop and shortage of labor, work continued until late November, when snows made it impossible to complete the harvest. During the summer of 1945, the 300 prisoners thinned and hoed 2,000 acres of sugar beets. Another 300 prisoners in the Ogden base camp were designated for sugar beet work in Davis and Weber counties.

In registering a need to employ prisoners of war, civilian applicants were required to indicate specifically when and where the work was to be done, the nature of the work to be performed, the man-days it would require, and what a civilian worker would be expected to accomplish in an average day. For planning purposes, applicants also reported the prevailing wage for the kind of work requested and the usual length of the work day for the specific work. They had to declare whether they would provide transportation to and from the camp, tools and equipment, and a noon meal for the prisoners. Once the application was approved, the civilian employer signed a contract with the War Department that restated the information included in the application, outlined the fiscal provisions of the agreement, and spelled out clearly the responsibilities of the government and the contractor. Some of these provisions were that the contractor had no authority to impose disciplinary measures on prisoners of war, that the government would provide the necessary guards and security measures, that government authorities would have access at all times to the work site in order to observe work conditions, that the contractor would furnish adequate training instruction and supervision but would not be responsible for disability compensation or medical care for the prisoners in his employ. If the prisoners caused damages that were not the result of fault or negligence of the contractor but that occurred because of willful misconduct by the prisoners, the government would pay for the damages.

Farmers were instructed to have everything ready so that the prisoners could begin work as soon as they arrived, to have drinking water easily available for the prisoners, to explain thoroughly what they wanted done, to show them how it was to be done, and to stay with them until they were performing their assignments as was expected. Responsibility for a good job performance rested with the farmers and how well they planned and supervised the work. Farmers were reminded that the guards were not responsible for supervising the fieldwork, but were there only to guard the prisoners. Finally, farmers were to encourage the prisoners in their work, treating them firmly but with consideration at all times.[30] The fiscal arrangements were somewhat complicated since the farmers paid the Box Elder Labor Association for the work and mileage plus 5 percent of the wages paid to help with expenses in running the POW camp. The association in turn paid the school board, the bus drivers, and the army and tracked the various credits from the army for camp and transportation expenses for the prisoners.[31]

In Cache Valley, the work in the sugar beet fields was demanding, and it was an effort for most prisoners to meet their daily quotas. The quota for each man was three tons of beets. Prisoners who worked to thin and weed the beets were expected to finish a half acre a day. Work details ranged from ten men for small farms to thirty for larger farms.[32] Some efficient workers assisted friends with their quotas, but Rudolf Weltin recalled, "It would not have been possible to help everyone who needed it. Otherwise, we would have had to work until early in the morning. It was such that the quota was so high that we had to work hard to reach it." According to Weltin, the prisoners in Cache Valley usually worked much longer than eight hours a day, often not returning to camp until 8:00 P.M. The long hours, coupled with short rations, led to protests by the prisoners and meetings with their spokesman and the camp commander. Because the prisoners were unable to determine what changes, if any, the camp commander could make on his own, the issues remained unresolved. Like their comrades in other camps, the Cache Valley prisoners turned to American civilians for help. "There were some farmers who understood what was going on. They gave us food to eat, and naturally we tried to repay them by working better." One of these farmers was Preston Alder, who "had a propensity toward people." He was one who "saw us as people, then prisoners. He spoke to us as normal people."[33]

Although the prisoners in Logan were employed primarily in the sugar beet fields, they were used to harvest potatoes, tomatoes, and beans as well as to assist in pea and turkey processing plants.

The Cache County extension-service agent concluded in his report for 1945 that the "quality of the work done exceeded the expectations of the farmers . . . [and] without prisoner of war labor, some crops would not have been harvested and could not have been planted."[34]

Prisoners assigned to the sugar beet fields were shown how to pull the beets from the ground and cut the tops off with a knife. They moved across the field pulling two beets at a time, knocking them together to dislodge the dirt, then tossing them in rows on either side. The beets were then loaded into trucks either by hand or by using motorized loading machines. However, the regimentation of army and prison life sometimes created confrontations between civilians in charge of the war farm-labor effort, army officers responsible for the prisoners, and local farmers. The farmers, with their traditional methods of working the fields, were caught in the middle, but were still obligated to pay for the services of the prisoners. Alder, the Cache Valley farmer, ran up against a tunnel-visioned authoritarian officer when the prisoners arrived at his field to thin sugar beets for the first time. The burly American officer announced: "These Krauts are going to work or I will use force to make them." Alder's response was that he wanted to see them work but that he was more concerned with their doing a good job. The prisoners were assigned the necessary rows to make their half-acre quota, and in short time Alder saw a problem. The inexperienced men, in order to meet their quotas, were scratching out the beets four or five feet apart rather than the required twelve to fourteen inches. When Alder complained to the officer in charge that the work was unacceptable and the quota unrealistic, the man bellowed, "You don't understand, mister. My problem is to make these men work. I am going to make them work or I will use this thing [his gun] on them." Alder retorted, "It is my job to grow sugar beets to make sugar. We have a sugar shortage in this country right now. My job is just about as important as yours." Alder issued an ultimatum that the half-acre quota be set aside at least until the men had some experience or the soldier could take the prisoners out of his fields. The officer reluctantly agreed; and after proper instruction, the prisoners completed the work to Alder's satisfaction.[35]

Morris Taylor, state farm-labor director for Utah during World War II, told of a colonel in Ogden complaining to him that the quota set for the prisoners was too high. To prove that the quotas were reasonable, Taylor took the colonel to a North Ogden sugar beet field to observe the prisoners at work. Their arrival brought the prisoners and guard stumbling out of the bushes alongside the field, where they had taken refuge from the blazing August sun. The colonel was incensed, but Taylor explained that the oppressive heat made work difficult and that if they were working the schedule a farm family would, they would weed early in the morning, lay off during the heat of the day, and resume work later in the evening. As it was, army policy called for work details to be carried out between 8:00 A.M. and 5:00 P.M.[36] Karl Altkruger found the work in the sugar beet fields to be torture. "You think that you can get used to something, but we never did get used to working in the sugar beet fields. The back pains were always there."[37]

The need for POW labor was serious for western agriculturists, and the inability of the Ninth Service Command to meet the demands led to frustration and confrontations with certain political leaders. Governor Charles C. Gossett of Idaho wired the state's senator in Washington, D.C., the secretary of Agriculture, and War Department officials, raising what some officials called "an unholy stink" about "crop suffering in the state of Idaho" and demanding that Idaho's POW allotment be increased.[38] In Utah, the sugar beet farmers criticized the way in which the War Department allocated POW labor, maintaining that there were not enough prisoners to harvest the beet crops. In a telegram to Elbert D. Thomas, his state senator in Washington, Frank G. Shelley, chairman of the Utah Agricultural Labor Advisory Board, complained that promised prisoners of war had not arrived although Utah farmers had planted crops believing that their labor would be available. Shelley warned that if the prisoners did not arrive there would be "drastic reductions of essential crops and . . . lack of confidence in government promises."[39] Army officials countered that there simply were not enough prisoners to meet the demand of sugar beet farmers. The situation was further compromised when plans to send an additional 150,000 German prisoners of war to the United States were canceled after VE Day. It was an additional blow to Utah sugar beet farmers when promises to make 1,400 prisoners available to help with thinning and weeding until June 15, 1946, did not materialize.

Utah farmers repeatedly praised the German prisoners for their good work, seeing them in a much more favorable light than they did workers brought in from Mexico or the Italian prisoners of war. According to one farmer, German prisoners "seemed to be just as good as the local boys, and did twice as much as the Italian prisoners. . . . The Germans seemed to be better workers and acted like they were more content to be here."[40] The prisoners could be called upon in a crisis, as Morris Taylor observed. When a heavy snowstorm struck on November 4, 1945, with sugar beets still in the fields, the Logan prisoners were outfitted with heavy clothing and hip boots and dispatched to the fields early in the morning. They pulled beets and threw them onto horse-drawn skids, since wheeled vehicles would have been useless in the mired field. "Without the German prisoners, they would never have gotten them out. . . . That is a heroic effort in my book, and I have to pat those prisoners on the back for what they did."[41]

The POW program was not without its critics, however. One Ogden resident asked, "Why bring any more German prisoners to America to be guarded and nursed and fed by us? It will take an army of soldiers and nurses to care for them." He proposed that the Allies should broadcast to Germany that after a certain date no more prisoners would be brought to the United States. Instead, responsibility for the captives would be given to German civilians to "feed and nurse or let starve." The result, he predicted, would be a general desertion by German soldiers seeking the care of the Allies.[42] There were complaints that the prisoners took jobs that civilians could do, such as potato harvesting which local boys and girls had previously been employed to do. One farmer had hired two brothers, thirteen and sixteen years old, to harvest potatoes; but after their first day on the job, he called their mother to say they were not needed because the German prisoners were coming to work for him. Other farmers turned down the boys' request for employment, choosing German prisoners instead, even though, according to the sixteen year old, some of the prisoners were no bigger than he was.[43] Other protests pointed at the number of able-bodied Americans needed to supervise and guard the prisoners, the number of Americans being shipped overseas to do work which the German prisoners in this country could do if they were in POW camps there, and the fact that 40 percent of the prisoners brought to America were assigned to work within the prison camps. "The net manpower gain to this nation must be very small."[44] In Utah, Local No. 869 of the National Federation of Federal Employees protested that prisoners were replacing civilians who had been released through a reduction-in-force program at Hill Field. The local secretary of the union, Boyd H. Ririe, declared that, despite denials by the base administration, the union could "supply facts and figures to prove definitely that they [the prisoners] are being worked in capacities for which civilian employees were released, some of whom are now walking the streets looking for work."[45] Maj. Guy E. Matheson was sent from Fort Douglas to investigate the allegations, and his report confirmed the union's charges. He recommended that prisoners of war employed at technical jobs formerly filled by civilians be removed and that qualified civilian labor be used instead.[46] Those prisoners who remained at Hill Field after September 1945 were used for policing the grounds and runways, garbage removal, and other work for which civilian employees were not available.

Despite these criticisms, available records disclose little dissatisfaction with the POW program in Utah. And, despite their complaint that there were too few prisoners to meet their needs, Utah farmers offered ample testimony that the POW labor was welcome, worth the money they had to pay for it, and—in a number of instances—made the difference between a lost or spoiled crop and a successful harvest. The Utah experience illustrates the national policy toward prisoners of war as it moved from a concern for security to an emphasis on their productive employment and reeducation toward an antifascist/prodemocratic outlook. Rather than simply emulating what was happening elsewhere in the country, Utah chose to be in the vanguard in demonstrating that prisoners of war could be used in technical service operations without an inordinate fear of sabotage and that productive work could be an effective means of managing and controlling enemy captives.

Rudolf Weltin dressed for his performance in the operetta "Im Weissen Rossl," produced by Austrian prisoners at Logan, Utah. (Photo courtesy of Rudolf Weltin)

TEN

Free Time

W*ith work as the primary activity for prisoners* of war, there was also a full range of recreational, educational, and religious opportunities available to the German prisoners in the larger camps, such as those in Ogden and Tooele. Support and encouragement of these activities by American authorities were consistent with the policy of strict adherence to the Geneva Convention. And, there were advantages in making prison life interesting and beneficial to those who were not out to give their captors trouble. The many activities engaged the diverse interests and talents that the captured soldiers brought with them into the prison compounds. Shortly after the Ogden camp was established, it boasted a library of nearly 400 titles consisting of German novels and history books, textbooks, religious works, classics and poetry collections, and a few English books. Less than a year later the number of books had increased sixfold to about 2,500 volumes. During May 1945, 75 percent of the books were in constant circulation and 60 percent of the prisoners used the library and reading room. Specific requests were for German classics by Goethe and Schiller and for local history books. The library was open daily except Sundays from 9:00 to 11:00 A.M., 2:00 to 4:00 P.M., and 7:00 to 9:00 P.M. Books could be checked out for a week, magazines for two days. Some of the available magazines were *Life, Time, Look, Newsweek,* and *Coronet.* Used magazines were sent over from the officers' club at the Ogden depot, and the men could subscribe to magazines and newspapers as well as purchase them in the compound canteen.[1]

Prisoners also had access to several radios and a phonograph within their compound. Although shortwave radios were prohibited, this rule was often ignored. Experienced electricians were able to adapt radios to shortwave with little difficulty. The rationale in allowing radios in the camp was explained as one way of letting the prisoners know that "Americans are not dictators, we are not slave drivers, we love people, we appreciate people, we respect people's rights. We are different from the dictators."[2] In some camps, loudspeakers were installed in each of the barracks, and news, music, and other programs were broadcast several hours during the day. One prisoner developed a distinct liking for western or cowboy music, recalling that some of his favorite songs were "Red River Valley," "Home on the Range," and "Oh, Susannah." Forty years later, Emil Blau still remembered some of the words to "Let Me Call You Sweetheart." At the camp in Roswell, New Mexico, the prisoner orchestra added "Pistol Packin' Mama" to its repertoire, and "The Yellow Rose of Texas" became the unofficial camp song. Understandably, the most popular American song in the German POW camps across the United States was "Don't Fence Me In."[3]

At the Ogden camp it took eight days to show weekly movies to all of the prisoners, including additional showings at 1:00 P.M. on Mondays and Tuesdays for those who worked the night shift. A prisoner trained as a projectionist traveled with Ogden's assistant executive officer, Calvin Bartholomew, in an effort to show movies twice a month in the branch camps. American films were shown for the most part, usually with subtitles, but some German films were also included. One former Ogden prisoner explained that those who could follow, in general, English dialogue would answer during the intermission the questions of those not so well versed in English.[4]

Before films became available for the prisoners, a thirty-man theater group was organized to provide entertainment. Two of its productions were *Silent Night, Holy Night*, by Karl Eiche, during Christmas 1944 and *Don Carlos* by Friedrich von Schiller in February 1945.[5] Another production, *The Robber* by Schiller, took four hours to perform. The staging of theatrical works often created opportunities for humor. On one occasion the prisoners were working on a play about gangsters, and had manufactured prop guns out of wood and sheet metal. The camp commander was concerned, and told the prisoners that they would have to be very careful since if spotted by the American guards, "the guards will throw their weapons away and run."[6]

In the Logan branch camp, the prisoners produced the Austrian operetta, "Im Weissen Rossl." Set in the resort area of the Austrian Salzkammergut region southeast of Salzburg, the operetta contains some of the best-known and -loved German melodies. The camp commander had given permission for its performance, and even assisted in locating clothing for costumes. The heroine of the story, Josepha Vogelhuber, the young and beautiful keeper of the White Horse Inn, was played by prisoner Rudolf Weltin, who was nineteen years old. There were several performances, which were enthusiastically received by the prisoners and the invited American spectators.[7]

A strong interest in music was demonstrated by the organization of orchestras and choirs. At Camp Warner the prisoners were so eager to get the essential instruments for an orchestra that they were willing to pay for them with their own money if they could be obtained locally. The Clearfield POW orchestra consisted of a piano, two violins, a trombone, a clarinet, two camp-made guitars, and twelve harmonicas. The highlight of the week for the hundred prisoners at Camp Deseret, the smallest POW camp in the state, was the Sunday concerts performed by their nine-piece orchestra.[8] In Ogden a twenty-four piece orchestra gave monthly performances and a fourteen-piece band played once a week. The music included classical, semiclassical, and popular American selections. A choir of sixty-five voices was also organized; arrangements were made for a music professor to visit the compound and give occasional lectures; and classes were offered in voice, piano, harmony, and music theory. Establishing the choir was not easy; only a few of the men had been members of singing clubs in Germany; and because there was no sheet music available, the songs had to be written out from memory.[9] The choir and orchestra were successful in offering programs of great musical variety. At Christmas 1945 the choir gave a concert with works by Verdi, Brahms, Mozart, Wagner, and Beethoven, followed a few days later by a New Year's concert in which the orchestra played music from Italy, North and South America, and Germany. There were foxtrots, slow waltzes, a tango, a carioca, and, as a climax, Johann Strauss's "Tales from

American officers and women view prisoner of war art exhibit at the
Ogden Defense Depot Officers' Club. (Public Relations Office, Ogden
Defense Depot)

Art and handicraft pieces made by German prisoners at the Ogden Defense
Depot offered for sale to American personnel and families. (Public
Relations Office, Ogden Defense Depot)

Typing class for German prisoners. (Public Relatons Office, Ogden Defense Depot)

Course certificate awarded Herbert Barkhoff at Ogden prisoner of war camp. (Courtesy of Herbert Barkhoff)

the Vienna Woods." Earlier in the year the choir, orchestra, and selected soloists had joined together for a grand two-part concert which began with a performance of the first movement of Beethoven's "Moonlight Sonata," followed by three selections by the choir, "Vespers," "Fahr Wohl der Goldene Sonne," and "Rasch Tritt der Tod den Menschen an. . . ." The first half of the program concluded with a reading about the life of Beethoven. The second part of the program opened with a violin solo of Franz Drdla's "Souvenir." Also on the program were selections from two Franz Lehar operettas, *Der Zarewitsch* and *Das Land des Laechelns*, and several well-known German songs by the chorus, including "Aennchen von Tharau" and "So Herzig wie mein Liesel." The concert ended with a performance of "Evening Prayer" from Humperdink's opera *Hansel and Gretel*.[10]

Arts and crafts were also popular with the prisoners. In the Ogden camp, space was available for sketching, painting, lettering, linoleum-block cutting and printing, wood carving, and model making. Leonhard Mombar, who had been a painter by profession, used a wooden box slab to carve and paint a medallion bearing an Indian head, encircled by the inscription "Zur Erinnerung an die Kriegsgefangenschaft, 1946, America." He had copied the figure from a photograph in a magazine. In Camp Douglas, Wyoming, four master violin makers were among the 3,000 prisoners. Arrangements were made with the YMCA to provide the appropriate woods and tools for the men to craft violins for use in the camp and for distribution to other prisoners. In Ogden, a prisoner made a violin and gave it to Calvin Bartholomew over his reluctance to accept such a priceless gift.[11]

Art was a favored recreational activity for the Germans. Erwin Schott, a Munich-born artist, conducted classes for his fellow prisoners and painted a number of pictures and portraits as gifts for the Americans with whom he worked. Some of his paintings were sent to an international exhibit of POW work held in Geneva, Switzerland. On April 22, 1945, an art exhibit, sponsored by the German prisoners, was held at the officers' club. The fifty works of art, painted by sixteen different prisoners at their own expense and on their own time, sold for about $5.00 each.[12]

Little is known about other creations by German prisoners in Utah camps; however, undoubtedly there must have been craftsmen equal to those in other camps where furniture, aquariums, animal cages and houses, and detailed replicas of old German castles, cathedrals, and other landmarks reminiscent of the homeland were built. Larger projects included chapels and smokehouses for sausages. One prisoner "actually built a complete Bavarian-style house within his compound and attempted to have it shipped home when he was repatriated!"[13]

Sports were very popular among the prisoners, with soccer the most favored. A shortage of soccer balls presented some difficulty at first, so prisoners were forced to be resourceful and make them out of small pieces of leather. In Rupert, Idaho, the prisoners attempted to manufacture their own Ping-Pong balls, an undertaking judged less than successful by camp inspectors. Later, the situation improved, and inspector Luis Hortal reported, "Sports and games could hardly be better." Ultimately, there were twenty-four soccer teams and sixteen "fistball" teams in the Ogden camp as well as eight tennis courts for approximately two hundred players. Boxing rings, badminton courts, billiard and Ping-Pong tables were available for a constant round of leagues and tournaments, giving the POW companies opportunities to cheer their teams.[14]

There was little interest in sports in the branch camps. As one former prisoner of war recalled, they had played on soccer teams in other camps, "but in Logan there was little time and little strength for soccer. Most of our free time was taken up with washing and taking care of personal needs." Logan prisoners longed for an excursion into the nearby mountains, but enforcement of strict policies precluded such a treat. Conditions were more lax at Bushnell Hospital, where some prisoners were permitted to go for hikes in the mountains at whose base their camp was located. The local wildlife, such as porcupines and deer, was of special interest, but guards warned the men not to wander too far from camp because they might come face to face with a wild bear.[15] If there was one additional activity the Americans could have allowed, especially in Utah, it would have been the privilege of hikes in the mountains.

Probably in keeping with tradition among prisoners of war everywhere, but perhaps also as a perceived need, a number of men undertook the manufacture of alcoholic beverages during their time in the United States. In Logan, Rudolf Weltin reported that they made wine from wild rosebuds mixed with sugar and water. "It was not much of a wine, but it was a little bit of alcohol."[16] Other prisoners were more inventive. Fritz Poes, a handyman and former railroad worker, used a water-filled fire extinguisher which he modified into a still. A mash of grapefruit or some other fruit was heated inside the metal cylinder, and the resulting alcoholic fumes then passed through a water-cooled coil, condensing into a homemade form of schnapps. There was some danger with this system. In Fort Lewis, Washington, before Poes's transfer to Utah, "the whole thing exploded and an entire wall was blown out between the heating room and the work room."[17] Ernst Luders described another method of alcohol production used by his comrades in Arizona. Among the men who shared a tent with Luders was the son of a wine grower from the Moselle region in Germany. The orange trees growing near the camp provided an adequate source of fruit, and when yeast stolen from the kitchen was added, several gallons of wine were produced. The smell of oranges fermenting attracted the attention of other prisoners, and soon nearly everyone was trying to produce orange wine. When it became obvious to the American authorities that the prisoners were engaged in making wine, they announced that such an industry was not allowed and that any homemade wine had to be disposed of within twenty-four hours. The consequences should have been predicted. Huge quantities of the homemade wine were consumed, leaving the prisoners drunk from overindulgence and crowding the latrines because they had diarrhea from the fermented fruit.[18] The prisoners were not always particular about some of the sources of alcohol. In Ogden it was necessary to remove bottles of hair tonic and after-shave lotion from the shelves of the canteen to keep the Russian prisoners from drinking them for their alcoholic content. "When the Russian prisoners celebrated, the way from the canteen to the barracks was strewn with empty . . . bottles."[19]

Although alcohol may have been the occasional temptress, education was the veritable mistress many prisoners turned to in their free time. In Camp Warner a well-organized educational program utilized POW instructors with classes in mathematics, German, English, Latin, French, Spanish, shorthand, bookkeeping, chemistry, geometry, literature, and writing. In May 1944, there were fifteen different classes available to the 600 German prisoners.[20]

In Clearfield the camp spokesman felt a strong need to give his fellow prisoners "the opportunity for education so that some day they could carry on their work in the Germany of the future." Nevertheless, like most young men, they were more interested in soccer or doing nothing at all than attending classes. The spokesman recognized the importance of teaching American history to the prisoners, but argued that it could not be fully understood without some comprehension of their own history. He lamented, "Could they but discover the right picture of their own history, it would mean everything to them." Since the teaching and writing of German history after 1933 had been "deluged with propaganda," only one side of German history had been presented, and those teaching German history to their fellow prisoners were doing so from what they remembered. The camp spokesman held that the most important books to be secured for the camp were those on German history written by well-known German historians before 1932.[21] The lack of sufficient equipment and textbooks was cited as the reason for difficulty in recruiting more prisoners to take classes offered in the camps. In other camps the loss of qualified and popular instructors through transfer deterred educational programs.[22] There were, however, individual success stories like that of Ernst Luders, who, with the assistance of the Red Cross, was able to secure textbooks and pamphlets from Germany on taxes in order to prepare himself for a profession as a tax accountant after the war. Officials in every POW base camp were strongly encouraged to offer a variety of classes for the inmates. However, classes were offered in only a few of the smaller camps. In Tremonton, for example, Charles C. Eberhardt reported: "Prisoners of war teachers are active in teaching English and French. Beyond this, the prisoners themselves have interest (but only slight) in such studies as geography or bookkeeping."[23]

In 1944 the provost marshal general authorized those prisoners with permission from their camp commander to enroll in extension courses offered by fourteen American universities, including DePaul University, Concordia Seminar, and the universities of California, Chicago, Michigan, Minnesota, Texas, Washington, Wisconsin, Colorado, Illinois, Indiana, North Carolina, and Virginia. There were obstacles to participation in such programs, mainly an inability to read and write English at the college level. Consequently, only 660 German prisoners throughout the United States were enrolled in the fourteen university programs in May of 1945.[24]

In August 1944 University of Utah President LeRoy E. Cowles was contacted by Dr. George F. Zook of the American Council on Education to determine if the university would like to be involved in an extension of the council's program for the education of prisoners of war. President Cowles responded that the university was very interested in the program, "but we are undermanned and would not have a great deal of time to devote to this project." Dr. Arthur L. Beeley, head of the Department of Sociology and dean of the School of Social Work, was designated as the university's representative in the project.[25] A month later, on September 28, 1944, Col. Francis E. Howard, director of the Prisoner of War Division, wrote to President Cowles suggesting that Professor Beeley visit the Ogden POW camp to meet with the camp commander and the prisoners who directed educational activities there. Colonel Howard's letter included three major conditions for the university's participation in an educational program for the prisoners: (1) the educational expenses, including Professor Beeley's visit, were to be paid by the prisoners themselves, (2) no civilians would be permitted to give lectures or to conduct classes for the prisoners, and (3) any plan developed by the university to assist the prisoners had to be submitted in writing for approval by the camp commander. Professor Beeley replied that he would be glad to cooperate in any way possible and suggested that he meet with Colonel Howard in Washington, D.C., while he was there to deliver a lecture to the National Police Academy. He would be available to visit the Ogden camp after his return to Utah at the end of the month.[26]

Eight months later, President Cowles was contacted again by army officials with a request for help with educational activities in the Clearfield camp. The university was asked to assist in the selection and procurement of appropriate American and German books; to loan visual aids and books from the university library; to advise the POW director of studies on addressing educational problems, including the organization of classes; and to provide any additional services that might be needed. Once again the university responded, agreeing to lend books from its library without charge and offering to send German-speaking professors when requested to "add . . . interest and efficiency to the classes, now being conducted by prisoner-of-war teachers." The German-speaking professors included Oscar J. Hamner, professor of history, to lecture on early American history and American government; Elden J. Facer, assistant professor of economics, whose topic was American industrial geography; and James L. Barker, professor of languages, who proposed to lecture on spoken English.[27]

Capt. Walter H. Rapp, in the report on his May 1945 visit to the Ogden camp, referred to the demand for American lecturers on United States history. He praised the help given by the University of Utah in supplying books, offering professional advice, and providing outlines for study. He also expressed a wish that the University of Utah might "be permitted to give correspondence courses to POWs at this camp. The prisoners appreciate this sponsorship and I feel it is a great asset."[28] Typical of such prisoners was Walter Leischner, who took correspondence courses in economics from the University of Utah. He would translate the study questions into German, answer them in German, and then translate the answers into English.[29]

Calvin Bartholomew, who was in charge of educational programs for both the prisoners and their American guards in the Ogden depot, noted a marked contrast in the interest of the two groups toward the educational opportunities offered by the military. For the Americans, Utah's universities offered free extension and correspondence courses for which they could earn credit. There was little interest, however, displayed by the guards; they gave priority to Ogden's notorious 25th Street for their off-duty time. Bartholomew deplored the fact that guards "were not interested at all in improving their minds or taking advantage of these opportunities." In contrast, the German prisoners were excited about the educational opportunities, even without earning credit. "Whatever they learned, they did for the love of learning."[30]

In an article in the November 1945 issue of the Ogden camp newspaper, *Unser Leben*, it was suggested that even behind barbed wire the prisoners could and should learn and work on their continued development. The words of Goethe that every day one should at least read a good poem and listen to something that is new were presented as a challenge to the prisoners. It was conceded that there were many prisoners who had not completed their education or learned a trade. The men were told that they needed above all a strong foundation in the basic subjects, especially the German language. "To master the German language is not only a duty and honor as a German but also is in one's own interest. Nowhere is the lack of education more painful and difficult as those situations relating to proper speech and correct writing." Judged second to the study of German was the study of the English language. "The study of foreign languages broadens one's knowledge and education and goes hand in hand with a deeper mastery of one's mother tongue." Finally, the prisoners were encouraged to study the geography and history of the United States so they could "return to the homeland with a knowledgeable picture of this land which stretches over an entire continent and is of tremendous importance to the world." Prisoners could expect that, once home, their friends and relatives would ask many questions about America; therefore, they should be concerned with learning enough to give intelligent answers.[31]

"Why American History?" was the title of another article published in *Unser Leben*. The article, taken from the Camp Cook, California, newspaper, *Der Lagerspiegel*, argued that as long as the German prisoners were in the United States they should make every effort to learn more about the country. Much could be learned by simple observation; however, some study of the past was required if the prisoners were to understand the cultural, political, and economic present as well as the mentality of the American people. The German prisoners knew a few things about American history, but for most of them it was quite a shadowy affair. Furthermore, during the past twelve years nothing had been done to rectify the situation. The article declared that a study of American history could be of great service, since "today we are suspended, politically speaking, in an airless room. We all feel that something new must be created, but what and how? We hope after a period of transition there will be a free and democratic Germany." In order to participate effectively as a free citizen in such a democracy, it was essential to develop a world perspective and the political acumen to identify any issues and trends that could jeopardize a new Germany. For this vision to become a reality, the study of the past was the key to success. The article concluded that perhaps the most beneficial aspect of studying American history would come from an analysis of the inner workings of democracy—how the ideas about democracy were first put into practice and how democratic ideals were able to hold the nation together during the tumultuous nineteenth century and bring the United States to a place of power and respect in the world.[32] Similar articles appeared in practically every issue of *Unser Leben* as part of an overall denazification program designed both to rid the prisoners of any loyalty toward nazism and to plant the seeds of democracy which would bear fruit after the men returned to Germany.

The German prisoners who arrived in Ogden in August of 1944 were not the hardened kind that seemed all too prevalent among those who had been taken earlier in North Africa. They were soldiers who had recently fallen into American hands in northern Europe, and many of them, including the POW spokesman, had experienced a difficult time in northern France and were likely "to remain tractable for some time."[33] As a result, there was progress in educating the prisoners to American democratic principles. In contrasting American democracy with European dictatorships, one Ogden prisoner observed, "In Europe when things go bad, the only thing left for a dictator to do is blame all the trouble on another nation. [But in America] when things go bad, the Republicans blame the Democrats and the Democrats blame the Republicans—and so you don't have to go to war with Mexico or Canada."[34] Many prisoners, sympathetic to the ideas of democracy that were stressed in the camp school, "grew up with Adolf Hitler in the schools and did not know anything else, and so some of us were somewhat for him, but afterward that disappeared very quickly. Democracy was something very different and new for us. The American people, they were something new for us, their generosity in all things, that was something we did not know."[35]

The prisoners' new visions about their personal and collective future that had developed because of the educational programs were reinforced through participation in religious activities and contemplating their relationship to a supreme being. Article 16 of the Geneva Convention gave prisoners the right to attend religious services. The policy of the United States encouraged such religious activity, but prohibited American personnel and prisoners worshiping together in religious services or sharing chapels. The shortage of qualified German chaplains among the prisoners presented problems to American authorities. There were only a handful of regular chaplains in the German army to begin with; most ministers and priests had been drafted as regular soldiers. Furthermore, among nine Catholic priests who had been assigned to the German army as chaplains and subsequently sent to the United States as prisoners of war, several were members of the gestapo or other political organizations and their assignments as chaplains were secondary to other duties.[36] Despite this situation, many prisoners had strong religious backgrounds that became manifest in the POW camps. In Clearfield, Karl Gustav Almquist, of the Swedish Legation, reported that in conversations with leaders among the prisoners he had found "a deep-lying interest in the [church] services and in Christianity, an interest which Christianity and the church once had impressed in the hearts of the men in their earlier days." Although there was not always an open display of religious interest, it was because "the men were too shy among the multitude of the others in the barracks." Still, the prisoners "were thinking deeply about Christianity."[37] In another camp, Almquist found that church attendance was small because the prisoners, who were very young, had been captured after only a few days in the German army. They "were rather young and were still seeking their way in life . . . [and] were not accustomed to going to church and attending services." Nonethless, the young prisoners "all were glad to have a pastor among them, which they demonstrated by looking him up for talks and advice on different matters."[38] For other young prisoners between the ages of seventeen and twenty-five, who only knew the political, military, cultural, and religious environment of the Third Reich, belief in anything was difficult. They were completely demoralized after Germany's defeat; they felt relatively helpless and alone, and were critical of every new political system and skeptical of any Christian endeavor on their behalf.[39]

In most large camps, the men's religious needs were well provided for, and some observers found that many of the prisoners "not only came into camp with their prayer book and rosaries, but used them in the most conscientious manner."[40] In addition to the Catholic and Lutheran chaplains who were among the prisoners, local clergymen were assigned to the camps, where chapels or other acceptable places of worship were provided. In the smaller branch camps, such as those at Salina and Orem, which were a considerable distance from the main camp in Ogden, only irregular visits by the clergy were made.

At first, Catholic services for the German prisoners in the Ogden camp were held in the open on the athletic field where an altar had been set up. When the Catholic chaplain was transferred, arrangements were made with the Catholic clergy in Ogden to provide religious services by saying mass on Sunday and holding devotional services on Tuesday and Saturday evenings. The services were under the direction of Father Girouf of St. Joseph's church in Ogden. Attendance was reported at about three hundred men a week, or about 20 to 25 percent of the Catholic prisoners.

Protestant services were arranged after the prisoners had been in Ogden for several months, with Pastor Schumann of Salt Lake City conducting the services. However, in a short time the assignment was given to Pastor Clement Harms, who was a Lutheran minister in Brigham City. Because of his small congregation in Brigham City, Pastor Harms seemed to welcome the opportunity to work among the German prisoners. A second-generation German-American, Harms spoke fluent German and took his work among the prisoners seriously. Karl Gustav Almquist spoke with him on July 10, 1945, about the spiritual needs of the prisoners and came away with a favorable impression of the pastor. Almquist observed that Pastor Harms spent considerable time after the services talking with the prisoners, who appeared to welcome the opportunity to "talk over their religious problems." Attendance at the Protestant services was reported at about two hundred men, or 15 to 20 percent.[41]

Pastor Harms began his work with the prisoners in Bushnell Hospital and gradually expanded his ministry to include the army depot in Ogden, the Clearfield naval depot, the branch camps in Tremonton and Logan, and on several occasions the branch camp in Preston, Idaho. Reflecting twenty years later on his experience in Utah, he recalled that the American camp personnel had been very cooperative in accommodating schedules and arrangements for religious services without any interference as to how they were conducted. As for the German prisoners who attended his services, they "were very appreciative . . . [and] happy that they could receive spiritual ministration." The prisoners in Brigham City showed their appreciation to Pastor Harms with a Christmas card designed by one of the men and signed by twenty of his comrades. The card, symbolic of the prisoners' belief that Christmas transcended the confines of the camp, portrayed a Christmas tree lighted with burning candles centered between six strands of broken barbed wire. Below the sketch was the scripture, "Glory to God in the Highest and Peace and Goodwill on Earth to Men." On the back of the card was a personal Christmas greeting to Parson Harms and his wife and an expression of gratitude from the German prisoners at Bushnell Hospital.[42] Despite the favorable report about Pastor Harms, it was suggested that the Ogden camp should have its own POW clergy. Camp personnel agreed that the right clergy could enhance the men's spiritual life very much. Col. Arthur J. Ericsson had tried to get Catholic and Lutheran chaplains for the camp, but had not yet succeeded. He asked Almquist's help in securing the transfer of qualified clergy to Ogden, again stressing the need for the right kind of people.[43]

Church attendance at Ogden was typical of most camps and better than some. In Papago Park, Arizona, out of a total of 1,870 men, only 30 Catholics and 25 Lutherans attended church regularly. One prisoner disclosed that those who attended church services were viewed as traitors by the staunch Nazis in camp. American officials reported that church attendance by the German prisoners seemed to increase following Germany's surrender.[44]

Although the needs of the Catholic and Protestant prisoners were of primary concern, some attention was shown to the religious needs of other prisoners. For example, camp officials gave a group of Mongolian prisoners from Russia permission to observe a religious holiday with a special ritual. Lt. Wayne Owens was assigned to purchase a goat, which was to be sacrificed as part of the religious ceremony.[45]

In meeting the social and religious needs of the prisoners of war, the YMCA performed a most important function. It brought an element of humanity to their experience that did not go unnoticed by the German prisoners. One prisoner wrote to the YMCA office, thanking the organization for its help and advice and crediting it with an increase in morale among the men. "You urged them to believe in humanity and to respect human dignity; and I am glad to say your efforts were not in vain."[46] In addition, the broadminded policies of American officials on matters of recreation, education, and religion contributed to the well-being of most prisoners of war in the United States and helped make their experience as captured soldiers the most humane in the history of armed conflict.

ELEVEN

German and American Relations

As former German prisoners of war and the World War II generation of Utahns reflect on their experiences with each other, one of the most compelling themes to emerge from both sides is the interaction among former German soldiers, American personnel, and American civilians. Often relationships transcended the wartime issues of bias, fear, loyalty, and hostility as well as the routine activities of work and recreation. The result was usually a testament of human goodwill as compassion, understanding, and friendship overcame the prejudice, hate, and violence associated with war. Language barriers presented considerable difficulty and prudence in dealing with the enemy demanded caution, but there were many situations when humanity overrode nationalism and fear and both captives and captors benefited from the common encounters.

Official policy sought to limit contact between prisoners of war and American civilians. Camp commanders were directed to institute measures to prohibit "fraternization, acceptance of hospitality by prisoners of war, and association with women." In Ogden both military and civilian personnel were reminded that the Germans were prisoners of war and "that fraternization and any dealings with them are absolutely prohibited." Furthermore, they were warned against approaching the camp fence and urged "to be constantly on the alert and report any irregularities or unusual incidents in connection with German prisoners."[1]

Civilian contractors were issued written guidelines outlining proper conduct toward the prisoners and their possible involvement if any escaped. The instructions warned: "If you fraternize with prisoners of war, or permit others to do so unnecessarily, give them clothing or other articles, accept or deliver mail for them and there is an escape, your action might tend to make it appear that you had aided in the escape."[2] Charged with carrying out the non-fraternization policy, guards had orders to thwart conversations between prisoners and civilians. Prisoners were told that any contact with civilians other than that necessary to carry out work assignments was not only discouraged but also forbidden. Although these security measures were not always possible or practical, especially when the prisoners worked for and with American civilians, care was taken to monitor POW contact with civilians.

For German prisoners the first contact with Americans was with soldiers who captured them and processed them for the trip to America. Arnold Krammer found that when army officials began using empty vehicles to transport prisoners back from the front, the convoys met with catcalls and jeers from the Americans en route to the front. However, when the Allies appeared to be winning the campaign, "resentment against enemy prisoners nearly disappeared . . . and as the POWs began to lose their initial fear of mistreatment at the hands of their captors, both sides began to relax."[3] There was a sense of shared experience and an unspoken mutual understanding between the Germans and the Americans. Some realized that their enemies were soldiers just like themselves who, because of fate, were fighting on the other side. As a concrete example of this mutual regard, American personnel donated blood for German prisoners when called upon to do so. In Ogden, Gordon Reeves volunteered his blood for a German prisoner who underwent an operation for a brain tumor in an unsuccessful attempt to save his life. Reeves then transported the body by ambulance to Salt Lake City and attended the burial services in the Fort Douglas cemetery. Georg Hirschmann, wounded near Anzio when the Allies landed on the Italian beachhead in January 1944, recalled how differently he felt about the enemy when he and a wounded American were lying side by side en route to a hospital ship. A few minutes before, they had been shooting at each other, trying to kill each other. Then it was suddenly different. The American pulled out a pack of cigarettes and shared them with his neighbors regardless of whether they were German or American. Vividly recalling the incident forty years later, Hirschmann summarized his reactions: "There are moments when you come to the realization of things you had not known."[4]

The period of initial capture, processing, and transportation to the United States offered little opportunity for extended associations to develop between German prisoners and American soldiers. But once the prisoners were assigned to camps and settled into a routine, the circumstances changed and friendships and a mutual trust became possible. In Continental, Arizona, Gerhard Graenitz was assigned to work as a cook with an American sergeant named Martinez who, because he had contracted malaria while serving in the South Pacific, had been reassigned to the small camp near his home. The two men drove together to Tucson every day to obtain supplies, and they always stopped to visit Martinez's fiancée, who lived five miles from the camp. Martinez would give the jeep and his wristwatch to Graenitz, instructing him to return in an hour. On his own and only a few miles from the Mexican border, Graenitz had no thought of escape. Instead, he spent his hour of freedom bouncing around the southern Arizona desert and offering rides to school girls. In December 1944, the two men drove by jeep from Continental north to the Grand Canyon to get Christmas trees for the camp. Equipped with a tent and supplies and armed with a Colt revolver and a Winchester rifle, they traveled for three days in their quest for the trees. Seeing the Grand Canyon was, as Graenitz related, "an experience out of this world. I had read about it in books, but one cannot imagine something like that. . . . The rocks, the sun, it is something I will never forget."[5]

Where Graenitz and other German prisoners took the opportunity to learn English from their American associates—albeit, as Granitz claimed in his case, "with a Mexican accent"—Americans were hesitant to learn anything more than a couple of words of German from the prisoners. An exception was Cpl. Lawrence Hood, company clerk for one of the four German POW companies at Tooele. Hood had been drafted in 1943 at the age of thirty-five; and after basic training in Camp Gruber, Oklahoma, and a brief assignment in Fort Lewis, Washington, he was sent to Camp Warner in January 1944. His arrival coincided with that of 1,000 German prisoners. With an interest in languages and plenty of spare time, he obtained a German textbook and tried to learn what he could

Fritz Enders, former prisoner of war at Salina, shortly after his return home. (Photo courtesy of Lorraine Nelson)

Inscribed photograph of German prisoner Fritz Noack given to his Salt Lake City friend.

Richard Boettger working with American women in an Ogden Defense Depot warehouse in 1945. (Photo courtesy of Richard Boettger)

Casket for Hans Gabriel, who died on August 13, 1945, at the Ogden Defense Depot when a metal box fell from a loading crane and crushed him. (National Archives photo)

Burial services for Han Gabriel at the Fort Douglas cemetery. (National Archives photo)

from the German clerk, Helmut Romaine, even though Romaine spoke English. He learned enough to fill out the payroll in German and carry on limited conversations. Nevertheless, he experienced frustration in learning to pronounce German, especially the words *nicht* and *nach*. "I could never get it the way they thought it should be. I would say 'nickt' and they would say 'nicht.' I would say 'nack' and they would say 'nach,' and I thought it sounded just like I had said it."[6]

Efforts by Germans to learn English from their captors can be exemplified by Heinz Richter's experience. Richter was responsible for cleaning tools and maintaining a fire in the stove. The American guard, who had nothing to watch outside, was drawn toward the inviting warmth of the stove inside the hut, and so spent the entire day in close association with Richter—who just happened to have an English-German dictionary. "I seized the opportunity to speak with him, using the dictionary. He was very patient with me. Sometimes he fell asleep, but I wouldn't let him sleep too long because I wanted to learn English."[7]

In Bushnell Hospital, Paul Hupfner became friends with an American soldier, who insisted that the German accompany him into Brigham City and even gave him his spare uniform to wear. Hupfner made friends not only with army personnel in Bushnell but also with the patients he served. One patient in particular, Frank Woods, who had lost his legs in the Pacific, developed such an affinity for Hupfner that he called for him whenever he needed something. Hupfner recalled forty years later that Woods had told him "that he loved me like a brother."[8]

Even the American guards showed some leniency in handling their German prisoners. Although instructed to do otherwise, they often turned their backs when farmers offered the prisoners soft drinks, candy bars, and food. Others developed sympathetic relationships with the prisoners. Before one guard left on furlough, prisoners working as mechanics in the motor pool gave his car an oil change and lubrication service before he left camp. In Salina, there was a guard who never seemed to have any money. In a gesture of friendship, the German prisoners approached the farmer offering to work an extra hour if he would give the extra pay to the guard. Dieter Lampe described the relationships with the guards in Salina as "somewhat leisurely and friendly." The prisoners were not supposed to take food or cigarettes that the farmers gave them back to camp; however, according to Lampe, some guards allowed the men to keep the gifts if they were shared with the guards.[9]

In the summer of 1945 the quality of American guards reportedly improved as soldiers returning from the battlefields of Europe were assigned to the POW camps. In Bushnell Hospital for example, approximately half of the guard detachment were veterans of overseas service.[10] As a consequence, when volatile situations arose, the conduct of the guards was usually more reasonable than that of "shooting first and asking questions later." Herbert Barkhoff wrote of one occasion when at 2:00 A.M. he could not sleep because of a personal crisis and, against camp rules, was out walking along the fence. The guards saw him, shined their spotlight on him, and telephoned their superior. Two soldiers were sent in a jeep to pick him up. After questioning him as to what he was doing, the guards returned him to his barracks and wished him a good night's sleep. Barkhoff was impressed not only with the way he was treated but also with the fact that the guards in the tower "did not shoot . . . [and] recognized that it was no attempt to escape but a foolish deed on my part."[11]

Although most American guards were flexible and lenient in their treatment of the prisoners, there were some who delighted in tormenting the German prisoners. And, there were others who "followed the book" on handling the prisoners. One Polish-born, German-speaking guard was the terror of the Ogden camp. According to one prisoner, "He was so bad that we called him the cannibal. None of us liked him. He was not a very good person." Then there was the other side of the coin. Some guards mistrusted the prisoners: "A German prisoner of war with a fork is more dangerous than an Italian POW with a machine gun" or "The Germans are in league with the devil!"[12] The Germans responded to tight control by playing tricks on their guards. "One of the things we did [in the Southwest] to get even with the guards who were always searching us is that one of the men put a cactus in his pocket and when the guard reached into his pocket to see what he had, he got the needles in his hand."[13] But American officers usually treated prisoners with fairness and consideration. When a patient in Bushnell Hospital repeatedly charged Paul Hupfner with being a gestapo agent because he had refused to wash the patient's underclothes and socks unless he was compensated—which was the usual practice—he complained to his supervisor and asked to be transferred. Instead, the medic put in a good word for Hupfner to the officer in charge and the recalcitrant patient was transferred and Hupfner remained at his assigned post.[14]

The prisoners also had ways of acknowledging those who treated them with fairness and consideration. When Wayne Owens, commander of the Sixth Prisoner of War Company in Ogden, was transferred to the First Prisoner of War Company, the men of the Sixth prepared a commemorative document listing their names and expressing deep regret that he was leaving. They offered best wishes and thanked him "for all . . . you have done to all of us in your understanding of all those things and troubles which are involved in a prisoner of war company. . . . Your firm but always correct treatment of the men of this company was recognized and always will be remembered as one of those things which made our stay in this country much easier." Three months later when Owens was promoted from first lieutenant to captain, the prisoners in his new company prepared a card of congratulations on his promotion.[15]

Indicative of the concern by camp officials for the prisoners of war, especially in the last months of their stay in the United States, is Col. Arthur J. Ericsson's 1945 Christmas letter to the Ogden prisoners. He realized that they would prefer to be with their families and friends at home, especially for Christmas, but urged them to find solace in the fact that their sojourn as prisoners of war was nearly over and that "this Christmas marks the last milepost on the way back to your loved ones and your homeland. For this reason alone you should greet this Christmas season as one of the most joyous of your life."[16] Colonel Ericsson was praised for his authoritative management of the camp, where "in spite of constant difficulties that present themselves, he always succeeds in finding a fair solution."[17]

During his inspection of the Clearfield Naval Supply Depot, Sture Persson found the German camp there to be one of the finest he had seen. He was impressed with the interest shown by the commanding officer, Capt. Homer O. Wood, in the welfare of the prisoners and with the good morale that was evident in the camp. On an inspection of the POW barracks, Persson was moved when Captain Wood "stopped and played a set of ping pong with one of the PWs. He made it . . . [such] that the men understood that he is their friend but at the same time their boss."[18]

As noted, interaction was not confined to prisoners with military personnel. In the smaller camps, such as Tremonton, Salina, and Orem, civilian doctors provided medical care for the prisoners when necessary.[19] Civilians worked with the prisoners, transporting them to fields and supervising their work in both agricultural and nonagricultural endeavors, providing opportunities for contact and exchanges. Leath Rasmussen of Salina was assigned to pick up the POW work detail in the morning and transport the men back to camp in the evening. He found the prisoners to be friendly and helpful. The prisoners would pile out of the vehicle to help change a flat tire or push the truck free if it got stuck. Rasmussen permitted the prisoners to ride in the cab with him despite questions about this practice from his associates. On occasion, when he was hauling sugar beets to the factory in Centerfield, he would stop at a little general store in Axtell, buy soda pop or candy bars for the twelve-man work detail, and distribute them when he returned to the fields. For this act of kindness and in remembrance of his stay in Salina, one of the prisoners gave him a large canvas painting of his home in Germany when he left.[20] Edwin Pelz recalled a variation of this experience. While traveling to and from the fields, guards and drivers would often stop at roadside stores or restaurants to go inside for a beer or soft drink, leaving the prisoners unattended in the back of the truck and subject to the attentions of local residents. Rather than insulting or harassing them, the people would "offer us cigarettes, then some of them would go into the store and buy us chocolates, candies, fruit, and such things."[21]

But not all civilian-German relations were cordial. Cobie Van der Puhl (now Wilson), who had befriended a number of prisoners in the Ogden depot, furnishing them with candy bars, sandwiches, and other items—despite official policy against such generosity and the fact that most of the articles were rationed—found the last group of prisoners assigned to her area the most difficult. On one occasion, when she asked a prisoner to fill a requisition, he turned to her with a look that said, "Lady, who do you think you are telling me what to do?" She got the message. "He just spit on me. . . . I wiped it off, but I didn't report him. I was ready to kick him."[22] And there was the opposite situation: civilians who showed no interest in or compassion for the German prisoners. Karl Altkruger recalled that, in Salina, prisoners were generally fed by the farmers; but if not, the guards would ask if the farmer would add something to supplement the men's meager ration. On one occasion when the guards showed a farmer the food that was to be the prisoners' lunch, he declared brusquely, "That does not interest me at all what they have to eat. I pay for their work, and they will not get anything to eat from me." Altkruger speculated that at the end of the day the farmer "must have been very angry, because we pulled almost everything out. . . . But we wouldn't have done that if he had brought us a little bread and butter, or some coffee."[23] Another account from Salina by Willi Klebe had a happier ending. A farmer had refused to provide the prisoners with fresh water on their first day of work. When they returned a few weeks later, they expected the same treatment. Instead, they were given lunch with a cake baked by the farmer's daughter. This turn of events came about because the farmer's nephew, who was a prisoner of war in a camp in Dusseldorf, had written to him that they ate better than the local citizens did. As an additional gesture of goodwill, the farmer brought out a box of large Brazilian cigars and gave one to each prisoner.[24]

More productive work was but one of the ways the prisoners acknowledged such acts of generosity. They also left mementos of their sojourn in Utah with the people who had treated them fairly. Floyd Johnson of Aurora, Utah, was given in exchange for cigarettes a small, wooden jewelry box made in the form of a German house. Prisoner D. Stern had made the box while at Camp Tonkawa, Oklahoma, and had carried it from there to Arizona and then to Utah.[25] Writing in her diary on October 26, 1945, Mrs. Dorothy J. Buchanan of Richfield, Utah, described her feelings when her husband arrived home from the farm with a gift from a prisoner. "A German prisoner had laboriously made a miniature of the home he left in Germany. He knows it has been destroyed. It is ingeniously and painstakingly made. I should add—lovingly. It is heartbreaking to look at it."[26]

Another Utahn acquired a painting by a former prisoner of war through unusual circumstances. A Utah Valley farmer, Rulon Nicholes was unimpressed with the lunch—two salami sandwiches apiece and black coffee—given to the ten prisoners thinning sugar beet plants in his fields. He drove to the house, got two gallons of milk and a freshly baked cake, and returned to share the food with the men. Two years later, he received a letter from Alfred Falke, one of the ten prisoners who had worked on his farm during the summer of 1945. The letter was addressed to "Lieber Ankel Nickels." Falke had apparently recalled a neighbor yelling to Nicholes, "How are ya, Uncle?" and had assumed that Nicholes's first name was "Uncle." The letter was translated from German to English by a woman who had immigrated from Germany before the war. Falke had written that he was an artist, and wanted to paint a picture of Mt. Timpanogos for Nicholes and his wife. He had a snapshot of the mountain, and he remembered how beautiful it was in the sunset. He asked Nicholes to send him some oil paints and a brush, so he could do the painting. It arrived in November

1948, and the gesture led to an exchange of letters as well as packages of food and clothing sent to Germany.[27]

There were occasions when the situation for the German prisoners had particular relevance in the lives of American families, especially for families whose sons were away in the service, missing in action, or held as prisoners of war by the enemy. A Salina farmer, expressing his anguish for his son, a pilot missing in the Pacific, was consoled by Herbert Barkhoff. "We encouraged him to have hope and wished him everything good for his son."[28]

Regardless of the quality of relations between Americans and Germans, the strongest indication of a significant change of policy in who worked next to whom was associated with German prisoners and American women. Early in the war the Tooele camp commander agonized over prisoners and women working in close proximity. He concluded that there would be no trouble because "the work is heavy manual labor and the women are apparently all in their forties."[29] By 1945, prisoners and women were working side by side in places like the Ogden army depot, and the women were supervising the prisoners as well. The situation was not without risk, however. Rumors circulated that some of the young American women felt sorry for the Germans at Tooele and that they were involved in illicit sexual relations. Some lost their jobs over it when they were caught. An Ogden guard found a woman's footprints going along a ditch bank and right into the POW compound. He was unable to locate the woman, however, and the prisoners denied that any females had been in their camp.[30] Beatrice Gappmayer Pyne recalled how concerned an American guard was when he found her, as an eighteen-year-old, in a building on her father's farm sorting plums with a German prisoner of war. Although she thought nothing of it at the time, when the guard came in, "he was not about to allow me and this guy to be alone in there."[31]

Another concern developed in the spring of 1946 when, because of a shortage of guards, some prisoners worked by themselves. The potential problem was compounded when farmers, who were obligated to pick up the prisoners at the camp and transport them to their fields, delegated this chore to wives and daughters.[32] Newspapers carried reports of misconduct, such as that of a Del Norte, Colorado, woman who had been involved for several months in a romantic affair with a German prisoner assigned to a nearby camp. In the evening the woman would drive her car out to a farm road where she picked up the prisoner and took him to her home in Del Norte.[33] Despite the danger of discovery and disgrace, some American women did show attention to the prisoners, sometimes on their own initiative, but usually with encouragement from the prisoners themselves. Still, a good measure of caution and circumspection was in order. As one former prisoner explained: "Once in a while there were small gifts, but they were not given to us directly; we were told for example, 'In box 10 there is a chocolate bar or a pack of cigarettes for you.' "[34] On other occasions, when prisoners came in contact with American women, there was a certain amount of curiosity, if not flirtation, on both parts. Herbert Barkhoff recalled such a situation. A group of young women at the Ogden depot were dressed in shirts and coveralls, causing the prisoners to joke about how it was often difficult to tell whether the civilian workers were male or female. One small, dark-complexioned worker aroused particular attention. Acting on a dare from his comrades, Barkhoff hung back until he and the object of curiosity were alone. In his best English Barkhoff inquired, "Are you a boy or are you a girl?" The American put both arms around the German prisoner, bent one leg at the knee, stood on tiptoe with the other in Hollywood fashion, planted a kiss on the lips of a surprised Barkhoff, and asked, "Now can you tell?"[35]

In Brigham City, prisoners attempted to establish contact with the young women working with them in a cannery by writing notes and slipping them into the peaches they were processing. Since most of the notes were written in German, there was a language barrier. But smiles and eye contact needed no translation, and at least one girl met a German prisoner in a nearby peach orchard during the lunch break. The two were caught. The prisoner was locked in the bus for the rest of the day and not permitted to return to the cannery. The young woman was fired and had her hair cut off for fraternizing with the German. However, threats of dismissal and having their hair cut did not deter the young women who traveled by car from Brigham City to Ogden to talk through the fence with prisoners who could speak some English.[36]

Whereas romance, flirtations, and sexual attraction were the reasons for many of the encounters between young American women and German prisoners, compassion and friendship was the foundation for other relationships. In Salina, sixteen-year-old Lorraine Nielson struck up a friendship with Fritz Enders, a tall, blond-haired, blue-eyed native of Bischleben near Erfurt, Germany. When he left Salina, Enders promised to keep in touch with her, even though army regulations prohibited prisoners of war corresponding with American civilians. Breaking this rule and taking advantage of another American friend he had made while working in Paso Robles, California, he wrote to her from California before his departure for Germany. The return address he used was that of his friend, W. N. McElwain, in Paso Robles. He wrote that "promises are made to be kept, not broken," and invited her to write him in care of McElwain. He urged her to be prompt, since they were scheduled to leave for Europe at the end of the month. He had been unable to write earlier because, after leaving Salina, he had gone to pick cotton for six weeks before being sent to Paso Robles. He continued: "Often I think of you, your dear parents and sister. I will never forget all the help and kindness which I had there." He was apprehensive about going home, and hoped to return to the United States soon. He included greetings for Boyd Nelson, her fiancé and future husband, and his family. He inquired if Boyd had become a soldier yet and whether the two had married. About the future, he wrote, "The political things aren't very well, but, I hope, that we never have such a terrible war again. The leaders of the U.N.O. have to be careful in the near future." Lorraine wrote Enders in care of his California friend, a letter that he answered on March 18, 1946, two weeks before his scheduled departure for Germany. He thanked her for the pictures she had sent and noted how clever she had been not to write on them. Since they could not be identified as those of an American citizen, he would be able to carry them back to Germany. He was still apprehensive about what he would find in Germany, commenting that he knew nothing of his parents.

Fritz Enders returned to find his father dead, his mother dependent on him, his home city under Russian occupation, no meat, no coal or wood for fuel, his countrymen freezing to death, and the prospects of losing his job in a bank to older men or war invalids. Still, he held out with conviction: "Come what may, time and the hour runs through the roughest day—I for myself will come through!" Lorraine and her parents sent packages with food, cigarettes, and clothes to Enders, and their correspondence continued until 1950. He asked that the Nielsons send coffee, which he presumably intended to sell on the black market. In return he offered to send pictures, stamps, wood carvings, and other items from the Old World, which he thought could be sold for a good price in the United States. The scheme did not work. Packages sent from Germany did not arrive, restrictions were placed on what could be sent to and from East Germany, and the Nielsons and newlyweds Boyd and Lorraine—like most Utahns—were limited in the amount of what they could package and send to Germany. Enders became more and more discouraged. In one letter he disclosed, "All the time, Salina, the camp and so on go through my head. . . . In dreams too I think back many times. One night I was dreaming the shooting. It was a bad night—maybe it would be better now if I was one of the dead boys." Still, America continued to hold the promise of a better life for Fritz Enders, and his correspondence with his Salina friends sustained him in times of despair. On another occasion he wrote, "Sometimes I think all is against us. But I know I have good friends too, that it is, why I always have the goodwill to make a life. My mother I have to help too. It is not so easy for an old woman to be left alone, else I would go out at once." Conditions worsened for Fritz Enders when he was bedridden with malaria in the fall of 1949. "All the worst things of war are coming through." His last letter to Lorraine was postmarked January 8, 1950, from Zendorf near Koblenz on the Rhein River. He was on a month-long visit to his cousin in West Germany. Unlike the previous letters, this one gave a clearer picture of the political situation under which he lived in East Germany. He warned his American friends not to write about politics or East Germany and the Russians. "It is very dangerous because I'm not a member of the party and have this way many difficulty." He reported that he did not have a good job in East Germany because he was not a member of the Communist party. He vowed: "We Germans . . . will never be a communist-people." But lest he be misunderstood, he wrote, "I'm always the same man like in Utah." He continued: "It is impossible for me to get out because I have to help my dear mother and brother. . . . Times will change. . . . My wish is still [the] U.S. One day I will be back." Lorraine and her husband responded to Enders's last letter, but because of the ominous warning about the political situation in East Germany and because there was no further word from him, they concluded that continuing the correspondence might create trouble for their anti-Communist German friend, and so they wrote no more.[37]

For another young woman, the right combination of circumstances—streetcar access to Fort Douglas, a clever and persistent prisoner of war, and lax security in the waning days before the last prisoners returned home—meant the beginnings of a romance with an Afrika Korps veteran who had been imprisoned in the United States for three years. Their story began on an April Sunday in 1946 when the young teenager and a friend attended a soccer game at Fort Douglas. Prisoner Fritz Noack was a spectator at the game; and when the American guards were not looking, he tossed a rock with a note wrapped around it to the young woman, requesting that she meet him behind the POW compound later that evening. Sympathetic toward the German prisoners and ripe for her first romantic adventure, she met Noack that night. Realizing that it was only a matter of days before he and his comrades would receive notice that they were to be returned to Germany, Noack wasted no time in deciding he would marry the young Utahn. Demonstrating his ability in English, he wrote, "Our hearts belong together forever and the first chance I find to come back to here for us to marry and to live with you." Their affection was sparked by twice-weekly clandestine meetings behind the POW compound and letters that they exchanged. The letters, Noack wrote, were a temporary balm for his loneliness until they could be together. As the camp interpreter and spokesman, Noack had access to a telephone. When he insisted, the young woman gave him her number. He took it down in German shorthand, in case "somebody looks through this book and finds these markings, he isn't able to read it." Lest anyone suspect he was a German prisoner, he proposed that he use the name Fred when calling her. The whole plan was aborted, however, when the young lady, exercising a good measure of caution, gave him a wrong number.

The romance was doomed to a rocky course. When the young woman's parents learned of the affair from FBI agents who had followed their daughter to and from the camp, they were incensed. Telephone calls were out of the question, and meetings in defiance of orders from her father became more circumspect. Noack asked if she could get some blue or brown dye so they could color his uniforms to look more like civilian clothes. He also proposed they slip into the city to go to a movie. When she found some elements of his conduct unacceptable, he apologized, "I'm not accustomed to your American customs. I imagined they would be the same like we have in Germany. Every country isn't the same, I have to realize that and I do so, but there can't be any difference in love." Perhaps the greatest challenge to their relationship was a scheme cooked up by Noack and his friend Sepp, who was interested in the young woman's friend. The two men, after three years of captivity and with only a few weeks until they would return home, proposed that the women escape with them to Mexico where they could be married. Noack explained the plan in a letter dated May 22, 1946. If they left after roll call on Saturday, they would have a twenty-hour head start before the Sunday afternoon roll call. The young woman was to get hold of a good map and see if she could borrow a car for the trip to Mexico. The young woman saw the pitfalls in such a venture and refused to go along with the plan. Noack did not try to push the scheme any further, and in his letter one week later he asked that she "please forget the plan we made up."

With the Mexican scheme abandoned, if not forgotten, the two continued to meet and write letters to each other. Their last meeting and exchange of letters was on June 12, 1946. Noack wrote that he had been busy mailing packages, turning in equipment, and preparing for their imminent departure. Reflecting on the past weeks, he continued: "It was the best time I ever spent in three years imprisonment. . . . I'm so grateful to you to have had a heart for a poor fellow who was so lonesome." He confessed that at night when he lay on his bunk to listen to the radio, "All our moments we spent together appeared in my thoughts and I had the desire . . . to know you close to me. But every time I have such a feeling I know that these ideas are only castles in the air. . . . I tried everything to stay here in the states, but the regulations say that we have to be sent back first, that's a hard deal." Noack admitted that "I can't forget you" and promised that "as soon as I reach my home I write you how the things are coming along and what we can do."[38]

The young woman never heard from her German prisoner of war again. One can only speculate whether Noack's correspondence from war-torn and Russian-controlled East Germany ever made it off the continent and, if it did, whether the young woman's parents intercepted the correspondence and destroyed it. Perhaps the distance from East Germany to Utah, the difficulty of returning to America, or other interests preempted Noack's return. He died in Hamburg Altona on February 23, 1987.

As the young women of Utah held an attraction for the German prisoners of war, so did Utah's children. They brought prisoners and Americans closer. When Robert Wenz and his comrades were picking cherries near Ogden, a three-year-old boy climbed into the baskets and started to stomp the cherries until they squirted. The farmer was angry that the prisoners were laughing instead of working until he saw the antics of his son and joined in the laughter. Audrey Godfrey, whose father had a farm in North Ogden on which the Germans helped harvest fruit, noted that her little brother with his blond hair, chubby cheeks, and dimples was loved by the men. "They would lift him in and out of the fruit trees. I suspect he reminded them of their own children back in Germany. They were very patient with him and liked to make him smile."[39] Delbert J. Olsen of Logan reported a similar incident. He had hired prisoners from the Logan camp to help harvest and load potatoes. On one occasion he had his three-year-old daughter with him and, busy with the work, was not paying much attention to what she was doing:

> I noticed that one of these men had her in his arms and it gave me a fright. I walked over to him and took the little girl by the hand but he didn't want to let her go. I could see the tears running down his face. The guard came running over. I don't know what he intended to do, and I said to him don't hurt that man for he has done nothing wrong. He could not speak to me nor I to him but he didn't have to. I knew that somewhere in this world he had a little girl that he may not ever see again. It showed to me that most men throughout the world have love and compassion in their hearts.[40]

Ed Cooper, a boy of nine or ten, whose father worked at the Broadfield Grain Elevators in Murray, Utah, became acquainted with several prisoners. On Saturdays young Ed went to the grain elevator to sweep, and there he met several prisoners who were unloading the trains. They treated him like their "kid brother"; and they taught him one of their German soldier songs, "The England Song." The lyrics, by Hermann Loens, a poet who had died in World War I, told of a soldier's farewell with his loved one as he prepared to sail against England. The boy's family was impressed that he had mastered the German lyrics and was singing the song with enthusiasm. However, their feelings about his education at the hands of German prisoners cooled considerably when his grandmother, who had come to Utah as a teenager from Wales and was familiar with the song, explained its message.[41]

For another young boy of ten, the prisoners of war in Logan, Utah, left an indelible impression. Reflecting on the summer of 1945, the wartime emotions, and what he learned about the prisoners, Hyrum Olsen described his hatred and fear of the Germans because they had killed so many of his neighbors and because they threatened to destroy freedom and democracy. He did not feel safe, even from the prisoners working in the fields under armed guards. "I was scared and would drive the cows to pasture as fast as I could past the fields of prisoners, then hurry home and watch to see if I had been followed." In August 1945 Olsen, accompanied by his father, attended his first rodeo at the Cache County Fair Grounds, where the Austrian prisoners were housed. He and his father had to walk past the prisoners toward the rodeo arena. "I could see their faces, their eyes and expressions. Some were indifferent to our being there; others were interested—maybe even entertained by our presence as we paraded by." Olsen continued his observations:

> I heard the melodic strains of music and saw a guitar being played and heard the sad sounding words being sung in his native tongue. One soldier played a squeeze box or accordion type instrument. At this moment the realization set in that they were really human beings with feelings, needs, desires and abilities not unlike the people of my world.
>
> The prisoners seemed older, subdued, and somewhat doleful. They were not the vicious enemy of my hatred. Their sad eyes penetrated my consciousness and I remember thinking maybe they have children my age at home. They probably have families and loved ones who want to see them.

In a few minutes, we were by and inside the rodeo arena where I was to witness my long-awaited first rodeo. Interestingly enough, I remember nothing of the rodeo itself. It is this close up observation of the German POWs that I remember so well.[42]

Some of the fascination children had with the prisoners of war led to unwise practices. According to an article in *The Hill Fielder* of May 3, 1945, Utah youngsters had been printing the initials PW on their clothing as a prank. The military did not see the humor, and declared it to be dangerous and ordered it stopped. The article warned that anyone wearing clothing marked with the PW initials ran the risk of being shot by military police as an escapee.[43]

Many German prisoners of war looked upon their time in America as an opportunity to learn about the country and its people. Utah, with its magnificent scenery, frontier history, and religious orientation, was of special interest to those whose vision extended beyond the mundane day-to-day routine as prisoners of war. An article of particular interest to the German prisoners that appeared in the January 1946 issue of *Unser Leben* was entitled "Utah, the Land, Its People, and Its History." It was three pages long and gave the prisoners a good overview of the state.

The article acknowledged that the prisoners knew very little about Utah, a state half as big as Germany, and set about correcting the situation so the men could later tell something about their experiences. The historical sketch included references to the Escalante expedition of 1776, the explorations of Father DeSmet, the discovery of the Great Salt Lake by James Bridger in 1825-26, the settlement by the Mormon pioneers in 1847, and the construction of the Mormon Temple in Salt Lake City. The usual geographical facts were given regarding the Great Basin, height of the Wasatch Mountains, origin of the word "Utah," land size, and population figures. Highlighted were the special attractions of Utah's canyon country—in particular Bryce and Zion national parks and the nearby Grand Canyon. Although few prisoners had seen or would see southern Utah's famous scenery, they were familiar with the area around Ogden. The article compared this region to a garden with orchards, fields, and lush meadows. For those who had seen "the hundred thousand peach trees in bloom around Brigham City, it was a moment never to be forgotten." Utah's poplar trees, planted in great numbers by Mormon settlers along the country roads, canals, and fields, gave the landscape a distinct character. "They form a windbreak for the meadows and fields and stand as loyal guards over the homes and barns of the farmers." The poplars reminded the author of the article of the German homeland: "[They] give a German like flavor to the landscape, and may be the reason why . . . [one] feels a touch of homesickness."[44]

A few prisoners remember Utah for a summer lightning storm that struck while they were in Bushnell Hospital recovering from gunshot wounds inflicted during the Salina incident. Willi Klebe had never experienced such a storm where the lightning seemed to come right through the electrical fixtures. Karl Altkruger admitted, "We screamed because of the pain in our injured limbs when the lightning struck. Then the nurses gave us tablets to calm us."[45]

Another feature of interest to the Germans was the Mormon culture and religion. Herbert Barkhoff recalled that, while a prisoner in Utah, he had learned about the Mormons, including the establishment of the Mormon church by Joseph Smith, his martyrdom, and the trek led by Brigham Young to the high mountains and the valley of the Great Salt Lake. He was given a copy of the Book of Mormon, but had to leave it behind when he returned to Germany. He was impressed with the Mormons and their state. "I was amazed at the irrigation systems. I rejoiced at the fruitful gardens and fields, and in the fall I tasted the wonderful peaches."[46] His only regrets about Utah were that he could not visit the Salt Lake Mormon Temple, which he saw only from the train, and that he did not have any contact with Utah citizens.

Although most former prisoners of war describe their experiences with American civilians in favorable terms, some Americans did not make a good impression on their German captive visitors. One German prisoner, basing his remarks on a conversation with a farmer, commented that the Americans did not know the population of their country, did not read newspapers, and were uninterested in politics. Instead, they were mostly concerned with "their meals, their automobile and as much comfort as possible." The prisoner castigated the American custom of driving into town on Saturday night to see a movie, and if it is "somewhat exciting, a little sentimental and of slightly bad taste, that's when it is of the right mixture for the U.S.A."[47] Another prisoner was generally unimpressed with American houses. "I remember the many wooden houses that we saw. They seemed quite simple to us. In Austria, by us, they were made of bricks."[48] Some prisoners were critical of American women's fashion. After his return to Germany, one former prisoner wrote to the parents of a comrade that their son had become acquainted with an American woman. He praised their son's good taste because she was "unlike most of the American women who paint their faces with all colors."[49] Others were shocked by the conduct of a Cache Valley farmer's wife, who left early in the morning, drove to the city, and returned in the afternoon to open a few cans for her husband's lunch, which was served on paper plates. The cans, paper plates, and other garbage was thrown out the kitchen window.[50]

The German POW experience in Utah was influenced by the state's dominant religion and, to a lesser degree, by the German American community within the state. Utah's German immigrants took special interest in the prisoners of war. On June 22, 1945, Kaspar J. Fetzer, president and general manager of the Salt Lake Cabinet and Fixture Company and spokesman for Salt Lake City's German community, wrote Senator Elbert Thomas. He reported that he had been approached by a number of faithful Mormons from Germany who had relatives scattered in POW camps throughout the United States. Since most of these prisoners were also good Mormons, their relatives and other German Mormons were anxious to have them sent to Utah so they might visit the men and so these men might nurture, through their affiliation with the Mormon church, the seeds of democracy. Senator Thomas contacted the War Department about the request, but army officials declared the proposal unfeasible: "Segregation on a basis of church membership would be a very expensive task, and would involve considerable time and be a burden upon transportation facilities."[51]

German Americans in Utah also sought to arrange for relatives who were in America as prisoners of war to remain in the country instead of being returned to Germany. One prisoner had lost his immediate family and home in Russian-occupied Germany. Another man, whose sister lived in Salt Lake City, had applied with his three brothers for immigration visas to move from Stuttgart to Utah in 1930. Although the visas were granted, the American consul had advised them to remain in Germany until they could find jobs in America. As a consequence, they did not immigrate. One did arrive at Fort Sam Houston, Texas, in 1945, but as a German prisoner of war.[52] Word circulated among the prisoners that if anyone wanted to come back to America, they should join the Mormon church because the Mormons would see to their return.[53] But, unlike the prisoners of war in America at the end of World War I, none of the prisoners in America in 1945 and 1946 were permitted to remain.

Missionary efforts among the German prisoners of war was of considerable interest to the Mormons. Those prisoners who were taking English classes were given pictures about the Mormons and asked if they wanted to know more about the religion. Two German-speaking Mormons who visited the prisoners in Fort Douglas were Kaspar Fetzer and Werner Lohner. Lohner, the younger of the two men, deferred to Fetzer, who spoke to the prisoners about the Mormon religion. The dozen or so prisoners who heard Fetzer's earnest and forthright comments about his firm belief in the Mormon faith listened politely, asked no questions, and were apparently uninterested in his message.[54] Rudolf Weltin recalled that in Logan there were people who talked about the Mormon church and that some tried to convert the prisoners. According to Weltin, the attempts at conversion failed. "We did not speak much about religion in camp. It was not interesting to me. We only wanted to do our work and go home. I never did see any prisoners who were ready to join the Mormon church." Dieter Lampe explained the lack of interest in the Mormon church and religion: The young prisoner "is much more interested in girls, smoking and perhaps drinking. As soldiers we hardly thought about anything else."[55]

But there were those prisoners who were touched by the Mormon faith and its practical application of Christian ideals in helping to provide the men with food and showing them other considerations. One Mormon farmer near Salina was so pleased with the prisoners' good work that he gave them a whole pig, which they smuggled into camp in their food cans and secretly cooked at night. Most Mormon farmers, however generous they might be in providing food, drew the line when it came to providing coffee. They did not want "to cook coffee for us at home, because if [people] smelled it in the house, [they] would say [the farmers] were not living their religion." Other prisoners observed different aspects of the local Mormon culture. Josef Becker was invited to eat lunch with a Mormon farmer in Tooele County, who insisted that "whoever works for me should eat with me." At the dining table were two glasses beside each plate, which Becker quickly learned were for water and milk, not beer and wine. Another prisoner recalled meeting people who said, "We are Mormons, and it is our responsibility to help where there is need." This experience stayed with him; he always remembered the Mormons as responsible, caring people.[56]

The German prisoners found friendship and compassion among non-Mormon Utahns as well. One American Italian, whose name was Anselmi, was especially attentive to Leonard Mombar and his comrades. He had come to America from the southern Tyrolean region near Bolzano, Italy, and he could speak German. He had worked seventeen years in the Utah mines, then purchased a farm. According to Mombar, "He looked at the food we had and said, 'My pigs get that,' and he gave us a wonderful meal. . . . In the evening he brought a jug and said [it was] some milk from [his] black cow. And he gave us red wine made from grapes he got from California." Mombar spent about five days working for Anselmi, getting good food and wine every day. Later, Mombar wrote to Anselmi from Germany, but did not receive an answer. Kurt Treiter was well cared for by an unnamed Japanese American who owned a farm between Orem and American Fork. He gave the prisoners working for him cigarettes and supplemented their noon meal with meat, chile beans, and bread. Aware of the treatment of his fellow American citizens in the relocation camps, the farmer declared, "I know how it is in the camps. By me the prisoners will be well treated."[57]

Roy Gappmayer had developed such a close friendship with the German prisoners who worked in his orchard, that he accepted a friendly challenge from a much younger Kurt Treiter to a wrestling match. Each man wanted to show the other how strong he was. According to Gappmayer's daughter: "The other prisoners thought it was a big deal. Here was a prisoner fighting with a farmer. The guards were all tensed up with their guns ready, but the wrestling match was all in fun and it drew the two of them closer together."[58]

As mentioned earlier, prisoners working on farms usually ate a lunch provided by the camp. The farmers, concerned about what looked like rather meager fare for working men, often gave them more food, with or without the knowledge of the guards. Most farmers reasoned that if the prisoners were well satisfied they would be better workers. Some farmers, concerned about the prisoners' health, would make a large bonfire at the edge of the field so the men, wet from working with the damp sugar beet plants, could dry out before being transported in an open truck back to camp. A. J. Buchanan, a Richfield farmer, learned of the sparse provisions issued to prisoners in the Salina camp when a group of them working for him came upon a dead pheasant and proceeded to prepare it so they could eat it. Disconcerted that the prisoners would cook and eat a pheasant that had apparently been dead for some time, Buchanan inquired about the quality of the lunches sent from the camp. He was moved to tears when one of the men disclosed that his lunch was two sandwiches of dry bread with cooked spinach as a filler. The Buchanans began supplementing the lunches brought from camp with chile, soup, and meat. When the Buchanans arrived with the extra food the prisoners would pretend they were unaware of its arrival until they were told to come and eat. "They were very well behaved people." On one occasion, the Buchanans wanted to invite the prisoners for a home-cooked meal of spaghetti, but the prisoners were denied that privilege.[59]

The prisoners who worked for Roy Gappmayer brought from camp what his family considered a miserable lunch: "Lukewarm tea, bread and sliced bologna . . . day after day with no variation." To supplement the prisoner's lunch, Gappmayer's wife always cooked something hot, which might include soup and hot rolls with honey and butter—which the prisoners insisted they had not tasted for years. And, for a prisoner's birthday, there was a large cake. The men ate outside at a table set up next to the Gappmayer home. Consequently, lunch at the Gappmayers' became a social event in which family members, guards, and prisoners participated in wide-ranging discussions.[60]

Although such conversations concerning the war, Hitler, and nazism were discouraged, they still took place. Floyd Johnson recalled that the prisoner who was the interpreter for the group assigned to his farm told him that they were not sympathetic toward Hitler. "These wars . . . come and go; something brings them on and you can't do anything about it. . . . We think a lot of the American people, and we don't . . . want to fight them." A German-speaking farmer remembered seeing prisoners cry when they sang about their homeland. Some of the songs carried a strong message of war weariness, if not pacifism. The farmer quoted a line from one of the songs: "In ein kleines weiss Hauschen wo kein Kugel wenden kann" (In a small white house where no bullet can come.) [61]

Along with eating together, discussing world affairs, and wrestling with each other, German prisoners and American civilians also shared the humor of the war which brought them together. A German prisoner, working under a hot, afternoon Texas sun, turned to his employer and smiled as he said, "Well, Hitler said we would be in America in 1945, and here we are—chopping cotton."[62] Many Americans remember the prisoners as being good natured and friendly. Floyd Johnson described his impressions of the German prisoners in Salina as "real nice, hardworking, respectable fellows . . . just the best . . . and who made me think a lot of the German people."[63]

Because of the basically fair treatment most German prisoners experienced during their sojourn in the United States, they left the country with a high regard for the American people. For some, friendships were established with Americans that would last a lifetime.

TWELVE

The Salina Tragedy

The 250 German prisoners of war at the branch camp in Salina, Utah, differed little from the 371,000 other Germans interned throughout the United States. Some had spent more than two years in America; others had arrived only a few weeks earlier and were among the last prisoners sent to the United States. Most were young men in their early twenties, but some were in their late forties—professional soldiers who had joined the German army before the invasion of Poland in September 1939 and others who had been drafted in the last days of the war in a hopeless attempt to stop the Allied forces pushing into Germany. The Salina prisoners of war who went to bed on Saturday night, July 8, 1945, had no reason to expect that the next morning would bring anything other than a well-deserved day of rest after six hard days thinning sugar beets. But before the night was over, the action of one man would leave nine prisoners dead and a horror seared into the consciousness of those who survived that would last a lifetime. As one former Salina prisoner reflected, "Utah, Lord, in normal times I'd never had known this state existed. But now I'll never forget it."[1]

Shortly after midnight on July 9, an American guard, Pfc. Clarence V. Bertucci, opened fire on sleeping prisoners with a .30-caliber machine gun mounted in a guard tower on the west end of the Salina camp. The bullets struck thirty of the forty-three tents before Bertucci was subdued as he reloaded his weapon. Six prisoners were killed outright, two died in the Salina hospital, and one died five days later in an army hospital. Nineteen prisoners were wounded. The residents of Salina reacted first with bewilderment, then with compassion for the dead and wounded prisoners, and finally with anger against the guard whose cold-blooded action had come two months after the collapse and surrender of Germany.

The twenty-three-year-old Bertucci was a native of New Orleans, Louisiana. A sixth-grade dropout, he had joined the army in 1940 at the age of eighteen. He had seen no combat duty, although he had served an eight-month tour in England with a field artillery unit. A problem soldier who suffered with arthritis of the spine, he was subject to military discipline on three different occasions for being absent without leave, refusing guard duty, and missing a train. Newspaper reports described Bertucci as "a quiet, reserved person, who made few friends," and noted that he had spent the hours before beginning his guard duty that night drinking beer in a local bar.[2] Earlier that evening he had had a cup of coffee in Mom's Cafe—a place he frequented—in downtown Salina. While in the cafe he was calm, but told the waitresses "something exciting was going to happen that night."[3]

Later, Bertucci confessed that he had committed the act because he did not like Germans and had been tempted on several other occasions to open fire on the prisoners. Stories circulated in Salina and elsewhere that Bertucci had acted in revenge for the death of a brother or a close friend who had been killed by the Germans in Europe. Newspaper reporters contacted Bertucci's mother in New Orleans. She expressed shock and sorrow at her son's deed and denied that a relative or close friend had been killed. She concluded that the shooting might be traced to an appendectomy he had undergone five years earlier and told a *New York Times* reporter, "Something must have happened to him as a result of the spinal injection, otherwise he would never have shot those men in Utah."[4]

Bertucci showed no remorse. Army officials eventually concluded that the premeditated action was that of an insane man. Capt. Wayne Owens, commander of an Ogden POW company, was assigned as the investigating officer for the shooting. In his report to the Ninth Service Command Headquarters at Fort Douglas, Utah, he concluded that Bertucci was sane and should be court-martialed for murder. Owen's Ninth Service Command superiors argued that he was not trained to judge whether Bertucci was sane or not, but

Owens maintained that a man was sane until he was proven insane. In the end, Owens scratched out his assessment of Bertucci's sanity, but still recommended that the man be court-martialed. Owens found no evidence that Bertucci had been drinking and concurred with the sergeant of the guard that Bertucci was fit for duty that lamentable night. Owens decided that Bertucci had committed a cold-blooded, calculated act for which he should be tried. Others disagreed; there was some public support for Bertucci, manifest in the number of telegrams which arrived, openly sympathetic to the guard and his deed.[5]

Twelve days after the shooting, Maj. Stanley L. Richter of the Prisoner of War Operations Division, Provost Marshal General's office, reported in a memorandum to the Special War Problems Division of the Department of State that a preliminary account of the Salina shooting had been received and that the investigation was continuing "with the view to the possibility of trying Private Bertucci by court martial."[6] Instead, Bertucci was found to be insane by a board of examiners at Bushnell General Hospital in Brigham City, Utah. Both the Ninth Service Command surgeon and judge advocate concurred in the finding. From Bushnell, Bertucci was sent to Mason General Hospital in New York.[7] How long he remained there is unknown, but Veterans Administration records indicate he died in 1969.

Established in June 1945, the Salina German POW camp received its first inmates when 250 Germans were sent from the large camp in Florence, Arizona. Arriving by train, the prisoners were marched up Main Street, where townspeople and school children saw for the first time soldiers of the German army—their enemy for the past three-and-a-half years. Many Salina residents were uncomfortable and locked their doors for the first time. Others, including Sharp Rassmussen, who lived adjacent to the camp, were not fearful of the situation, realizing that the prisoners were under careful watch and posed no real threat.[8]

Salina families were aware of what some of their husbands, sons, and brothers who were serving overseas thought of Germans. Writing from Nuremberg to his parents in Salina, Keith Crane explained that his unit had just left Frankfurt am Main, where the German people "thought they were pretty well off. . . . We changed their minds—we drove them out of their homes . . . and it was easy the way they had treated the French. . . . We soon took over and made good use of all their modern conveniences. Most every one of us have a radio, a good mattress, and when we left, we took the things we could use."[9] Naturally, Salina citizens considered such actions normal in wartime conditions.

Many residents recalled World War I, which had killed some of their men and wounded others. Armistice Day became an important local holiday and was celebrated by barbecuing elk that had been shot in the nearby mountains. In the first few years after the war, the celebration had a distinct anti-German flavor, with an effigy of Kaiser Wilhelm II hung from a hay derrick at the east end of Main Street, not far from where the POW camp would be located a quarter of a century later. The effigy, labeled "Kaiser Bill," was marched west along Main Street and set on fire to the cheers of participants and onlookers.

When World War II German prisoners marched the full length of Main Street that quarter of a century later, they got a subdued reception. Local residents were notified that they were not to go to the branch camp unless it was absolutely necessary; under no circumstances were they to contact the prisoners personally. The Germans were not to be bothered or molested in any way, nor were they to be looked upon or treated as a curiosity.[10]

The Salina camp consisted of forty-three tents, which housed the prisoners, enclosed by two barbed-wire fences. Guard towers were located on the east and west ends. Outside the compound were several long, frame buildings which housed the guards and camp personnel, a small infirmary, and an administrative center.

The prisoners were detailed out to farmers in Sevier and Sanpete counties to assist primarily in sugar beet thinning and harvesting. Since the men were noncommissioned officers, they had not worked while interned in POW camps. After Germany's surrender, however, the situation was reassessed and American authorities concluded that noncommissioned officers should work. Salina was their first work camp.

The shooting by Bertucci was completely unexpected. The prisoners had been sleeping for about two hours when the American guard started firing into the compound. Sharp Rassmussen, whose house was located on the west edge of the prison camp, was an eyewitness. That night he and his wife had been in bed only a short time when he heard the shooting and screaming. "I jumped out of bed and ran out to the front porch in my underwear. . . . They had a big light over the barracks and I could see that gun ejecting the shells, just a rainbow of copper shining in that light."[11] Watching the horror, Rassmussen realized that the guard might swing the gun around, which would put him in the line of fire; he ducked behind the corner of the porch until the guard was subdued. The shooting woke up nearly every citizen in Salina. Many feared that the "Nazis" were attempting to escape until word circulated about what had actually happened.

Although civilians were prohibited from entering the camp, a short time later Rassmussen went into the camp with Dean Nielson, supervisor of the prisoners' work assignments for the sugar beet farmers, where he saw the blood-soaked and bullet-ridden mattresses stacked awaiting transportation to the city garbage dump. The shots, the screams and yells, the rainbow of discharging shells, the dusty and bloodied mattresses were indelibly etched in Rassmussen's memory.

Willi Klebe recalled that before going to bed, he and others had washed their clothes and hung them to dry between the tents. He was asleep when the shooting started. "I was hit in the foot, and my comrade, who loved to play chess and who lay with his head toward the center of the tent, got a whole salvo in the back and was dead immediately. Adolf Paul was his name. We cried because of him. He was a fine person." Another man killed in Klebe's tent was a boxer. "He was shot in the stomach and his intestines were hanging out." The shooting for Klebe was beyond words: "What it was like, I simply cannot describe."[12]

Gottfried Gaag heard the shots and raised up in bed just as the bullets passed through his tent. He was shot through the lungs, fell off his bed, and rolled outside the tent. At first the others could not locate him; when they did, he was still alive, although the air coming from his chest wound made a terrible sound. Gaag died before he reached the hospital. Two of the other five men in Gaag's tent were struck by bullets. One man was hit in the foot by an explosive round and another had a splinter over his left eye, which burned badly and caused considerable bleeding.[13]

Some prisoners threw mattresses against the tent walls in the desperate hope that it would offer some protection from the machine gun bullets.[14] Others were just plain lucky. Karl Altkruger was seriously wounded in the foot, but as he fell off his bed he grabbed his sea sack. Later, he found a flattened bullet inside a shoe-polish can. "That bullet would have hit me in the breast. It went into the sea sack, but then stopped in the shoe polish can. The shoe polish was smeared everywhere. But it did save my life."[15]

The casualties were severe. The wounded and dead, many of whom were still lying on their cots, were transported by truck to the Salina hospital. There were only four empty beds in the hospital, so the wounded were placed in the hallway and the waiting room; several had to be treated outside on the lawn. The dead were placed on the west lawn of the hospital grounds to await transportation to Bushnell General Hospital. Dr. Rae E. Noyes, director of the Salina hospital; Merle Lau, the night nurse on duty; and two other aides cared for the wounded while armed guards encircled the hospital to keep the curious away.[16]

The guards were especially cautious about talking with news reporters. Wesley Cherry, editor of the *Salina Sun*, and his wife were at a dance four miles away in Redmond with a camp sergeant and his wife. The sergeant was notified to report back to the camp, so Cherry drove him to the camp and then went to the Salina Hospital. He took his camera hoping to document the hospital scene, but he was restrained by the guard and ordered to stay away from the hospital even after he offered to put the camera away.[17]

Inside the hospital most of the Germans were in shock; others screamed out in agony and frustration. Willi Klebe, who was among the wounded, recalled an example of the compassion shown the men. While the wounded were lying on the hospital floor, a woman came in and gave each of them a lighted cigarette. Although he did not smoke, the astonished Klebe accepted the gesture of goodwill. "We had been captured in the desert, and had been in prison for two years without seeing a civilian, then all of a sudden a woman opens the door and gives each of us a cigarette. I cannot describe how good it seemed."[18]

There were no Catholic or Lutheran clergy on hand to comfort the injured; however, according to one account, local Mormon church leaders, referred to as "elders," were permitted inside the hospital and, following the practice of the Mormon faith, anointed and blessed one or two of the wounded Germans. The prisoners reportedly had requested the presence of the Mormon elders, but since none of the wounded were Mormons or knew about the practice, it seems more likely that they arrived on their own initiative or by mistake when the German cries of "meine Eltern," meaning "my parents," were misunderstood as cries for "the elders."[19]

Dr. Noyes lamented that for the two prisoners who died in the Salina hospital, "There wasn't much we could do for these other than give them sedatives to ease the pain."[20] Five days later, Friedrich Ritter died at the Kearns army hospital. The few days that Ritter lived were pure agony. He was hit in the head by a number of splinters from exploding rounds and was in a great deal of pain. He "called or screamed either for his mother or for someone to 'give him a bullet.' There was nothing to do for him."[21]

Thirteen prisoners were seriously wounded: Gustav Harnisch, Kurt Banse, Herbert Barkhoff, Willi Echner, Willi Schlesinger, Heinz Pickel, Herbert Babst, Artur Burckhardt, Arno Backmann, Max Brendamour, Emil Steng, Friedrich Behrenz, and Richard Hermann. Four were moderately wounded: Willi Klebe, Dieter Lampe, Hermann Diederich, and Karl Altkruger. And two were slightly wounded and, after treatment, returned to the camp: Emil Blau and Werner Gruber. Newspaper reporters who visited the wounded prisoners in the Kearns army hospital on Sunday wrote poignant descriptions of them. One prisoner, still clad in his blue POW dungarees, "lay on a crumpled bed. . . . A small white patch covered his left eye and he held a bloody towel over his mouth. From time to time he was shaken by convulsions."[22] The other wounded looked "tired and resigned." Six of them agreed to meet with reporters, although none of them spoke English, and to pose for photographs. The encounter was frigid. The prisoners were seen as "unhurried, disinterested, and uncooperative" when the cameramen began giving them instructions so they could take their pictures. One officer saw fit to comment that this behavior was typical of them: "Temperamental as all heck. If they don't want to do something they just don't do it."[23] As Herbert Barkhoff explained forty-two years later: "Before noon, reporters came to us. They did interviews with us. That was something we were simply not used to. We probably did not conduct ourselves as very good press agents."[24] Perhaps the Americans did not realize how seriously the men had been physically wounded and how emotionally shaken they were by the incident. More than a month after the incident twelve of the wounded were still in the Ogden POW camp hospital.

Reflecting on the tragedy, Hans Fertig, spokesman for the Salina prisoners, said that although there had been no previous threats or shots, guards armed with machine guns were a concern to the prisoners, who feared that a tragedy might result. Apparently the machine gun had been installed only a few days prior to the shooting, despite the fact that the war with Germany had ended two months previously. Furthermore, the prisoners complained through Fertig as their spokesman about the machine gun and requested that at least the ammunition belts be removed from the weapon.[25]

The nine men who had been killed came from all over Germany and ranged in age from twenty-four to forty-eight. Six were captured in Tunisia in 1943, two in France shortly after the Normandy invasion, and the last at Bad Wildungen, Germany, on March 30, 1945, one month before the surrender of Germany. Four of the nine were husbands and fathers. At forty-eight, Ritter was the oldest but most inexperienced prisoner of the nine. He was one of the last German prisoners sent to the United States from Europe. He arrived in Florence, Arizona, on June 4, 1945, and a few days later was sent to Salina. He was undoubtedly called to military service in the last months of the war when old men and young boys were recruited in the defense of Germany. Like so many of his generation, Ritter had probably seen action as a soldier during World War I. He left a wife and three children.[26]

After the shooting, Hans Fertig, as camp spokesman, requested that the men be permitted to forgo their regular work for a few days. Colonel Ericsson refused, however, convinced that the prisoners would be better off working "than brooding over the attack in their tents."[27] Ericsson agreed to a second request that a prisoner delegation be allowed to attend the burial service for their eight dead comrades, which was to be held on July 12 in the Fort Douglas cemetery. The men were buried in unopened military caskets, wearing khaki uniforms rather than their German ones. No flags covered the caskets since the Nazi swastika was barred from the service and the German national flag was unavailable. Instead, each casket was decked with two wreaths of roses, gardenias, and carnations purchased by prisoners of war at Ogden and perhaps elsewhere. Fifteen prisoners representing the Salina camp were in attendance, and a chorus of seventeen prisoners from the Ogden camp sang three songs: "Song from the Monks" by Beethoven, "Good Comrade," and "Down in the Valley." American officials took unnecessary precautions to insure that no Nazi songs were sung. Hans Fertig spoke a few words at the service. In appropriate military fashion, he "stepped forward, facing the graves, addressed the dead soldiers briefly, clicked his heels, and returned to his place." Fertig's words, translated by an interpreter, expressed sorrow that the men had died by accident and would not return to their homeland; he declared that the misfortune had been God's will. The service ended with the sounding of taps, a three-volley salute by a six-man squad, and Chaplain Frank Edwards committing the bodies to the graves. Their final resting place overlooked the Salt Lake Valley and the graves of American soldiers buried there since the 1860s.[28] Two days earlier, a funeral mass in memory of the dead prisoners had been held in the Ogden camp. A second service was held for Friedrich Ritter, who died in the Kearns hospital on July 14.

There could easily have been more than nine dead in Salina; the nineteen wounded men cheated death by only inches. Although they received excellent medical care, their recovery was neither fast nor complete. Karl Altkruger suffered a great deal of pain with his injured foot, which had a hole in it "the size of a fist."[29] The doctors at Bushnell Hospital told him that if the foot were amputated, the pain would soon disappear. However, they wanted to save it, so he endured the pain and returned to Germany with a complete, if not perfect, foot. Later, he was told by German doctors that he had been lucky. "If a German army doctor had cared for me, he would have amputated my foot." According to Altkruger, the bullet "exploded in my foot. Everything was destroyed. It has healed quite well, but the stiffness in the joints will never go away. I always have pain when I walk. Two toes are gone on [that] foot."[30]

Herbert Barkhoff recalled vividly his medical treatment in Bushnell Hospital under the care of a doctor of Polish or Lithuanian descent, who spoke German and talked a great deal about his home and family and in whom the wounded prisoners developed complete trust. X rays were taken of Barkhoff's wounded foot, but when the doctor began to probe for a painful metal splinter, he could not locate it. "That was a cause for more drops of sweat on both our heads." Barkhoff was taken back for a second X ray, which located the splinter more precisely. "The local anesthetic had worn off. The doctor asked me again and again if it hurt. . . . After a short time he handed me the metal as a souvenir."[31]

Dieter Lampe took six shots through his right arm, including one explosive shot. He was given morphine, penicillin, and a transfusion of blood that was donated by Americans, including a woman lieutenant. When he came to in the hospital, she was lying next to him with blood running through a tube from her arm into his. He "had a private room and next to it was a washroom and a toilet. Everything for me, that was unbelievable. Then I had a ward boy and then a nurse, her name was Jane, my loved one. Everything was there. . . . That made a deep impression on me at that time because we were not used to such things." Utah doctors promised that the arm would heal completely; but after several months, Lampe was transferred to Tennessee and then back to Germany before he recovered fully. He realized that it would have been impossible to receive the same care in Germany that he had been given in America. "There was no penicillin in Germany. They would have immediately taken off my arm." Even after his return to Germany, there was still doubt the arm would be saved, and "a professor in Hamburg told me that . . . the best thing to do would be to amputate my arm immediately."[32]

Some men who recovered from their wounds returned to the routine life of prisoners of war without any special consideration for their brush with death. Following his stay in Bushnell Hospital, Herbert Barkhoff was sent to the Ogden POW camp, where he had the good fortune to be assigned to a barracks whose leader was from his home area, Goettingen. After two weeks rest to allow his foot to recover, he was assigned to help manufacture wooden pallets.[33] Emil Blau, who was slightly wounded in the head by a piece of an exploding bullet, went from Salina to California—first to Camp Lemore and then Camp Lakeland. He then went by train to New York and sailed to Antwerp, Belgium, where he spent a few days before leaving for England on January 25, 1946. He remained in England until May 28, 1947, when he boarded a ship for Cuxhaven, Germany, and eventually made his way home to Trier on July 1, 1947, nearly two years after the Salina shooting and four years after his arrival in the United States as a prisoner of war.[34]

The Salina shooting affected German prisoners in other camps who heard about it; they expressed concern and fear that a similar tragedy might occur in their camps.[35] When Karl Gustav Almquist of the Swedish Legation visited the Ogden camp two days after the shooting, the incident was fresh in the minds of the staff there. Somewhat to Almquist's surprise, the assistant executive officer, Lt. Keimet P. Stover spoke of little else, expressing his deep regrets "that such a thing could happen, especially in a country which . . . wanted to live up to the Geneva Convention and considered it an honor to observe its rules literally."[36] Public response to the tragedy and its effect on America's image appeared in a *Salt Lake Tribune* editorial on July 10, 1945, describing the shooting as an "unfortunate, unprovoked and unpardonable . . . crime so cowardly and irrational that immediate action should be taken to punish the killer or to commit him to some sanitarium for the insane." Bertucci's action had "betrayed the trust he accepted . . . to be a protector of his government's good name as well as of its security from enemies . . . [and had] shamed his comrades, embarrassed his countrymen and disgraced the army."[37]

Eric Kososik, who was in Ogden in July 1945, recalled that the prisoners were very depressed and concerned. "It bothered me very much and for a long time I was unable to sleep." When Kososik left Ogden for a small agricultural camp near Billings, Montana, which was similar to the Salina camp, his fear increased. The prisoners were crammed together and the camp was surrounded by towers with machine guns. "There was no protection or no defense. . . . I was very frightened. During the daytime when you went to work, there was no problem, but at night when you came back to the compound, then is when it started."[38] In Ogden, a group of German prisoners were considering what could be done in retaliation for the shooting. They discussed abducting an American and hanging him. "But then we came to the conclusion that it would not help and that it was not right to execute an innocent American for the shooting." After the initial anger passed, "it did not take long before it was forgotten, and we were content with the resolution."[39]

In the Logan branch camp, circumstances were such that the prisoners came within a hair's breath of being machine-gunned. The problem arose when quotas were increased. According to

Rudolf Weltin, "We came back to camp at 8:00 P.M. or later and we were cussed because we had not done enough, and we were told that we would have to work longer. We protested through our camp leader." While the spokesman was meeting with the camp commander and the 300 weary but potentially threatening prisoners waited for an answer, "the guards followed what was happening and one of them said, 'Shall I shoot into the camp?'. . . The captain gave him to understand that he was not to do it, and he was relieved. . . . He could have shot at 300 men. He said he would do it, but whether he would have done it, we do not know."[40]

Delays in notifying family members in Germany of the deaths of the nine men surely caused additional grief. American families who have had no word of relatives missing in action in Southeast Asia know the torment that existed for the German families who received no letters from or about their loved ones, saw other prisoners of war return from America to their families, and heard that all prisoners had left America. But inquiries to American authorities from the families of the Salina dead met with a cold, often imprecise response. Antonio Liske did not learn of her husband's death until three years after the shooting—and then the news came from a returned soldier who gave her an inaccurate account of the incident. He maintained that Georg Liske was with seven fellow prisoners inside a tent when an American guard burst into their quarters and, without the slightest reason, dispatched them with a machine gun. On behalf of Liske's widow, a German official wrote to American officials, asking that the "assassination" of Georg Liske be verified by an official confirmation and, if the report of wanton murder after the cessation of hostilities were true, that provisions for indemnification be made for the widow and orphan. Responding to the inquiry, Col. J. L. Harbaugh, Jr., of the judge advocate's office, avoided mentioning the circumstances of Liske's death. He also managed to avoid addressing specifically the issue of compensation for murder after the cessation of hostilities with a fancy bit of legal footwork. Colonel Harbaugh explained that prisoners who were incapacitated from illness or injury while on the job received medical attention and compensation benefits. Those who died were provided a proper burial, but all payments and benefits ended. No fund existed to pay survivors' benefits after the death of a prisoner; he conceded, however, that money due prisoners for their labor would be transmitted to the Provost Marshal Division in Europe for payment to rightful heirs. Four months later, $13.28 owed Georg Liske was transferred to the Provost Marshal Division to be paid to his widow.[41] Available records do not disclose whether she received the money or whether she was even notified of its existence or the method of payment. At a different time and under different circumstances, a guilt-ridden America may have been more generous in handling this affair.

On December 26, 1946, Richard Wiskow wrote the Provost Marshal General's office in Washington, D.C., about the fate of Hans Meyer, his brother-in-law. The family had received no official word about the fate of young Meyer, but one of his comrades, who was with him in the Salina camp, had told a mutual acquaintance of his death. Wiskow asked for confirmation of whether the report was true or false. There was no response to his letter. In 1947, a friend of Meyer's, Johanna Luedtke, wrote the International Red Cross in Geneva, Switzerland, for information on him. The Red Cross responded, describing the details of his death. There was also the suggestion that the family was owed a substantial sum of money for work done by Meyer before the shooting. After a series of letters—the last written by Meyer's sister, Elisabeth Wiskow, on November 13, 1949, in which she reported that the family still had not received any form of communication from the U.S. Government regarding her brother—the director of the Enemy Prisoner of War Information Bureau, Maj. Joseph O. C. Ducharme, finally responded on June 15, 1950, explaining that it was the responsibility of the German government, with the assistance of the International Red Cross, to inform the next of kin of deceased prisoners of war. Enclosed was the long-awaited check—in the amount of $13.70—for Hans Meyer's work prior to his death. Meyer's relatives must have been disappointed in the small amount; they had anticipated that the thrifty young Hans would have saved considerable money with the intention of sending it home to his mother as he had done before being taken prisoner. Furthermore, in order to cash the check, Meyer's family would have to travel from their home in Luebeck to Berlin, more than two hundred miles away.[42]

Nearly two years after the Salina tragedy, the parents of Gottfried Gaag still had not been notified of their son's death. They inquired about their missing son, but there is no evidence of a response. They continued to hope, however. A postcard sent through the Red Cross dated March 16, 1947, and postmarked from their new residence at Weihenzell in Middle Franconia read: "Dear Gottfried, Our best greetings from our new homeland. We are anxious to hear from you. We await with great longing seeing you again. Parents."[43] Like Gaag's parents, Mrs. Joseph Paul, mother of Adolf Paul, received no official notice of her son's death until after she wrote the commanding officer at Camp Tonkawa, Oklahoma. In her letter she reported having received a card from him, sent April 30, 1945, from the Oklahoma camp. Since then she had received no word from him. A recently returned prisoner had informed her that Adolf had been killed in an accident—presumably at Camp Tonkawa, since that was his location when last she heard. Distraught and in desperation, she was seeking any news of his fate. Suffice it to say that the U.S. Government did not respond to the needs of the families of the Salina slain in a manner usually expected of it by its citizens.

Most of those wounded in Salina returned home without their families being aware that they had been wounded. And, once back in Germany, some of them sought compensation from the U.S. Government. For Karl Altkruger, it was a frustrating, unsuccessful endeavor. Considered a disabled soldier by the German government, he was told that Germany had signed an agreement not to make any demands of the American government and that all he should expect was the same compensation paid all disabled German veterans. "When I tried to bring up the matter because it had taken place after the capitulation, I did not get anywhere. . . . I received so many papers I did not know where to start."[44]

Writing in the early 1950s, Dieter Lampe expressed both the bitterness and the hope that the U.S. Government would recognize an obligation to provide some compensation to the wounded:

> I bear no grudge against him who let it off [fired the machine-gun burst]. And yet, I want to be honest! I bear a grudge against his country. What happened to me did not take place in the war, it was an accident. I bear a grudge if some people nowadays push things off on the war which do not go on its bad account. Damages resulting from accidents are usually settled by some sort of redress, at least the attempt is made at it, materially and out-

wardly. The "artificial joint" has long since been forgotten. But the cool, negative hand of bureaucracy, which not only seems to exist in our country, embitters. . . . "America will take care of you", Cherrio! Up to now, it has forgotten me and I would so much like to conquer this bitterness and be able to believe in the good and in promises. But I work, wait and hope. I bear my burden for the rest of my life, at least I'll try. Maybe the day will finally come.[45]

In time, Lampe did come to grips with his life-changing wound. He married a young woman who had waited for his return and who accepted his injured arm without hesitation. When she learned that he had been wounded, "it was nothing really special. Many men and even women were injured and wounded. I took him as he was. No one could persuade me otherwise." With no profession or training, he landed a job as an errand boy for a Hamburg radio station and from there went on, with hard work and opportunities, to become one of Germany's most respected radio announcers. In retirement, he pushed for the construction of a golf course near his home and actively pursued his hobby, playing with a backhand swing using his left arm.[46]

Recognizing the courageous personal adjustments demanded of those caught in a tragedy that happened nearly fifty years ago, Herbert Barkhoff wrote, "The widows and the orphans, the family members, the seriously wounded who never regained their full health, the others who were injured, they carried and carry the burden that was brought during the night of 9 July 1945."[47] Karl Altkruger took comfort in the realization that "there were many who had it much worse than we did. For me, personally, things could have been much worse than they are. That has been a comfort to me."[48] Dieter Lampe also looked back on his life with an injured arm: "I always try to hide my arm, so that people cannot see it. . . . I was wounded when I was 23 years old, and now it has been 43 years since it happened. I have been nearly twice as long a cripple as I was whole. You get used to it. You try to do things with one arm and you don't think about what happened anymore. . . . The time as a prisoner of war is a small episode in one's life. I had some bad luck, but life continues."[49]

The Salina incident is a blemish on an otherwise outstanding effort by the United States to provide for the well-being and good health of war prisoners. With hindsight and removed a considerable distance in time from the propaganda-fueled hatreds, the cheapness of life, and the intensity of a war that engulfed humanity, we should ask whether it was absolutely necessary to arm guards with deadly machine guns to watch 250 German prisoners of war two months after their country had capitulated—particularly when those prisoners were located in one of the most remote parts of the United States. The Salina incident demonstrated that an unstable man with a deadly weapon could perpetrate an act of violence that could not only kill and injure unsuspecting victims but also taint America's honor. Americans were both incensed and pained by the death of the nine German prisoners. Also, had Americans known of the delays in notifying the next of kin and the callous way in which inquiries about money due and possible indemnification payments were handled, it is hoped they would have felt an even deeper shame.

THIRTEEN

Home

Two thoughts were foremost in the minds of the German prisoners of war in camps spread across the United States—the homeland, and when they would return to it. The end of the war came as both a shock and a blessing to most German prisoners. In Ogden, P. Schnyder, who inspected the camp on May 30, 1945, reported the men as "rather depressed and affected by the defeat of Germany."[1] Frederick Weber recalled, "The end of the war really ripped the heart out of us. . . . Some were so overcome emotionally that they didn't think they could take it." Indeed, one man was so despondent over the loss of the war that he tried to hang himself in a room used for drying clothes. The American camp commander was empathetic toward the man's feelings; he told the prisoners that if there were others who were as disheartened about the situation they should let the Americans know so they could work with them to try to prevent any more suicide attempts.[2]

A former prisoner described the decline in morale that followed Germany's capitulation and the realization that the prisoners were no longer under the influence of German officers or obligated to keep their oath to Adolf Hitler. What had been presented as a united front dissolved as prisoners split up into small groups, argued, and fought with each other. "We were usually sick and tired of each other's company, except for a few of your chosen friends that you stuck together with, and there wasn't much of a common feeling anymore."[3]

Edwin Pelz perhaps expressed best how most German prisoners reacted when they heard that the war in Europe had ended. He wrote that it was "a bitter blow," even though they had expected, even prayed for, an end to the war. Some cried for joy that the war was over, but most were stunned and said nothing as they reflected on what the war meant to them personally. For Pelz: "I was sad. The friends I had lost in Europe came to mind. And the millions of dead on both sides. It was all for nothing—all the fears, prayers, and tears. It was in that moment that I realized our generation in Germany had been misused and betrayed."[4] For Eric Kososik: "At the end of the war there was a lot of disappointment, but there was also the feeling of getting everything over and going home and starting a new life."[5] In Ogden, Ernst Hinrichs wrote, "The end of the war was a day of salvation for us. There was not a great shout of joy, but we were glad that the terrible slaughter in Europe had come to an end. The hope of a quick return home was awakened."[6]

A longing for home was common to all soldiers, but the stigma of defeat and the total lack of morale and purpose made the days of waiting hard to bear for the German prisoners. The anxiety about going home was enhanced when their normal routine was interrupted, and holidays, especially Christmas, magnified the personal turmoil for everyone. The anguish and hope at Christmas of 1945 among the prisoners in Ogden is apparent in a poem written by Friedrich Hensel for his friend and bunkmate Ernst Hinrichs:

> Through German lands death moves;
> In German houses need gnaws;
> German honor is trampled in filth.
> > O my homeland.

> Night. Grim Night. How long you are!
> Torn hearts sigh with fear;
> It rings from the homeland—the muffled sound.
> > It is Christmas today!

> Peace on Earth? Vulgar scorn?
> The Son of God is born?
> The darkness will soon be light
> > from the bright glow.

You German brothers in a foreign land:
The child that is found with you in need
Stretches to you from his cradle—
    A saving hand.

Break the Misery! Bind the wounds.
Bring good hope to troubled hearts.
God is with you, In league with man.
    Christ the Savior is here![7]

The despair felt with delays in leaving the United States and the homesickness for one's family are evident in a letter written by Fritz Poes from Ogden on April 1, 1946, to his wife in Idar-Oberstein after he met two acquaintances already on their way home: "It is now four years since we have seen each other, but some time the day will come when we are permitted to see each other again. Do not despair my dear, and be brave and raise my children well. I love you all so much. It was a beautiful time when we were together in love."[8]

The editors of the Ogden camp newspaper *Unser Leben* were attuned to the prisoners' low morale, and they sought to describe the situation in their articles and help their comrades deal with the homesickness and listlessness that permeated the camp. One writer attributed much of the low morale to their status as "on-lookers"; although the men were much concerned about the future, they could only watch from afar as the course of world history unfolded without their being permitted to take part. He observed: "Life demands much of people. Often it strikes us as very hard and we believe at first that we will not be able to endure the coming days. How happy therefore are those who find a way out and one who has learned something always finds the possibility to master life."[9]

The German prisoners were encouraged to be active in sports and to find purpose in their lives, especially through the educational programs which not only offered something to occupy their time but also helped to prepare them for the future. Even in defeat, nationalism could be used to buoy sagging spirits and reinforce their individual and collective worth as Germans. Their country's historic buildings were important: "Our memorable buildings through their age and the events with which they are associated, the 'History in Stone,' which remains in our castles,

German prisoners leaving America en route to Vienna and home. (National Archives photo)

Released German prisoners of war arriving at the Huetteldorf train station, happy to be back in their Austrian homeland. (National Archives photo)

An Austrian woman shows pictures of her son to returning prisoners, hoping they can give her some word about him. (National Archives photo)

Messages were left for and by returning Austrian prisoners in Vienna in order to reestablish contact between the men and their families. (National Archives photo)

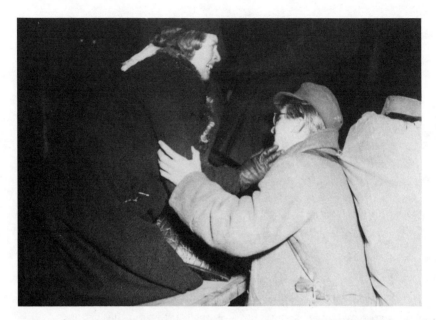

A Viennese woman and returning prisoner weep for joy at their reunion. (National Archives photo)

Honoring dead German prisoners of war buried in the Fort Douglas cemetery. (Allan Kent Powell photo)

churches, monasteries, convents and other institutions, has for us a great and comfort-filled meaning." The prisoners were told to look at the positive contributions made by German culture, where they would find not only a part of the homeland but also encouragement for the future. Music, in particular, was important; the lives of Germany's great composers, whose music would be "like a burning torch during the march into a dark and uncertain future," offered a key to understanding the German people. In the words of Wilhelm Furtwaengler, "If one wants to know what the Germans are, he must ask Germany's music. The music gives a deeper and clearer testimony of us than we can imagine. Wherever Germans live in the world, they will find themselves in German music and once again recognize themselves."[10]

Although the editors of *Unser Leben* sought to avert melancholy and homesickness in their comrades, their newspaper covers betrayed their own longing for home. The cover for the January 1946 issue was a sketch of a German house beside a brook, with pine trees growing on the flanks of towering mountains. Another cover had a prisoner with a spyglass sitting on a mountain range labeled *Utah* and looking eastward to a rising sun labeled *Europe*. A poem, "In Honor of the Homeland," expressing the men's feelings, was published in an issue:

> In my homeland I returned once again
> It was still the old homeland.
> The same air, the same songs,
> and still everything was different.
>
> The waves roared as before.
> On the wooded path deer still sprang,
> and in the distance rang the evening bells.
> The mountains gleamed out from the sea.
>
> But in front of the house, where for years
> our mother always greeted us. I saw
> foreign people, with strange behavior.
> How it hurt me to look on.[11]

Although dreams and thoughts of the homeland filled the minds of most prisoners of war, news of the situation in Germany was of particular importance. To some degree this information was available by radio or through newspapers to those who could read and understand English. They in turn shared the news with their non-English-speaking comrades. But most of them longed for first-hand news from Germany. According to Herbert Barkhoff, even though the prisoners were informed through newspapers of what was happening in Europe, "the fate of our own families lay hidden." His father was employed by the railroad and, aware of Allied air attacks on the tracks and transportation facilities, he wondered if his father was still alive. He summed up the one all-important frustration among the prisoners: "What the Americans could not take from us was the concern for our families in Germany. Every prisoner of war was, more or less, affected by the war. After the end of the war, we received no more mail and could not write home."[12]

When Karl Gustav Almquist visited Bushnell General Hospital on July 13, 1945, he spoke with German patients and left with this impression of the prisoners: "It is surprising . . . how easily they open up their hearts. How they have time to think over deep things. The anxiety for their relatives at home is a main concern. In such cases men's words are nothing; only God's own word can bring consolation."[13]

Letters from home containing glimpses of conditions in Germany and the impact of the war on family and acquaintances would have been kept and reread many times, adding to the growing anxiety felt by the prisoners once the war with Germany was over. Writing to her son on November 2, 1944, Herbert Barkhoff's mother revealed that "We must spend some hours in the hole in the ground in our garden" and that "There have been many changes here in the village. I cannot tell you everything. There are many dear families that have the same fate as you and in other ways have been touched." She reported on two friends: "Otto is seriously wounded and Gerhard, the dear young man, met a hero's death in the east." Despite the trying circumstances, she held out hope of victory and a reunion with her son. "[Let it] last as long as it must, we will let everything pass over us if only it comes to good and the victory is ours. The main thing is that we all, including you, stay healthy and that we see each other again in our dear homeland."[14]

Contemplating his country's defeat, yet looking ahead with guarded optimism to the prospects of a new Germany, a prisoner writing in the camp newspaper at Camp Atlanta, Nebraska, gave a sensitive yet realistic summary of many prisoners' perspectives during the winter of 1945–46. Germany's collapse had been a tremendous disappointment, but as individuals their own future was still tied to what their beloved fatherland would become. "We are looking toward democracy and can see a bright light at the end of the darkness. However, looking at the reports that are coming from home, there are all kinds of domestic and political problems which have yet to be overcome and suddenly the light does not look so bright anymore. It will take time, but there is hope.[15]

Knowledge of the conditions in their homeland and the level of concern felt by Utah's German prisoners for their countrymen are apparent in their generosity in donating money to the American Red Cross for relief work in Germany. The campaign to collect funds was launched with an article in _Unser Leben_ entitled "The Homeland Calls!" It was proposed that a contribution in dollars which would ease suffering, comfort those in doubt, and save lives was not much to ask of men who had a full table, warm rooms, and clothes as well as the peace and comfort that many took for granted. The article reminded the men:

> We are a part of our people, a splinter of the nation which because of the war has been separated into a foreign land. But we have not lost our connection with the entire whole and therefore the developments in Europe and in our homeland touch us. It is our sincere prayer that the Almighty will not entirely withhold his hand from us and it is our righteous desire to help with everything we can. The current collection will, without doubt, show the result that our duty and honor as German men demands. . . . When in later years the catastrophic winter of 1945–46 is spoken of, then the conduct of German war prisoners in America will be cited as an example of true sacrifice to our countrymen.[16]

Prisoners in the Ogden camp donated nearly $53,000 for the relief work, or approximately the equivalent of one month's pay for all the men. In his expression of thanks, the camp spokesman wrote, "The most important thanks for us is the knowledge that with our offering, many tears will be dried, hunger pains quieted, suffering eased, [and] women, children, and the sick helped. Thereby we have not forgotten our duty to the homeland."[17]

If conditions in the homeland were severe, most prisoners of war still longed to return to Germany as quickly as possible. By spring of 1945, few prisoners still believed that Germany would win the war, although some did hope for a super weapon that would turn the tide in Germany's favor. The die-hard prisoners captured in 1943 had seen enough of America in nearly two years of captivity to recognize the tremendous size and resources that the United States was bringing to bear on the German nation. Those recently captured in France knew the Allies were advancing rapidly on Germany and sensed it was only a matter of time before Germany would be forced to capitulate. Still, when the end came, some found it hard to believe. For Georg Hirschmann, the style of American radio contributed to the confusion. He was able to understand what was being reported about the end of the war, but in the end found it unbelievable since the announcement was followed by a commercial for toothpaste.[18]

Learning how quickly American prisoners of war were being liberated from the camps in Germany and returned to the United States, some German prisoners thought they, too, would be repatriated expeditiously. As soon as was possible, many American prisoners were airlifted from Germany to French ports, and most of the nearly 100,000 Americans were on their way home by May 8, 1945, the date of Germany's formal surrender.[19] The impact of the rumors and talk of returning home was predictable. One prisoner wrote, "There is talk about us being shipped back home, but nothing is certain and no one can tell us. It makes us very impatient and homesick."[20]

The immediate repatriation of all German prisoners was impossible because of the lack of transportation facilities; the inability to process such a large number of prisoners for release in Europe; the chaotic conditions in Europe; America's preoccupation with the war against Japan; and the request by American farmers, especially cotton and sugar beet farmers, to keep prisoners in the United States to help with the 1946 crops. Statistics indicate that approximately 57,000 German prisoners left the United States before the end of 1945 and the remaining 314,000, by July 1946. German prisoners in Utah were among the last to leave the United States for home.

Ernst Hinrichs recalled that when he boarded ship in New York City, "We had to go up and down the gangway with our sea sacks, and were photographed. The next day in the newspaper, which we saw, it said that the German prisoners of war came with empty hands and were returning home with full sea sacks."[21]

The German historian Hermann Jung ends his account in *Die Deutschen Kriegsgefangenen in Amerikanischer Hand/USA* (*The German Prisoners of War in American Hands/USA*) with a quote from the diary of a prisoner on the day of his departure from America. Jung considered the quote representative of what most German prisoners felt toward the United States, including those who came to Utah. "Halt, be careful. Now you will take your last step on American soil. Perhaps forever—perhaps. How was it stranger, on my sod? Oh, you know, it was pleasant and perhaps I will realize sometime that I have learned a great deal here and perhaps I will become homesick for you—perhaps. But you know that now I am going home. Farewell and thank you—farewell."[22]

One of the most difficult experiences for the prisoners at the end of their sojourn in America was saying good-bye to friends they had made among their fellow prisoners. As one prisoner recalled when his friend left for Austria, "Our parting was very painful. We had been together for years and had shared much. He was like a father and a brother and best friend to me." He saw it as God's will at work. "He separated us at this time so I could get strong by myself and stand on my own two feet when I returned to Germany."[23]

Reports that returning prisoners were not going straight to Germany, but were being turned over to the English or the French for work assignments to help rebuild war-torn European countries caused further depression. These reports were soon followed by disconcerting rumors sweeping through some camps that the Americans were even considering turning German prisoners over to the Russians. As a matter of fact, Americans were sympathetic to the idea of German men spending two or three years in Russia to help rebuild the cities destroyed by Hitler's army. A Gallup poll published in March 1945 disclosed that 71 percent of Americans favored the idea; two months later, a similar poll showed that the percentage had risen to 82 percent.[24] Despite the polls, prisoners were not sent to Russia; 123,196 German prisoners did go to England and another 55,000 were required to stay in France after crossing the Atlantic. Others spent time in Belgium. Nearly 50 percent of the prisoners experienced this kind of delay at the hands

of America's allies. The men were threatened that if they misbe-
haved or were uncooperative they could count on remaining
prisoners of war once they reached Europe. For these men, the
time seemed to stretch on forever. Richard Boettger, who served
as a soldier for only four months before his capture in Normandy,
spent nearly three-and-a-half years as a prisoner of war—a year and
a half in the United States and two years in England. He did not
leave England for his home in Reutlingen until November 1947,
over two-and-a-half years after Germany's capitulation.[25]

American officials either did not know for sure that the
prisoners under their care in the United States were destined for
work camps in France or Great Britain or were simply not forthright in their reassurances that the prisoners were to be sent straight
to Germany. A Red Cross delegate in Belgium reported in May 1946
that the repatriated German prisoners declared they were not
properly informed of the fate that awaited them and that the American camp officers themselves were not told what would happen
with their prisoners. He stated that one could easily imagine the
prisoners' disappointment and disillusionment when, after years
of imprisonment, they were being sent to a work camp in England
instead of home to Germany.[26]

The German prisoners sometimes were mistreated by the
French and British. Eric Kososik recalled, "The French people really
treated us bad. They threw stones at us as we were traveling in open
trucks." Their black uniforms did present problems for some of
the returning prisoners. Frederick Weber said that when they arrived in England, the local population thought they were all SS
troops and screamed and threw stones at them.[27] Later returnees
were accompanied by an American officer through France into Germany to prevent them from being seized by the French, having
their discharge papers destroyed, and being assigned to work details in France.[28]

Compared with what they had when they arrived in America,
prisoners acquired considerable property during their stay. War
Department officials had two possibilities for dealing with property that belonged to the prisoners, and it was important to avoid
the appearance of indiscriminate confiscation. The first was to consider some items as fully used and being abandoned by the
prisoners on their return to Europe. The second involved recog-

nizing the prisoners' rights to personal property they had acquired—usually purchased with money earned in work details. If the government did not offer free transportation of these items back to Europe, it would be the same as confiscating them. A compromise was reached by allowing each prisoner to take fifty-five pounds of personal property plus ten pounds of books and printed material purchased in canteens or from the War Department as orientation material. The sixty-five pounds had to fit in one barracks bag.[29] Most of the returning prisoners were well supplied with cigarettes, clothes, and other items from the camp canteens that were intended for their families once they reached Germany. Few were able, though, to keep these possessions. If unscrupulous guards and officials did not seize the items, then the returnees were pressured to share their goods with German prisoners who had not been sent to America and had had no access to such things as cigarettes, candy, or clothing.

Cigarettes were the most valuable item that the prisoners took back with them because they could be put to good use on the black market or bartered for essential services. Ernst Hinrichs used the American cigarettes he sent home to entice the local doctor, a habitual smoker, to make regular house calls on his sick mother. Josef Becker used part of the tobacco he sent home to purchase a Paris wedding dress for his new bride. Gerhard Graenitz traded cigarettes on the black market for clothing and enough furniture to furnish a complete house when he married.[30]

Although the men who returned with some American goods were envied, they were not greeted as heroes. As Josef Becker recalled, "I arrived home that evening with my sea sack and my bundles. I went through the village because we lived on the edge. No one recognized me. In six years a boy becomes a man."[31]

Homecoming was traumatic for children of prisoners of war returning from America. Willi Klebe's wife recounted the dilemma for their six-year-old son as his father returned home still limping from the bullet wound in his foot suffered at Salina and wearing a navy jacket, *Luftwaffe* pants, and an old infantry hat. When Klebe rang the doorbell his son refused to open the door, mistaking his father for a beggar. When Frau Klebe recognized her husband, the boy still refused, declaring, "No, we will not let the old man in. He is too dirty." Even after the joyful reunion between his parents, it was still more than a week before the six-year-old Roosie would go to his father.[32] On his return to Germany, Ernst Hinrichs found that his parents, brothers, and sisters were alive and still living in the home he had left. But everywhere in the cities and the rural areas were foreign people who had been driven from their homeland. They had lost everything but their lives and were housed in barracks, schools, and private houses. "These people had no work, practically nothing to eat, and hardly any clothes."[33] Many returning prisoners soon joined the ranks of the refugees described by Hinrichs. Life was a struggle. Prospects were dim, and the only comfort lay in realizing that they had survived the greatest calamity in world history. Others, like Hinrichs, returned to the homes, family, and surroundings they had always known. To be sure, they were deeply touched by the war, and yet home provided a solid foundation on which to build a future.

After nearly a decade of war and aggression during which individual lives were melted in the furnace of violence and reshaped on the forge of a totalitarian system fighting for its survival, returning prisoners did experience a sense of rebirth. Most had gone to war strongly believing in Germany's ultimate victory. They knew chances were great they might lose their lives, but they knew their sacrifice was matched by that of thousands of other soldiers and patriots. If fate destined them to death on the battlefield, they would play out that destiny as best they could. For some, it carried them into the depths of Russia as prisoners of war; for others, it meant internment in the New World.

Once they returned to Europe, a number of former prisoners wrote to American farmers for whom they had worked. The Hoffmann family of Smithfield in northern Utah had employed a group of Austrian prisoners to work in their sugar beet fields during the summer of 1945, three of whom wrote from Austria to reestablish contact with the Hoffmanns. The letters described the conditions the men found in Austria and expressed appreciation for the hospitality shown them while in Utah. Wilhelm Haimbock, who returned to his home in Vienna on September 17, 1946, wrote the following month, "There is much misery and destruction! There is very little food, especially when one has three children, and who are always hungry even though we have nothing. I hope that you remember me."[34]

A few of the prisoners were remembered because of their interest in the Mormon church. During one of his visits to Logan, Calvin Bartholomew was asked by the camp spokesman to tell the prisoners about the Mormon faith. He spoke to the prisoners for about an hour telling them of the church founder, Joseph Smith, and his search for a true church. Questions followed; and on subsequent occasions, several prisoners asked for more information about the church. After the prisoners had been transferred to California, Bartholomew learned that he had been instrumental in converting several prisoners to the Mormon faith.[35]

Some former prisoners tried to maintain contact with Americans they met, intending to return to the United States with their help. It is estimated that about 5,000 returned to the United States as postwar immigrants or refugees.[36] Several men returned to Utah, some of them because of their ties to the Mormon church. Frederick Weber was introduced to Mormonism while working in the American Can Company cannery in Ogden by O. B. Hadlock, an Ogden area high school principal who had been in Germany as a Mormon missionary before World War I. The two men discussed the Mormon religion and became friends. They corresponded after Weber returned to his home in Dusseldorf, where he continued his interest in the Mormon church. He was baptized a Mormon in 1947, and in 1951 he began the application process to immigrate to America. Hadlock served as his sponsor, and two-and-a-half years later, he and his family arrived in Utah. A stone sculptor by profession, Weber got a job with the Buehner Block Company polishing marble. From time to time he was able to put to good use his training as a sculptor. When a vandal damaged the statue of Christ in the Salt Lake Mormon Temple visitors center in 1982, Frederick Weber repaired and restored it.[37]

The experiences of German prisoners of war in America were retold in Germany and in some cases became the catalyst for others to immigrate to the United States. Walter Koch was captured by the Russians on May 8, 1945, and remained in Russian POW camps until his release on September 15, 1949. During that time he dug peat in the summer, tore down destroyed buildings, cleaned bricks during the winter, and carried out a variety of other jobs during his more than four years as a prisoner. Hunger, not work, "was our all-time worst problem. In all these years I didn't drink one drop of milk, didn't eat one egg, a piece of meat or piece of cheese, not an apple or carrot." When he returned to his home in Dusseldorf, he met Frederick Weber, who told him of his experiences as a prisoner in America. Koch recalled, "When I compared his experiences with mine, it was like the difference between Heaven and Hell. . . . When I heard how he had lived . . . while the war was going on, I couldn't believe it." Koch reasoned that if prisoners of war were so well treated in America during wartime, then America would be an even better place to live in peacetime.[38]

Eric Kososik was one of the former prisoners not affiliated with the Mormon church who returned to Utah. Born in Rumania in 1926, he left the country with his parents in 1939 when the Russians took over the region. Drafted into the German air force in January 1944, he finished his training in May and was sent to Normandy, where he was captured a short time after the Allied invasion. After a three-week stay in Liverpool, he was sent to the United States, where he spent twenty-one months in Ogden and another three months near Billings, Montana, before returning to Germany in 1946. Unable to return to his home in Rumania, he stayed in West Germany, married a refugee from Lithuania in 1947, and in 1950 decided to emigrate to the United States "because I had so many acquaintances here and I love the country, and because things were so bad in Germany." The decision was very difficult. "It was very hard to leave my parents and my wife's parents." Although his status as a former prisoner of war in the United States slowed the process, he and his wife were fortunate in securing the help of the Lutheran World Federation, which contacted the Ogden Lutheran church and arranged a sponsorship for the Kososiks. Since both of them had been born outside the political boundaries of Germany, they were able to emigrate as displaced persons and not under the quota system which limited the number of German immigrants coming into the United States. At the time of departure from Bremerhaven, the family included a three-year-old daughter and a one-year-old son. The passage to New York was financed by selling most of their possessions in Germany; train tickets from New York to Ogden were purchased with money loaned by the Lutheran Federation, which Kososik paid back within two years.[39]

Another former prisoner of war who found his way to Utah came not because he had been interned in the Beehive state, but because of the influence of a Utah serviceman whom he met while both were at Fort Benning, Georgia. Otto Liebergesell was captured by American soldiers shortly after the Normandy invasion. Before the war he had studied animal husbandry, with a special emphasis on poultry. At Fort Benning, he was fortunate to be assigned to care for pigeons used by the Signal Corps. One of his duties was to work with American paratroopers, who used the pigeons to send messages from the field back to headquarters, since radios were sometimes damaged in the jumps. A paratrooper from Utah, Earl Jackson, became good friends with Liebergesell. When Jackson learned of Liebergesell's interest in emigrating to the United States, he offered to sponsor him. Jackson also offered a partnership in establishing a poultry farm, and persuaded his German friend that Utah, with its clean air, magnificent mountains, and moderate temperature was the best place for such an endeavor. Returning to Germany in 1946, Liebergesell emigrated to Utah in 1951, which turned into a much more difficult experience than Fort Benning had been. When he arrived in Wayne County, he discovered that neither he nor Jackson were financially able to establish the poultry farm. While in Wayne County, he had his first introduction to Mormonism and was perplexed as to why many of those he met were anxious for him to give up Catholicism for Mormonism.

With no prospects for employment in Wayne County, he moved to Ephraim, in Sanpete County, where he worked hauling and bagging grain. He also worked for a time laying brick for a local contractor and then took on a small project by himself for a local Mormon bishop. The project was a bitter experience: the bishop refused to pay him, claiming the work was unsatisfactory; and the bishop's wife lectured him about why he should join the Mormon church. As it turned out, the bishop owed money to several people in Ephraim, and Liebergesell's efforts to seek legal redress failed due to local politics.

After a few months, Liebergesell saw clearly that there was no future for him in rural Utah. It was difficult enough to earn a few dollars to take care of himself; it would be impossible to provide for his wife who was to follow after he settled in Utah. Although he was impressed with the friendliness and goodwill of most Mormons he met, he was uncomfortable with the pressure from others to join the church. He sensed that some people were disappointed that he was already married, since there were young Mormon women who would be suitable for the handsome German and who would insure that his conversion to Mormonism was complete. Recognizing that the rural Utah life-style was too different from what he was used to back in Germany, he moved to Salt Lake City.

Once in Salt Lake City, Liebergesell wrote to a Catholic priest he had met on board the ship bringing him to America and who had contacts in the city. The priest put him in touch with the administrator of Holy Cross Hospital, who arranged for him to do maintenance work at the hospital. He was subsequently able to send for his wife. The cultural opportunities and religious diversity of urban Salt Lake City, the birth of a child, the purchase of a home, good neighbors, and a permanent and enjoyable position at the hospital were the events that changed his status from former prisoner of war to citizen of the United States.[40]

Although many prisoners talked about returning to the United States, few did. Ernst Luders expressed what was probably a typical sentiment for many men once they returned to their homes. "We learned about America, but it was always a foreign land for us. . . . It was a very different mentality, which does not mean it was better or worse than the German mentality, but it was different. . . . When you saw your school friends, and your brothers and sisters, and everyone, then the feeling of belonging returns. . . . That is the middle point." He also said, "Immigration to America would have been a possibility only if I did not have roots here in Germany."[41]

Former prisoners have come as tourists and visitors, however, to see the places where they spent time as prisoners, to renew old friendships, and to rekindle memories of a distant past. In 1980 Richard Boettger, accompanied by his wife and three of their four children, was able, through a large measure of good luck, to reestablish friendships he had made in Ogden thirty-five years before. Hoping to contact Cobie Van der Puhl, he went to the Ogden address he had for her. The Van der Puhls were no longer there according to a neighbor, who invited the German tourists into his home. He did not know where Cobie was nor did he know anyone else who might know. Discouraged, the Boettgers tried one more possibility—Edith Cannon. She also was no longer at her old address, but the Boettgers were told that the Cannons had moved just across the street. There was a great reunion as Edith Cannon recognized one of her boys. The next day as the Boettgers were ready to leave their hotel to catch the plane back to Germany, Edith Cannon called to say she had located Cobie Van der Puhl, now Wilson, since she was married. Although their reunion was brief, Richard Boettger and Cobie Wilson reestablished ties that were broken when he left the Ogden camp in 1945. The two families have become good friends, exchanging frequent letters and telephone calls, and enjoying visits with each other.[42]

In the summer of 1986, Ernst Hinrichs returned to Utah with his daughter to visit friends. "I had the chance to see my old work place and the mountains of Ogden. In the Depot we had the opportunity to participate in a parade. There I stood, a former prisoner of war, forty years after I had carried these letters on my clothing. Memories were awakened."[43]

Painful memories were reawakened for Dieter Lampe, who was wounded during the shooting at Salina, when he returned to Utah in 1977 with his wife to visit. He visited the site of the former POW camp, now occupied by a rodeo arena, but with a few of the administration buildings from the Civilian Conservation Corps and World War II eras remaining. The Salina hospital, now a senior citizens center, brought back bitter memories associated with his stay there for his torn and shattered arm. A drive around the former sugar beet fields, now mostly hayfields, helped recall more pleasant memories of working and joking with his comrades and their encounters with the Sevier County farmers the summer of 1945. During his visit, Lampe met Dean Nelson, under whose direction the prisoners had worked in Salina, and Merle Lau, who was the nurse on duty the night he and twenty-three others were brought into the Salina Hospital. Everything seemed to intensify the memories associated not only with Salina and the tragic shooting but also with his life since then and the adjustment to a crippled arm. His visit was reported in the *Salina Sun, Richfield Reaper,* and the *Salt Lake Tribune,* but the headlines were upsetting to Lampe: "Former Nazi POW Recalls Night of Horror in Salina Prisoner Camp Shooting during Visit to Sevier Area," and "Ex-Nazi POW Visits Site of 1945 Utah Tragedy." He took offense at the use of the word "Nazi" in the headlines, claiming instead that he was a former German prisoner of war. Obviously sensitive to the implications of the word "Nazi" and incensed that American journalists chose not to use "German" either out of ignorance or as a ploy to create a more sensational headline, he declared, "It made me very angry. . . . I finally had to decide that the Americans were dense and just to leave it at that, but I did not find it very good."[44]

On October 26, 1988, two other victims of the Salina shooting returned to Utah. Karl Altkruger and Herbert Barkhoff were honored guests at the rededication of the German POW memorial in the Fort Douglas cemetery. During their three-week visit, the men and their wives took the opportunity unavailable to them as prisoners to visit Utah's national parks and other points of interest. Perhaps the highlight of their visit was their return on November 9 to Salina, where they toured the former camp site and hospital. As an expression of his thanks for the good care and treatment the prisoners had received in Salina, Barkhoff placed flowers on the graves of nurse Merle Lau, Dr. Rae Noyes, and work supervisor Dean Nelson. A special program was held in the North Sevier High School auditorium, at which Barkhoff told the 500 people in attendance that he felt no anger or resentment—then or now—toward the American guard who fired the shots during the night of July 8, 1945. He hoped that God would give the man strength to carry his burden. He explained, "I was a soldier, and I learned that especially in a war situation one winds up at a point where 'hosanna' and 'crucify him' are no longer two terms, but become one. Right and wrong are not that clear." He concluded his remarks to the residents of Salina with this wish: "After 43 years, allow us to thank all of those who stood by us, took care of our wounds and pain— thank you from the bottom of our hearts. Let us now join together and work for peace. May the symbols of Utah along with the Stars and Stripes stand together over the land of the free."[45]

It is clear from the experiences of men like Herbert Barkhoff, Frederick Weber, Eric Kososik, Dieter Lampe, Richard Boettger, and others cited in this study that both individualism and personal drama marked their stories. In examining the events involving those Germans and Utahns who shared most of 1944, 1945, and 1946 together, it is important to keep in mind that some experiences were similar and many were different; but as long as there are people willing to share their experiences of the World War II era, the story of German prisoners of war in Utah will continue to unfold.

FOURTEEN

Conclusion

In May of 1944 Georg Hirschmann, from a small German village south of Nuremberg, lay in an American aid station on the Anzio beach in southern Italy nursing a leg ripped by an artillery explosion and waiting for transportation to an American hospital ship. Despite the wound and his capture by American troops, one thought crowded everything else out of his consciousness: "Now I have won the war!" Forty years later, that conviction remained with him as he related his experiences as a prisoner of war in America and recalled that of the thirty houses in his home village "not one house . . . was spared the loss of a son. One or two died from every house. Most of them fell in Russia." His younger brother was among those who died fighting in Russia. He maintained that the majority of German prisoners sent to the United States saw their capture as a personal victory since the alternatives were death on the battlefield, returning home with a serious wound, or capture by the Russian forces.[1] Karl Groeger, a former prisoner from Austria, expressed a similar sentiment in a letter written in June 1947 to a Utah farmer: "We were well off in all cases. The good food and good cigarettes, . . . that is only in America, and here in this land [Austria], I will never forget it nor you, Mr. Hoffmann. . . . It was prison but we had it very good. It was nice and good with you and I am very thankful that we returned home healthy and strong and not like the others."[2]

The German prisoners did return to their homeland in good health and as survivors of a world war that claimed the lives of forty million human beings during the fighting in Europe. Germany lost

6 percent of its prewar population, including 3,250,000 military personnel and 3,640,000 civilians. Of all Germans born in 1924, the year Georg Hirschmann was born, 25 percent were dead by the end of the war and 31 percent had been wounded.[3] Given these incomprehensible statistics—even though Hirschmann, Groeger, and others could not have known the precise figures—it is understandable why these men considered it a victory to be prisoners of war in America. The humane treatment of World War II prisoners was not an isolated development of the 1940s; its roots can be traced to the early Christian era when one was taught to love one's enemy and to practice a more considerate treatment of prisoners rather than requiring their death or their enslavement when ransoms could not be met. But throughout most of European history this ideal was not applied universally, and it was not until the late eighteenth century that prisoners of war ceased being considered the property of their captors and were regarded as ordinary men once they surrendered and therefore entitled to the care and protection of the capturing nation.

During its fight for independence, America faced the question of the treatment of prisoners of war, and the Continental Congress of 1776 adopted measures for the compassionate treatment of prisoners. British mistreatment of American prisoners, however, meant that the declared principles were not always practiced on British prisoners. Concern for humane treatment of prisoners led to an 1785 treaty between the United States and Prussia addressing the issue. The treaty remained in effect and was "the only effective agreement between the United States and Germany on the treatment of prisoners of war during World War I."[4]

Building on the World War I experience, the International Red Cross began work on a new POW code in 1921. Eight years later, the Geneva Convention of 1929 addressed the issue of prisoners of war and their treatment. The ninety-seven articles adopted at the convention outlined the duties and responsibilities of captors and captives alike. During World War II, adherence to the Geneva Convention was a matter of honor and priority by the United States and most Germans, at least toward their American and British captives.

America's humane treatment of prisoners of war has a lengthy history (with the exception of the American Civil War and the Indian wars), but its first international test in modern-day warfare came during World War I. The 3,200 German naval and merchant marine personnel who were interned in America between 1917 and 1919 presented the United States Government with issues and problems similar to those faced three decades later when more than a hundred times that number arrived as prisoners of war between 1943 and 1945. Initially, military officials in both wars were uninterested or even opposed to the transportation of German soldiers from the battlefields of Europe to the United States. During World War I, Gen. John Pershing had resisted public pressure to send captured German soldiers to the United States until the war ended. During World War II, the United States allowed England to bear the burden of caring for German and Italian prisoners until it could do so no more. Although there were public arguments about the military and economic advantages in sending the prisoners to the United States, military leaders seemed to hope the POW problem would take care of itself.

The German naval prisoners interned in America during World War I were, in many ways, different from the German soldiers who began arriving in 1943. Few in number, many had visited or lived throughout the world, and although loyal to the Kaiser beyond question, they had been away from Germany since the war began. The concept of "total war" did not yet exist, and although the Germans were fervent nationalists, they were not infused with the ideology of fascism that seemed to call for action even beyond the more rational voice of patriotism. The prisoners sent to Utah had already sat out the war in considerable comfort in Guam and Hawaii, and most expected to resume their lives as seamen once the conflict was over. In a cursory comparison of World War I and World War II prisoners, the former were surprisingly more active in trying to escape and seemed to be more troublesome. Perhaps it was because there were so few of them or because their presence in the United States was generally unknown. Perhaps their travel in foreign lands gave them confidence that they could blend into the milieu of America. Hence, they dug tunnels and plotted escapes. It may also have been the strong convictions and leadership of such naval officers as Capt. Adelbert Zuckerschwerdt that made the difference.

It should be noted, however, that American treatment of the naval prisoners often seemed to encourage such behavior. In Utah, for example, there were almost no recreational activities, there were no meaningful work opportunities and no way to earn money, and the military prisoners were integrated with civilians arrested as enemy aliens. At Hot Springs, North Carolina, the prisoners not only had considerable freedom but also received $5 to $10 dollars a month, and were permitted to undertake a number of construction projects to improve life in the camp. Under these conditions, the Hot Springs inmates seemed much more content than the men at Fort Douglas, Utah, and Fort McPherson, Georgia.

In retrospect, the World War I experience in dealing with prisoners of war in the United States should have provided answers to basic questions in dealing with World War II prisoners. Should prisoners of war be sent to the United States? What kind of food and shelter should be provided? To what extent are prisoners a threat to internal security and peace? What level of security should be maintained? How should the men use their time? What work could they perform and should they be paid? Where should the prison camps be located? Should contact with civilians be permitted? After the war, what would be appropriate policies for those who wanted to stay in the United States or who could not return to their former homes?

By the time it became necessary not only to ask these questions but also to seek the answers, the World War I experience had either been forgotten or did not seem relevant to the situation in the 1940s. As policy makers outlined the World War II approach, there was no apparent attempt to draw on past history. Had they done so, they would have undoubtedly proceeded with a greater confidence that their basic ideas and objectives were correct. America's participation in World War II produced a POW policy that eventually touched nearly every state in the union. In Utah, two factors brought the German prisoners to the state. First was the development of the military and naval supply depots at Ogden, Clearfield, and Tooele. Second was the use of prisoners of war primarily in the sugar beet fields and to a lesser degree in other agricultural and horticultural activities. Both segments of Utah economy—defense and agriculture—benefited significantly, and despite a few complaints about the enthusiasm for or commitment to the work, most defense depot workers and almost every farmer who employed the prisoners gave them high marks for their work.

As Americans interacted with the German prisoners, there was always the question of how American prisoners were being treated in Germany. Comparison between the two groups is difficult because the circumstances were different. Approximately 95,000 American prisoners were held captive by the Germans as contrasted with 371,000 Germans held in the United States. But where the Germans were in camps scattered from Maine to California and from Washington to Florida, the Americans were held in German territory that was about the size of Texas. The number of American prisoners held in Germany and Austria was small compared to the number of Russian, French, and British prisoners, plus the forced laborers sent to Germany from Poland and other conquered nations, to say nothing of the Jewish and political prisoners sent to concentration camps. The operation of POW, forced-labor, and concentration camps occupied the time and resources of the Third Reich much more than did the incarceration of the Germans in the United States. German citizens were more accustomed to seeing foreign prisoners and workers than Americans were. But, in America, German prisoners had more opportunities for interaction with civilians than did American prisoners with German civilians. Where many Germans not only took back with them names and addresses of Americans they had met but also maintained some level of contact, few if any Americans became acquainted with German civilians. There were a number of reasons for this—paramount being the strict control over American prisoners even when they were sent out on work details among the Germans. Also, learning German held little interest for the Americans, and those Germans who spoke English and may have wanted to be friendly toward the Americans ran the risk of being viewed as informers. With the bombings and the struggle for survival, life was lived on a much thinner edge in Germany than in America. Americans were released, processed, and on their way home within a few weeks of the end of the war; Germans remained in the United States several months after Germany's surrender. Recall that it was during the summer and fall of 1945 that many German prisoners worked on the farms and in factories and military installations, where they came in contact with American civilians who no longer saw them as the hated enemy. A frequent, if not typical, event occurred when the German prisoners left Roy Gappmayer's orchard in the fall of 1945. He had his daughter type a card for each of the twelve men on which he expressed his appreciation for their work, gave them his address, and asked them to write and keep in touch with him. Several of the men did and today their children keep up the contact.

The care and treatment of American and German prisoners was in stark contrast, but primarily because of conditions in wartime Germany. American prisoners were underfed and ill-nourished, but so were the German soldiers and civilians. The Americans were generally better fed and cared for than other prisoners—especially the Russians. Despite the fanatical and insane objectives of the Nazis, adherence to the Geneva Convention was important as a test of German honor. As one former American prisoner declared, "I know of no other nationality, including Americans, so concerned with being regarded as honest (inherently honest) in all things as the Germans. If I ever wanted to taunt and anger any of my captors, all I had to do was to refer in an off-hand manner to his dishonesty." This code of honor and obedience to orders explained why the Germans would "deliver Red Cross food and supplies to us when they themselves were hungry and when their transportation system was taxed to the breaking point to sustain their war effort."[5]

The psychological experience was different for German and American prisoners of war. Although many German prisoners held fast to the hope of a new wonder weapon or ingenious strategy that would bring victory to Germany, by the time they reached the United States, it was clear that the tide had turned against Germany. They had failed to hold North Africa; the offensive on the eastern front had stalled on the outskirts of Moscow, with a loss of 330,000 men of the German Sixth Army in the defeat at Stalingrad. The Russian counteroffensive, launched against the Germans in the summer of 1943 just as the prisoners from the Afrika Korps were settling into their camps in the United States, meant a dramatic change in Germany's strategy from acquiring more territory to trying to hold captured territory.

Although none could openly admit Germany was losing the war, German prisoners in America realized that things were going badly, that America had tremendous resources and strength, and that it would take a miracle for Germany to win. Their concern for families and homes and insecurity about the future brought a certain submission in the thinking, if not conduct, of German prisoners which grated against their training and self-image as soldiers. As a result, the kind of "goonbaiting" of guards developed to a high art in some American POW camps in Germany was absent among the German prisoners in the United States, where protests were staged either en masse or individually by theft, the prankish use of the swastika symbol on flags or carved into peaches, the wearing of Nazi uniforms, or the display of pictures of Adolf Hitler. More subtle ways were debates with reeducation officers and teachers about America's failure to live up to the ideals of democracy. When defeat did come, it was bitter, but three factors seemed to ease the sting: the prospect of returning to their loved ones in a short time, the challenge of helping rebuild Germany, and a retrospection on the great German contributions to culture.

American prisoners lived with a different anxiety. Confident that the Allies would win the war, it was unclear how they would individually survive Germany's defeat. Most expected to be liberated from their camps, but there was concern that the gestapo might execute them in a mad gesture of the insane total war to which they had committed. Others, in the eastern camps, feared the rigors of long marches if the Germans forced them to flee before oncoming Russian forces. Most worried that their health would be permanently affected by poor rations and unsanitary conditions. Some, like Benjamin Gabaldon, who worked in the bombed-out houses and rubble piles of Munich expected to die in an Allied bombing raid. Yet, American prisoners were free of the worry over the safety and well-being of family members back home, which the Germans were not.

As those Germans who were prisoners in America reach their late sixties and seventies, two general categories seem evident. The largest category includes those who put their experience in the context of the horror and destruction of global war and look back with gratitude on their being in the United States as prisoners. They have a positive view of the United States and her citizens, and because of their sojourn here, feel that the land has become a part of them. A smaller group includes those who see their time as prisoners of war as inseparable from the war and the loss of family, friends, homes, and homeland; the difficult postwar readjustment; and, perhaps, a reality in their last years with which they are not yet reconciled. Germans held in Russia seem more likely to fall into this group. Given the treatment, poor conditions, and longer stay, they do not have the same feeling for Russia as others have for the United States.

As a category, former American prisoners seem to fall in the middle. For them, Germany remains a strange and foreign place, unembraced in the way former German prisoners speak of America and their time here, and an element of distrust lingers. Few individual deeds of goodwill are recalled, but the food shortages, poor conditions, mistreatment of others are vivid memories.

Unfairly and often unconsciously, there is sometimes a stigma associated with being a captured prisoner when your side wins. For Americans—especially those who were captured in their first days of combat, sometimes without even seeing the enemy—acceptance of their fate as prisoners of war to the loosing side came with difficulty. Some family members equated their capture as a manifestation of cowardice, and some people drew a clear but discriminatory distinction between soldiers and prisoners of war.[6] Probably few Germans have had to explain the circumstances of or apologize for their being taken prisoner by the Allies. Apparently some Americans have felt a need to explain their capture by the Germans. For those shot down in bombing missions, the explanation was usually easily understood. For those captured in Italy, during the Battle of the Bulge, or in other encounters with the Germans, the explanation became more complicated.

The experiences of Utahns as prisoners in Germany and Germans as prisoners in Utah were not unique when compared with the larger picture. The examination of one state, however, like Utah, provides a case study for the larger global experience of war and its repercussions nearly five decades later. For Utahns, their encounter with German prisoners was not only a part of the worldwide saga of war but also an aspect of war's primary impact at home, the nationalizing of life in the Beehive state. The POW experience was a further manifestation of the impact of federal policies and programs on an insular state that under normal circumstances would not have attracted many Germans except as immigrant converts to the Mormon church. In addition to these distinctions, the Utah story is important as part of the Germans' experience in America because of circumstances and events that were unique to Utah. These include the Germans' encounter with the American West, with Mormons, with Italian prisoners, with wounded American soldiers at Bushnell Hospital, and with civilians at the defense depots. Finally, the shooting at Salina—although an isolated event, the like of which occurred in no other camp—was a sobering illustration to a nation whose land and citizenry had not felt the fury of world conflict nor witnessed the millions of other incidents whose individual threads of death and misery wove a huge and gruesome tapestry. In the death of nine sleeping prisoners and wounding of nineteen others, it was clear that war-inspired hate brought no honor or glory—only injustice, suffering, and shame.

Notes

INTRODUCTION

1. Leonard J. Arrington and Thomas G. Alexander, "The U.S. Army Overlooks Salt Lake City: Fort Douglas, 1862–1965," *Utah Historical Quarterly* 33 (Fall 1965): 344.

2. Edward John Pluth, "The Administration and Operation of German Prisoner of War Camps in the United States during World War II" (Ph.D. diss., Ball State University, 1970), 421.

3. Ray Allen Billington, *Land of Savagery, Land of Promise: The European Image of the American Frontier* (New York: W.W. Norton, 1981), 54–56.

Chapter 1. THE KAISER'S MEN: GERMAN PRISONERS OF WAR IN UTAH DURING WORLD WAR I

1. George G. Lewis and John Mewha, *History of Prisoner of War Utilization by the United States Army, 1776–1945*, U.S. Department of the Army, Pamphlet 20–213 (Washington, D.C., 1955), 51–52. The first to write about the German naval prisoners at Fort Douglas was Raymond Kelly Cunningham, Jr., in "Internment 1917–1920: A History of the Prison Camp at Fort Douglas, Utah, and the Treatment of Enemy Aliens in the Western United States" (M.A. thesis, University of Utah, 1976), 87–96. In conjunction with his research, Cunningham located important reports and documents relating to the camp and activities of the naval prisoners. Copies of these papers were deposited in the Marriot Library, University of Utah, and are included in the Raymond Kelly Cunningham, Jr., Collection in the library's Special Collections. I am indebted to Mr. Cunningham for his work in locating the records and his generosity in making them available to other scholars.

2. Lewis and Mewha, *Prisoner of War Utilization*, 52–53.

3. Cunningham, "Internment," 4.

4. *Salt Lake Tribune*, 22 June 1917.

5. Ibid., 10 June 1917.

6. Ibid.; *Deseret News*, 10 June 1917.

7. *Salt Lake Tribune*, 21 June 1917.

8. Ibid., 20 June 1917.

9. Ibid., 21 June 1917.

10. Barbara W. Tuchman, *The Zimmermann Telegram* (New York: Bantam Books, 1966), 55.

11. Karl P. Huebecher and Charles Vuillenmier, "Inspection Report of Fort Douglas," 20 and 21 November 1917, Record Group 407, Box 76, Folder 6, p. 1, "Report of the Inspection by the Swiss Commission, Ft. Oglethorpe, Ft. McPherson, and Ft. Douglas," National Archives, Washington, D.C.

12. *Salt Lake Tribune*, 25 January 1918.

13. Ibid., 4 October 1917.

14. Huebecher and Vuillenmier, "Fort Douglas," 1.

15. Ibid., 7.

16. *Salt Lake Tribune*, 10 and 11 June 1917.

17. Ibid., 11, 13 June 1917.

18. Ibid., 11 June 1917; Huebecher and Vuillenmier, "Fort Douglas," 6–7.

19. *Salt Lake Tribune*, 16 October 1917; Huebecher and Vuillenmier, "Fort Douglas," 7–8.

20. See Ernest Clements, Chief of Welfare Committee, to U.S. War Department, 27 November 1918, National Archives, Cunningham Collection, University of Utah; John Munz to U.S. War Department, 18 April 1919, National Archives, Cunningham Collection, University of Utah; Adjutant General to Hon. James H. Brady, United States Senate, 18 July 1917, Record Group 407, Box 79, Folder 27, "Parole, Releases, Transportation on Release, Exchange War Prisoners and Enemy Aliens," National Archives, Washington, D.C.

21. *Salt Lake Tribune*, 26 October 1917; Lewis and Mewha, *Prisoner of War Utilization*, 54.

22. W. B. Wilson, Secretary of Labor, to Secretary of War Newton D. Baker, 25 January 1918, National Archives, Cunningham Collection, University of Utah; Adjutant General, Memorandum for the Chief of Staff, 1 February 1918, National Archives, Cunningham Collection, University of Utah.

23. William B. Glidden, "Internment Camps in America, 1917–1920," *Military Affairs* 37 (December 1973): 139.

24. *Salt Lake Tribune*, 25 January 1918.

25. Huebecher and Vuillenmier, "Fort Douglas," 13.

26. *Salt Lake Tribune*, 14 September 1917. The names of the dead prisoners buried at Fort Douglas in 1917 and 1919 are Stanislaus Lewitski, 13 September 1917, fractured spine; Henry L. Zinnel, 1 June 1918; Herman German, 16 July 1918, toxemia; Adolph Wachenhusen, 17 September 1918, apoplexy; Frank Benes, 6 November 1918, pneumonia; Herman Leider, 18 November 1918, pneumonia; Rojo Zilko, 23 November 1918, pneumonia; Joseph Fiskolo, 23 November 1918, Spanish influenza; Max Leopold, 24 November 1918, Spanish influenza; Maximillian Kampmann, 26 November 1918, influenza complicated by pneumonia; Felix Behr, 29 November 1918, pneumonia; Chas Morth, 1 December 1918, pneumonia following influenza; George Schmidt, 2 December 1918, pneumonia following influenza; Emil Laschke, 3 December 1918, cause not given; Walter I. Piezarek, 6 Decem-

ber 1918, pneumonia; Erich Leavemann, 9 December 1918, pneumonia following influenza; Carl Johan Blaase, 14 December 1918, pulmonary tuberculosis; Arthur Rube, 22 December 1918, bronchopneumonia; Frederick Otto Hauf, 25 December 1918, suicide by hanging; Frank Stadler, 21 January 1919, chronic asthma; Walter Toppf, 16 May 1919, pulmonary tuberculosis. Information on the dead is found in notices sent from Fort Douglas to the Adjutant General, Record Group 407, Box 73, Folder 23, National Archives, Washington, D.C.

27. *Salt Lake Telegram*, 2 October 1917.

28. Huebecher and Vuillenmier, "Fort Douglas," 7.

29. *Deseret News*, 12 June 1917.

30. Ibid.

31. Ibid., 13 June 1917; The *Salt Lake Telegram*, 12 June 1917, gave a slightly different version of the incident noting that Addison had the first finger of his left hand shot off. Identified as a respectable citizen, Addison said he had no idea how he came to be in the vicinity of the camp. He was permitted to leave the fort with a severe reprimand.

32. *Salt Lake Telegram*, 15 June 1917.

33. Huebecher and Vuillenmier, "Fort Douglas."

34. F. M. Caldwell to the Adjutant General, "Investigation of Complaints of War Prisoners, Fort Douglas, Utah," 15 February 1918, National Archives, Cunningham Collection, University of Utah; Glidden, "Internment Camps," 138.

35. See documents dated 10 October 1917, Record Group 407, Box 79, Folder 27, National Archives, Washington, D.C.

36. Col. George L. Byram to the Adjutant General, 15 February 1918, Record Group 407, Box 74, Folder 28, National Archives, Washington, D.C. See also draft of letter dated June 11, 1918, apparently sent from Fort McPherson, ibid.

37. Cunningham, "Internment," 24.

38. Ibid., 109.

39. Erich Brandeis, "Birds in a Barbed Cage," Record Group 407, Box 79, Folder 22, p. 2, National Archives, Washington, D.C.

40. University of Utah, Cunningham Collection (National Archives), "Testimony Expected in the Case of United States vs. the (28) Interned Aliens Whose Names Appear on the Joint Charge Sheet," Salt Lake City.

41. Brandeis, "Birds in a Barbed Cage," 2.

42. It was found that the cost of transferring the 517 naval prisoners would be $52.26 each. Fifty guards would be necessary, and they could each travel round trip from Salt Lake City for $80.00. The total cost would have been $31,018.42. Adjutant General to Captain Sheriden, 29 September 1917; Adjutant General to the Secretary of War, 13 March 1918, Record Group 407, Box 79, Folder 27, "Parole, Releases, Transporation on Release, Exchange War Prisoners and Enemy Aliens," National Archives, Washington, D.C.

43. Adjutant General to Secretary of War, 13 March 1918.

44. Frederick Oederlen and Louis H. Junod, "Fort Douglas War Prison Camp Inspection," 19, 20, 21 December 1918, p. 2, National Archives, Cunningham Collection, University of Utah.

45. J. T. Van Orsdale to the Adjutant General, 8 May 1918, Record Group 407, Box 74, Folder 28, "Escape," National Archives, Washington, D.C.

46. Maj. Harry T. Matthews, "Report of Investigation of Escape of Ten (10) German Prisoners from, and General Conditions of, War Prison Barracks, No. 1 at Fort McPherson, Georgia," 13 November 1917, Record Group 407, Box 76, Folder 7, "Inspection of War Prison Camps in the United States," National Archives, Washington, D.C. See also Adjutant General to Chief, Military Intelligence Branch, Executive Division General Staff, 26 July 1918, Record Group 407, Box 74, Folder 28, "Escapes," National Archives, Washington, D.C.; L. W. Redington to General McManus, 25 September 1919, National Archives, Cunningham Collection, University of Utah.

47. Adjutant General to Commander, War Prison Barracks, Fort McPherson, Georgia, "Naturalization of Prisoners of War," 14 June 1919, Record Group 407, Box 79, Folder 25, "Naturalization," National Archives, Washington, D.C. The names of the seventy-three men admitted to the United States found on a list in Record Group 407, Box 79, Folder 28, National Archives, Washington, D.C. 48. Walter Engelbrecht had been an officer of the North German Lloyd ship lines from 1904 until 1914; but as a reserve naval officer, he had been ordered to active duty on board the *Cormoran* and was interned in Guam. After the end of hostilities, he contacted officials of the North German Lloyd Company about the possibilities of returning to his former position. The response from Germany about employment, however, was anything but encouraging, so he decided to stay in the United States, become an American citizen, and try to make a living here. Erich Fratzscher, also a lieutenant on the *Cormoran*, followed a similar course. Before the war he was an officer in the Hamburg American Line. He had been to the United States many times before the war and had worked in New York City for a time. He planned to become an American citizen and was confident that with his experience and familiarity with America, he would have no difficulty finding employment. Walter Engelbrecht and Erich Fratzscher to Commandant, War Prison Barracks #1, Fort McPherson, 13 May 1919, Record Group 407, Box 83, Folder 20, "Release of German Prisoners—Naturalization," National Archives, Washington, D.C.

Among the naval prisoners at Fort Douglas were four men who had immigrated from Germany to New Guinea in 1911 and were drafted into service aboard the gunboat *Geier* when war broke out in 1914. At the end of the war, the four men, Heinrich Koch, Walter Jungmann, Heinrich Kessler, and Fritz Metzner, requested that they be sent to the former German colony of New Guinea by way of San Francisco. They declared that if they were sent to Germany they would be penniless since all of their property was in New Guinea and that there was no one in Germany on whom they could depend for help. Furthermore, since it was their intention to return to New Guinea, it would be almost impossible to do so from Germany. American officials honored their request and they were among the seventy-three who were not repatriated to Germany. Heinrich Koch to the Adjutant General, 30 April 1919, National Archives, Cunningham Collection, University of Utah.

49. F. B. Davis to Commandant, Fort Douglas, 4 June 1919, National Archives, Cunningham Collection, University of Utah.

Chapter 2. FROM SOLDIERS OF THE THIRD REICH TO PRISONERS OF THE UNITED STATES

1. George G. Lewis and John Mewha, *History of Prisoner of War Utilization by the United States Army, 1776–1945*, U.S. Department of the Army, Pamphlet 20–213 (Washington, D.C., 1955), 90–91.

2. U.S. Provost Marshal General's Office, "Prisoner of War Operations," Historical Monograph, vol. 1, 28, microfilm, Library of Congress, Washington, D.C.

3. Arnold Krammer, *Nazi Prisoners of War in America* (New York: Stein and Day, 1979), 2; Judith M. Gansberg, *Stalag: U.S.A.* (New York: Thomas Y. Crowell, 1977), 4–5.

4. Lee Kennett, *G.I.: The American Soldier in World War II* (New York: Charles Scribner's Sons, 1987), 183.

5. Eric Kososik interview by Allan Kent Powell, 18 March 1987, Ogden, Utah.

6. Richard Boettger interview by Allan Kent Powell, 6 May 1987, Reutlingen, Germany.

7. W. Stanley Hoole, ed., *And Still We Conquer: The Diary of a Nazi Unteroffizer in the German African Corps . . .* (Tuscaloosa: Confederate Publishing, University of Alabama, 1968), 32.

8. Josef Becker interview by Allan Kent Powell, 25 April 1987, Idar-Oberstein, Germany.

9. Ernst Hinrichs, "History," 1, copy at Utah State Historical Society, Salt Lake City.

10. Hoole, *And Still We Conquer*, 34.

11. Boettger interview.

12. Kurt Treiter interview by Allan Kent Powell, 20 and 21 February 1984, Mutterstadt, Germany.

13. Hinrichs, "History," 2.

14. Patrick G. O'Brien et al., "Stalag Sunflower: German Prisoners of War in Kansas," *Kansas History* 7 (Autumn 1984): 183.

15. Jennie M. Thomas, "History of the Prisoner of War Camp, Ogden, Utah," 76–79, Historical Branch, Headquarters Control Division, Utah Army Service Forces Depot, 1945, Weber State College Library, Manuscript Collection, MS 29, Box 1, Record Group "Defense Depot, Ogden, Chronologies, 1930–1971."

16. Anton H. Richter, trans. and ed., "A German P.O.W. at Camp Grant: The Reminiscences of Heinz Richter," *Journal of the Illinois State Historical Society* 76 (Spring 1983): 64.

17. Krammer, *Nazi Prisoners of War*, 28.

18. John Hammond Moore, "Hitler's Wehrmacht in Virginia, 1943–1946," *The Virginia Magazine of History and Biography* 85 (July 1977): 268.

19. Quoted in Arnold Krammer, "When the Afrika Korps Came to Texas," *Southwestern Historical Quarterly* 80 (January 1977): 255.

20. Frederick Weber interview by Allan Kent Powell, 26 February 1987, 9, 16 March 1987, Salt Lake City, Utah.

21. U.S. War Department, *Enemy Prisoners of War*, Technical Manual 19–500, ch. 2, sec. 5, Supplies, par. 17 (Washington, D.C.: U.S. Government Printing Office, 1945).

22. Boettger interview.

23. *The Centerville Newsette*, May 1945, 4. Copy provided by Professor Richard Roberts, Weber State College, Ogden, Utah.

24. Lewis and Mewha, *Prisoner of War Utilization*, 111.

25. Edward John Pluth, "The Administration and Operation of German Prisoner of War Camps in the United States during World War II," (Ph.D. diss., Ball State University, 1970), 123–27.

Chapter 3. UTAH CAMPS AND ENEMY PRISONERS

1. DeKoven L. Schweiger, "Report of Visit to Prisoner of War Camp, Ogden, Utah," 10–12 December 1943, National Archives, Microfilm 365.45, Utah State University.

2. E. Tomlin Bailey, "Ogden Prisoner of War Camp Report," 21 October 1944, Record Group 389, Box 2668, Folder "Other Inspection Reports—Ogden," National Archives, Washington, D.C.

3. G. S. Metrauz, "Camp Ogden, Utah," 25 November 1944, Record Group 389, Box 2668, Folder "Other Inspection Reports—Ogden," National Archives, Washington, D.C.

4. Ernst Hinrichs interview by Allan Kent Powell, 27 April 1987, Shortens, Germany.

5. Lt. Col. Earl L. Edwards, Assistant Director, Prisoner of War Division, to Commanding General, Ninth Service Command, Fort Douglas, Utah, 7 January 1944, National Archives, Microfilm 365.45, Utah State University.

6. Leonard J. Arrington and Thomas G. Alexander, "They Kept 'Em Rolling: The Tooele Army Depot, 1942–1962," *Utah Historical Quarterly* 31 (Winter 1963): 3–25.

7. Leonard J. Arrington and Archer L. Durham, "Anchors Aweigh in Utah: The U.S. Naval Supply Depot at Clearfield, 1942–1962," *Utah Historical Quarterly* 33 (Spring 1963): 109–26.

8. John E. Christensen, "The Impact of World War II," *in* Richard D. Poll, et al., *Utah's History* (Provo: Brigham Young University Press, 1978), 500.

9. Leonard J. Arrington and Thomas G. Alexander, "Sentinels of the Desert: The Dugway Proving Ground (1942–1963) and Deseret Chemical Depot (1942–1965)," *Utah Historical Quarterly* 34 (Winter 1964): 37.

10. Rudolf Weltin interview by Allan Kent Powell, 5 May 1987, Frohenleiten, Austria.

11. Charles C. Eberhardt, "Prisoner of War Camp, Utah Army Service Forces Depot, Ogden, Utah, Branch Camps: Logan, Tremonton, Orem, Salina," 13 August 1945, Record Group 389, Box 2668, Folder "Other Inspection Reports—Ogden," National Archives, Washington, D.C.

12. Hermann Jung, *Die Deutschen Kriegsgefangenen in Amerikanischer Hand/USA*, vol. 10/1, in *Zur Geschichte der deutschen Kriegsgefangenen des Zweiten Weltkrieges* (Bielefeld, Germany: Verlag Ernst und Werner Gieseking, 1972), 35.

13. G. S. Metrauz, "Camp Rupert, Idaho," August 1945, Record Group 389, Box 2671, Folder "Other Inspection Reports—Rupert, Idaho," National Archives, Washington, D.C.

14. Kurt Treiter interview by Allan Kent Powell, 20 and 21 February 1984, Mutterstadt, Germany.

15. Paul Hupfner interview by Allan Kent Powell, 12 March 1986, Inzinglen, Germany.

16. Eric Kososik interview by Allan Kent Powell, 18 March 1987, Ogden, Utah.

17. Rudolph Fischer, "Prisoner of War Camp, Ogden, Utah, Army Service Forces Depot, Ogden, Utah," 4, 5 April 1945, Record Group 389, Box 2668, Folder "Ogden, Utah, Inspection and Field Reports," National Archives, Washington, D.C.; Jennie M. Thomas, "History of the Prisoner of War Camp, Ogden, Utah," 82, Historical Branch, Headquarters Control Division, Utah Army Service Forces Depot, 1945, Weber State College Library, Manuscript Collection, MS 29, Box 1, Record Group "Defense Depot, Ogden, Chronologies, 1930–1971."

18. Thomas, "Prisoner of War Camp, Ogden," 81–83.

19. Karl Gustav Almquist, "Report of Visit to Prisoner of War Camp, Bushnell General Hospital, Utah," 13 July 1945, Record Group 389, Box 2657, Folder "Other Inspection Reports—Bushnell," National Archives, Washington, D.C.; Jung, *Deutschen Kriegsgefangenen*, 138–48.

20. Fischer, "Prisoner of War Camp, Ogden," 4, 5 April 1945.

21. *Unser Leben*, April 1945.

22. P. Schnyder, "Camp Clearfield Report," 31 May 1945, Record Group 389, Box 2658, Folder "PMGO Inspection Report—Clearfield, Utah," National Archives, Washington, D.C.

23. Josef Becker interview by Allan Kent Powell, 25 April 1987, Idar-Oberstein, Germany.

24. On June 15, 1945, a thirty-five-year-old noncommissioned officer, Hermann Mass, died at the Ogden camp. Born to a working-class family in Ilshoven near Schwaebisch-Hall, he studied at the University of Tubingen, the University of Munich, and the University of Berlin, where he completed his Ph.D. work in natural history with a study of archaeological sites and discoveries relating to the early German period. At the beginning of World War II, he gave up his position at the Kaiser Wilhelm Institute and joined the army. He fought first in France, then Russia, where he earned the Iron Cross, Second Class, during the bitter winter fighting of 1943–44. After the invasion of Normandy in June 1944, he was ordered back to France, where he was taken prisoner and sent to the United States. As a prisoner he was known to his comrades for his love of books and music, his interest in the theater, and the poetry that he wrote. He was characterized as a man of few words and willing to shoulder his load as a prisoner. Plagued by a weak heart, he died on June 15, 1945. His fellow prisoners were deeply moved by his death. They regretted that he would not see his beloved family and homeland again and that he would be buried in a foreign land. They recognized him as one who had shown high regard for his comrades and as a man who had lived a pure life. *Unser Leben*, August 1945.

The twenty German prisoners who died in Utah were:

Paul Eilert, 38 — 8 June 1944, cancer of the intestine

Alfred Malinowski, 19 — 27 December 1944, crushed when forklift he was driving went off loading dock

Fritz Wienken, 45 — 18 January 1945, brain tumor

Paul Karl Schaeffer, 32 — 4 May 1945, suicide by hanging

Hermann Mass, 35 — 15 June 1945, heart disease

Walter Vogel, 32 — 8 July 1945, shot at Salina

George Liske, 31 — 8 July 1945, shot at Salina

Gottfried Gaag, 29 — 8 July 1945, shot at Salina

Adolph Paul, 28 — 8 July 1945, shot at Salina

Otto Bross, 25 — 8 July 1945, shot at Salina

Hans Meyer, 24 — 8 July 1945, shot at Salina

Fritz Stockmann, 24 — 8 July 1945, shot at Salina

Ernst Fuchs, 21 — 8 July 1945, shot at Salina

Frederich Ritter, 48 — 13 July 1945, shot at Salina

Heinz Rascher, 25 — 20 July 1945, unstated cause

Karl Heinrich, 35 — 28 August 1945, chronic nephritis

Hans Gabriel, 20 — 13 August 1945, crushed by falling metal box

Erich Raschke, 43 — 28 August 1945, arteriosclerosis

Paul Heimerdinger, 30 — 13 September 1945, unstated cause

Hans Wieland, 30 — 30 January 1946, acute meningitis

Of the more than 371,000 German prisoners in the United States, only 491 died while interned. Of the total, 265 died of natural causes; the other 226 deaths were: suicide 72, murder 4, manslaughter 3, execution 14, struck by falling trees 12, drowning 17, use of firearms 40, motor vehicles 43, other 21.

25. Maj. Stephen Farrand, Prisoner of War Operations, Provost Marshal General's Office, to Special War Problems Division, Department of State, n.d., Record Group 389, Box 1340, Folder 13, National Archives, Washington, D.C.

26. Nicholas Bethell, *The Last Secret* (New York: Basic Books, 1974), 8; George G. Lewis and John Mewha, *History of Prisoner of War Utilization by the United States Army 1776–1945*, U.S. Department of the Army, Pamphlet 20–213 (Washington, D.C., 1955), 148.

27. Thomas, "Prisoner of War Camp, Ogden," 77–78.

28. Bethell, *Last Secret*, 22–23.

29. Ibid., 24–25.

30. Ibid., 26–27. Other Russian prisoners returned to Russia from Portland, Oregon, on the S.S. *Dzerjinsky* on April 30, 1945. A month earlier, fifteen Russian-protected personnel were sent to Portland from Camp Rupert "for immediate transfer to ships for embarkation to Russia." It is not known whether the fifteen sailed before the departure of the *Dzerjinsky*; however, included in the March 31 transfer of Russian prisoners to Portland were ten Russian ambulatory cases sent from Bushnell General Hospital in Brigham City. Two of the ten were identified as civilians; six were listed as privates; and two were sergeants. Three of the men had been captured in North Africa, the other seven in France. W. P. Fischer to Commanding General, Fort Douglas, Utah, 4 April 1945, Record Group 389, Box 1578, Folder "IX Service Command Correspondence," National Archives, Washington, D.C.

31. Georg Hirschmann interview by Allan Kent Powell, 23 February 1984, Puelheim by Altdorf, Germany; Wayne Owens interview by Allan Kent Powell, 26

June 1987, Fargo, North Dakota; Erwin Schott interview by Allan Kent Powell, 6 May 1987, Munich, Germany.

32. Metrauz, "Camp Ogden, Utah"; Owens interview.

33. Albert Gewinner to Commanding Officer, Prisoner of War Branch Camp, Tremonton, Utah, 23 June 1945, Record Group 389, Box 2483, File "Ogden, Utah, 1942–46," National Archives, Washington, D.C.

Chapter 4. AMERICAN POLICIES AND PRISON CONDITIONS

1. Edward John Pluth, "The Administration and Operation of German Prisoner of War Camps in the United States during World War II" (Ph.D. diss., Ball State University, 1970), 64–65, 202–3, 330–32.

2. Ibid., 107, 134, 171–75.

3. J. L. Kingsley, "Proposed Intellectual Diversion Program for PW Camp Douglas, Wyoming," 3 January 1945, National Archives, Microfilm 365.45, Utah State University.

4. U.S. War Department, *Enemy Prisoners of War*, Technical Manual 19–500, ch. 2, sec. 10, Discipline and Control, par. 58 (Washington, D.C.: U.S. Government Printing Office, 1945); Rudolf Weltin interview by Allan Kent Powell, 5 May 1987, Frohenleiten, Austria; Richard Boettger interview by Allan Kent Powell, 6 May 1987, Reutlingen, Germany; Herbert Barkhoff, manuscript history, 53.

5. Kennard Bybee interview by Allan Kent Powell, 14 April 1987, Salt Lake City, Utah.

6. Ernst Hinrichs interview by Allan Kent Powell, 27 April 1987, Shortens, Germany.

7. Boettger interview.

8. Hermann Jung, *Die Deutschen Kriegsgefangenen in Amerikanischer Hand/USA*, vol. 10/1 in *Zur Geschichte der deutschen Kriegsgefangenen des Zweiten Weltkrieges* (Bielefeld, Germany: Verlag Ernst und Werner Gieseking, 1972), 114–18, 129.

9. Dieter Lampe interview by Allan Kent Powell, 28 April 1987, Grossensee, Germany; interview with Karl F. *in* Joseph Frederick Doyle, "German Prisoners of War in the Southwest United States during World War II: An Oral History" (Ph.D. diss., University of Denver, 1978), 67.

10. U.S. Provost Marshal General's Office, "Prisoner of War Menu and Messing Guide," Prisoner of War Circular #35, 1 July 1944, 3–9; Wayne Owens interview by Allan Kent Powell, 26 June 1987, Fargo, North Dakota; Walter Hahn, conversation with Allan Kent Powell, 13 April 1987. Dr. Hahn, a native of Germany and employed in the Bushnell Hospital personnel office was asked by army authorities to talk with the prisoners to find out why morale seemed so low. He learned that they simply wanted more potatoes with their meals.

11. Ernst Luders interview by Allan Kent Powell, 7 May 1987, Bad Oldesloe, Germany; Georg Hirschmann interview by Allan Kent Powell, 23 February 1984, Puelheim by Altdorf, Germany; P. Schnyder, "Camp Clearfield Report," 31 May 1945, Record Group 389, Box 2658, Folder "PMGO Inspection Report—Clearfield, Utah," National Archives, Washington, D.C.

12. Interview with Herman K. *in* Doyle, "German Prisoners of War," 160; Jennie M. Thomas, "History of the Prisoner of War Camp, Ogden, Utah," 86, Historical Branch, Headquarters Control Division, Utah Army Service Forces Depot, 1945, Weber State College Library, Manuscript Collection, MS 29, Box 1, Record Group "Defense Depot, Ogden, Chronologies, 1930–1971"; Maj. Edward L. Shannahan and Capt. W. J. Bridges, Jr., "Report of Inspection of War Camp, Rupert, Idaho, and Branch Camps," 5–18 June 1945, National Archives, Microfilm 365.45, Utah State University.

13. Barkhoff, manuscript history, 36; Weltin interview.

14. Pluth, "German Prisoner of War Camps," 279; Thomas, "Prisoner of War Camp, Ogden," 71.

15. *The Salt Lake Telegram*, 19 March 1945.

16. U.S. Provost Marshal General's Office, "Prisoner of War Operations," Historical Monograph, vol. 1, 77–78, microfilm, Library of Congress, Washington, D.C. Jung, *Deutschen Kriegsgefangenen*, 50.

17. Jung, *Deutschen Kriegsgefangenen*, 314–15.

18. Luders interview. The restriction on tobacco was part of an army-wide rationing of smoking tobacco which was implemented on 3 June. The Dugway Proving Ground newspaper, *Sand Blast*, reported in its 18 May 1945 issue that four kinds of ration cards would be issued: "Orange for military personnel and their dependents; green for civilians employed by the War Dept and their dependents; pink for Italian Service Unit members and buff for Prisoners of War." Military personnel in the continental United States were limited to six packs of cigarettes or twenty-four cigars a week or approximately four ounces of tobacco a week. ISU members and prisoners were provided only half the military ration, and orders were given that prisoners were not to be sold cigars and cigarettes, but "must roll their own."

19. Thomas, "Prisoner of War Camp, Ogden," 91.

20. Jung, *Deutschen Kriegsgefangenen*, 72.

21. John H. Ortner, "Camp Warner," 11 May 1944, National Archives, Microfilm 365.45, Utah State University.

22. P. Schnyder, "Camp Ogden, Utah," 30 May 1945, National Archives, Microfilm 365.45, Utah State University.

23. Cobie Van der Puhl Wilson interview by Allan Kent Powell, 1 June 1987, Clearfield, Utah.

24. Jung, *Deutschen Kriegsgefangenen*, 89–90.

25. Willi Klebe interview by Allan Kent Powell, 28 April 1987, Hannover, Germany.

26. Barkhoff, manuscript history, 64; Mrs. Barkhoff to Herbert Barkhoff, 26 December 1944, copy at Utah State Historical Society, Salt Lake City.

27. Fritz Poes to Annchen Poes, 30 June 1944, copy at Utah State Historical Society, Salt Lake City.

28. Col. A. M. Tollefson, Director, Prisoner of War Operations, correspondence, 5 June 1944, Record Group 389, Box 1587, Folder "IX Service Command, Correspondence Transcripts," National Archives, Washington, D.C.; Frederick Weber interview by Allan Kent Powell, 26 February 1987, 9, 16 March 1987, Salt Lake City, Utah.

29. Jung, *Deutschen Kriegsgefangenen*, 91; Kurt Treiter interview by Allan Kent Powell, 20, 21 February 1984, Mutterstadt, Germany.

30. Quoted in Kurt W. Boehme, *Geist und Kulture der Deutschen Kriegsgefangenen im West* (Bielefield, Germany: Verlag Ernst und Werner Gieseking, 1968), 119.

31. Barkhoff, manuscript history, 71.

32. Fritz Noack to _____, 14 May 1946.

33. Boehme, *Geist und Kulture*, 18, 115.

34. Gerhart H. Seger to Elbert D. Thomas, 30 June 1944, *in* Elbert D. Thomas Papers, Utah State Historical Society, Salt Lake City. Attached to the letter was a "Memorandum on the Re-education of German prisoners of war in the United States of America" by Gerhart H. Seger.

35. Kaspar J. Fetzer to Elbert D. Thomas, 22 June 1945, *in* Elbert D. Thomas Papers, Utah State Historical Society, Salt Lake City.

36. Jung, *Deutschen Kriegsgefangenen*, 235.

37. Arnold Krammer, *Nazi Prisoners of War in America* (New York: Stein and Day, 1979), 202; John Hammond Moore, *The Faustball Tunnel: German Pows in America and Their Great Escape* (New York: Random House, 1978), 233.

38. Schnyder, "Camp Ogden"; Luis Hortal, "Prisoner of War Camp, Bushnell Hospital," 11 August 1945, Record Group 389, Box 2657, Folder "Other Inspection Reports—Bushnell," National Archives, Washington, D.C.

39. Krammer, *Nazi Prisoners of War*, 203–4; Jake W. Spidle, "Axis Invasion of the American West: POWs in New Mexico, 1942–1946," *New Mexico Historical Review* 49 (April 1974): 105–6; John Hammond Moore, "Hitler's Wehrmacht in Virginia, 1943–1946," *The Virginia Magazine of History and Biography* 85 (July 1977): 268.

40. *Unser Leben*, April, January 1945.

41. Hinrichs interview.

42. Krammer, *Nazi Prisoners of War*, 174, 180; Jung, *Deutschen Kriegsgefangenen*, 231.

43. Calvin Bartholomew interview by Allan Kent Powell, 14 June 1987, Provo, Utah.

44. Paul Neuland to Director, Prisoner of War Special Projects Division, 17 May 1945, National Archives, Microfilm 365.45, Utah State University; Paul Neuland, "Report of Visit to Prisoner of War Camp, Douglas, Wyoming," 16–17 February 1945, Record Group 389, Box 2660, Folder "Other Inspection Reports—Douglas, Wyoming," National Archives, Washington, D.C.

45. Paul Hupfner interview by Allan Kent Powell, 12 March 1986, Inzinglen, Germany; Hirschmann interview.

Chapter 5. AMERICAN PRISONERS OF WAR IN GERMANY

1. Arnold Krammer, "When the Afrika Korps Came to Texas," *Southwestern Historical Quarterly* 80 (January 1977): 256.

2. David A. Foy, *For You the War Is Over: American Prisoners of War in Nazi Germany* (New York: Stein and Day, 1984), 37–43.

3. *The Hillfielder*, 1 March 1945.

4. Ray T. Matheny, *Die Feuerreiter: Gefangenen in Fliegenden Festungen* (Munich: Alberecht Knaus, 1987), 171-77. In his book about the American experience in Germany, *For You the War Is Over*, David Foy found treatment such as that of Ray Matheny to be "the exception rather than the rule. . . . That the vast majority of parachuting airmen were treated fairly by both the German civilian population and enemy armed forces is, at best, inaccurate," 38.

5. Matheny, *Feuerreiter*, 183–85.

6. Ibid., 185-91.

7. Foy, *For You the War Is Over*, 59.

8. Benjamin Gabaldon interview by Allan Kent Powell, 25 November 1987, Salt Lake City, Utah.

9. Wallace Butterfield interview by Allan Kent Powell, 28 May 1987, Salt Lake City, Utah.

10. Harvey Sundstrom interview by Allan Kent Powell, 14 January, 13 May 1987, Lewiston, Utah.

11. Stanley Davis Blackhurst interview by Allan Kent Powell, 13 November 1987, Salt Lake City, Utah; Matheny, *Feuerreiter*, 193–94; Gabaldon interview; Foy, *For You the War Is Over*, 56.

12. Blackhurst interview.

13. Foy, *For You the War Is Over*, 114.

14. Ibid., 71.

15. Sundstrom interview; Matheny, *Feuerreiter*, 250; Blackhurst interview.

16. Matheny, *Feuerreiter*, 250.

17. Foy, *For You the War Is Over*, 154.

18. Blackhurst interview.

19. Sundstrom interview.

20. Gabaldon interview.

21. Sundstrom interview; Blackhurst interview.

22. *The Transcript-Bulletin*, 15 December 1944.

23. Foy, *For You the War Is Over*, 93.

24. Ray T. Matheny interview by Allan Kent Powell, 3 December 1987, Provo, Utah.

25. Foy, *For You the War Is Over*, 88.

26. Blackhurst interview; Butterfield interview.

27. Matheny, *Feuerreiter*, 213–14.

28. Foy, *For You the War Is Over*, 107–8.

29. Butterfied interview; Blackhurst interview; Gabaldon interview.

30. Butterfield interview; Blackhurst interview; Matheny, *Feuerreiter*, 279–83.

31. Sundstrom interview.

32. Gabaldon interview; Blackhurst interview; Sundstrom interview.

33. Sundstrom interview.

34. Foy, *For You the War Is Over*, 140.

35. Matheny, *Feuerreiter*, 275.

36. Foy, *For You the War Is Over*, 151–52.

Chapter 6. ITALIAN PRISONERS OF WAR IN UTAH

1. John Hammond Moore, "Italian POWs in America: War Is Not Always Hell," *Prologue: The Journal of the National Archives* 8 (Fall 1976), 141–51.

2. Jennie M. Thomas, "History of the Prisoner of War Camp, Ogden, Utah," 7–8, Historical Branch, Headquarters Control Division, Utah Army Service Forces Depot, 1945, Weber State College Library, Manuscript Collection, MS 29, Box 1, Record Group "Defense Depot, Ogden, Chronologies, 1930–1971."

3. Ibid., 11.

4. Ibid., 11–13, 62.

5. Ibid., 42–43. The Italian prisoners grew amazing quantities and a wide variety of produce on the fifty acres. Included in the harvest were, for example, 3,765 pounds of rutabagas; 4,617 pounds of turnip greens; 5,821 pounds of swiss chard; 46 pounds of parsley; and 21,680 pounds of watermelons.

6. Thomas, "Prisoner of War Camp, Ogden," 47.

7. *History of Ogden Air Technical Service Command*, CY 1945, vol. 2, 95, Hill Field History Office, Ogden, Utah.

8. Thomas, "Prisoner of War Camp, Ogden," 52.

9. Francis E. Bierstadt to Army Service Forces, Office of the Provost Marshal, 9 February 1944, National Archives, Microfilm 365.45, Utah State University; Howard W. Smith to Commanding General, Ninth Service Command, 30 October 1944, National Archives, Microfilm 365.45, Utah State University.

10. M. A. Maffeo to Captain Spencer, 20 January 1945, National Archives, Microfilm 365.45, Utah State University.

11. Paul Neuland and Walter H. Rapp, "Report on Visit to Prisoner of War Camp, Ogden, Utah," 16 May 1945, Record Group 389, Box 2668, Folder "Other Inspection Reports—Ogden," National Archives, Washington, D.C.; Thomas, "Prisoner of War Camp, Ogden," 92.

12. Thomas, "Prisoner of War Camp, Ogden," 55, 66–67.

13. U.S. Provost Marshal General's Office, "Fort Douglas, Utah, pt. 3, Remarks," PMG Form #27, Fort Douglas, Utah, Period ending 15 June 1945, Record Group 389, Box 2530, Folder "Fort Douglas," National Archives, Washington, D.C.

14. Thomas, "Prisoner of War Camp, Ogden," 66.

15. Maffeo to Spencer, 20 January 1945; Luis Hortal, "Report of Visit to Prisoner of War Camp, Hill Field, Utah," 12 August 1945, Record Group 389, Box 2663, Folder "Other Inspection Reports—Hill Field," National Archives, Washington, D.C.

16. Philip Notarianni conversation with Allan Kent Powell, 9 August 1986, Salt Lake City, Utah.

17. Moore, "Italian POWs," 149.

18. Thomas, "Prisoner of War Camp, Ogden," 27.

19. Floyd Johnson interview by Allan Kent Powell, 1 November 1986, Aurora, Utah.

20. Thomas, "Prisoner of War Camp, Ogden," 53, 56–57.

21. Ibid, 63, 66.

22. Moore, "Italian POWs," 147–48.

23. Mary K. Fredricksen, "Some Thoughts on Prisoners of War in Iowa, 1943 to 1946," *The Palimpsest* 65 (March/April 1984): 77.

24. U.S. Provost Marshal General's Office, "Prisoner of War Operations," Historical Monograph, vol. 1, 146–47, microfilm, Library of Congress, Washington, D.C.

25. Gene Miconi interview by Allan Kent Powell, 17 June 1986, Ogden, Utah.

26. Ralph A. Busco and Douglas D. Alder, "A History of the Italian and German Prisoner of War Camps in Utah and Idaho during World War II," *Utah Historical Quarterly* 39 (Winter 1971): 64–65.

Chapter 7. LOYALTY AND RESISTANCE

1. Edward John Pluth, "The Administration and Operation of German Prisoner of War Camps in the United States during World War II" (Ph.D. diss., Ball State University, 1970), 157–58.

2. Richard Boettger interview by Allan Kent Powell, 6 May 1987, Reutlingen, Germany; Dieter Lampe interview by Allan Kent Powell, 28 April 1987, Grossensee, Germany.

3. Lt. Col. Frank E. Meek to Commanding General, 7 March 1944, Record Group 389, Box 2486, Folder "Tooele," National Archives, Washington, D.C.; Maj. Edward L. Shannahan, "Report of Visit to POW Base Camp, Tooele, Utah," 20–21 April, 9 May, 1944, Record Group 389, Box 267A, Folder PMGO Inspection Reports, Tooele, Utah, National Archives, Washington, D.C.

4. Col. Arthur J. Ericsson, quoted in Jennie M. Thomas, "History of the Prisoner of War Camp, Ogden, Utah," 80, Historical Branch, Headquarters Control Division, Utah Army Service Forces Depot, 1945, Weber State College Library, Manuscript Collection, MS 29, Box 1, Record Group "Defense Depot, Ogden, Chronologies, 1930–1971."

5. William L. Shea, ed., "A German Prisoner of War in the South: The Memoir of Edwin Pelz," *Arkansas Historical Quarterly* 44 (Spring 1983): 46.

6. Hermann Jung, *Die Deutschen Kriegsgefangenen in Amerikanischer Hand/USA*, vol. 10/1, in *Zur Geschichte der Deutschen Kriegsgefangenen des Zweiten Weltkrieges* (Bielefeld, Germany: Verlag Ernst und Werner Gieseking, 1972), 131.

7. Herbert Barkhoff, manuscript history, 67, copy at Utah State Historical Society, Salt Lake City.

8. Reporter Jack House of the *Birmingham News*, quoted in Stanley W. Hoole, "Alabama's World War II Prisoner of War Camps," *The Alabama Review* 70 (April 1967): 114.

9. Interview with Karl F. in Joseph Frederick Doyle, "German Prisoners of War in the Southwest United States during World War II: An Oral History" (Ph.D. diss., University of Denver, 1978), 68.

10. U.S. War Department, *Enemy Prisoners of War*, Technical Manual 19–500, ch. 2, sec. 10, Discipline and Control, par. 62 (Washington, D.C.: Government Printing Office, 1945).

11. From *Die Brucke*, POW newspaper from Camp Breckenridge, Kentucky, No. 19, quoted in Kurt W. Boehme, *Geist und Kulture der Deutschen Kriegsgefangenen im West* (Bielefeld, Germany: Verlag Ernst und Werner Gieseking, 1968), 13; Paul Neuland and Walter H. Rapp, "Report on Visit to Prisoner of War Camp, Ogden, Utah," 16 May 1945, p.2, Record Group 389, Box 2668, Folder "Other Inspection Reports—Ogden," National Archives, Washington, D.C.

12. Sture Persson, "Report of Visit to Prisoner of War Camp, Rupert, Idaho," 13–14 March 1946, National Archives, Microfilm 365.45, Utah State University.

13. Paul Hupfner interview by Allan Kent Powell, 12 March 1986, Inzinglen, Germany.

14. U.S. National Archives, "Prisoner of War Agreement," n.d., Record Group 389, Box 2660, Folder "Camp Douglas," Washington, D.C.

15. Pluth, "German Prisoner of War Camps," 329; Maj. Edward L. Shannahan, "Report of Visit," 20 April 1944, Record Group 389, Box 1578, Folder "IX Service Command Correspondence Transcripts," National Archives, Washington D.C.

16. Josef Becker interview by Allan Kent Powell, 25 April 1987, Idar-Oberstein, Germany; Frederick Weber interview by Allan Kent Powell, 26 February, 9, 16 March 1987, Salt Lake City, Utah; Heinz Siegel interview by Allan Kent Powell, 18 February 1984, Niederbierbach by Neuwied, Germany.

17. Eric Kososik interview by Allan Kent Powell, 18 March 1987, Ogden, Utah.

18. Becker interview.

19. P. Schnyder, "Camp Ogden, Utah," 30 May 1945, National Archives, Microfilm 365.45, Utah State University.

20. Quoted in Terry Paul Wilson, "The Afrika Korps in Oklahoma: Fort Reno's Prisoner of War Compound," *The Chronicles of Oklahoma* 52 (Fall 1974): 367–68.

21. Arnold Krammer, "When the Afrika Korps Came to Texas," *Southwestern Historical Quarterly* 80 (January 1977): 269; John Hammond Moore, *The Faustball Tunnel: German POWs in America and their Great Escape* (New York, Random House, 1978), 217.

22. Moore, *Faustball Tunnel*, 147–48.

23. Lawrence Hood interview by Allan Kent Powell, 18 August 1986, Tooele, Utah.

24. Capt. DeKoven L. Schweiger, "Report of Visit to Camp Warner," 8–10 March 1944, Record Group 389, Box 2674, Folder "PMGO Inspection Reports, Tooele, Utah," National Archives, Washington, D.C.

25. Shannahan, "POW Base Camp, Tooele."

26. Karl Altkruger interview by Allan Kent Powell, 23 April 1987, Hannover, Germany.

27. Shea, "Memoir of Edwin Pelz," 46.

28. Jung, *Deutschen Kriegsgefangenen*, 117, 129.

29. Pluth, "German Prisoner of War Camps," 333.

30. Paul Brickhill, *The Great Escape* (New York: Crest Book, 1950), 61.

31. Becker interview.

32. Boettger interview; Ernst Luders interview by Allan Kent Powell, 7 May 1987, Bad Oldesloe, Germany; Georg Hirschmann interview by Allan Kent Powell, 23 February 1984, Puelheim by Altdorf, Germany; Neuland and Rapp, "Prisoner of War Camp, Ogden," 2.

33. Neuland and Rapp, "Prisoner of War Camp, Ogden," 2; Weber interview; Luders interview.

34. Ernst Hinrichs, "History," 4, copy at Utah State Historical Society, Salt Lake City; Leonhard Mombar interview by Allan Kent Powell, 22 February 1984, Langlau by Gunzenhausen, Germany.

35. Hirschmann interview; Kososik interview.

36. Luders interview.

37. *Unser Leben*, January 1946, first issue.

38. Rudolf Weltin interview by Allan Kent Powell, 5 May 1987, Frohenleiten, Austria.

39. Hirschmann interview.

40. Jung, *Deutschen Kriegsgefangenen*, 226.

41. Weber interview.

42. Siegel interview; Judith M. Gansberg, *Stalag: U.S.A.* (New York: Thomas Y. Crowell, 1977), 103–4.

43. *Unser Leben*, August 1945.

44. Boehme, *Geist und Kultur*, 119.

45. Kososik interview.

46. *Unser Leben*, November 1945.

Chapter 8. ESCAPE

1. Frederick Weber interview by Allan Kent Powell, 26 February, 9, 16 March 1987, Salt Lake City, Utah.

2. The best account of German POW escape attempts and the apprehension of the sixteen who were still at large in 1947 is in Arnold Krammer, *Nazi Prisoners of War in America*, ch. 4, "Escapes" (New York: Stein and Day, 1979), 114–45. John Hammond Moore's *The Faustball Tunnel: German POWs in America and Their Great Escape* (New York: Random House, 1978) deals with the escape of twenty-five German naval officers and seamen from their compound at Papago Park, Arizona, in December 1944 by means of a tunnel. The following select list of articles deals with escape attempts in specific areas and states: Stanley W. Hoole, "Alabama's World War II Prisoner of War Camps," *The Alabama Review* 70 (April 1967): 89–90; Jake W. Spidle, "Axis Invasion of the American West: POWs in New Mexico, 1942–1946," *New Mexico Historical Review* 49 (April 1974): 106–8; Terry Paul Wilson, "The Afrika Korps in Oklahoma: Fort Reno's Prisoner of War Compound," *The Chronicles of Oklahoma* 52 (Fall 1974): 368; Arnold Krammer, "When the Afrika Korps Came to Texas," *Southwestern Historical Quarterly* 80 (January 1977): 272–74; John Hammond Moore, "Hitler's Wehrmacht in Virginia, 1943–1946," *The Virginia Magazine of History and Biography* 85 (July 1977): 262–63; John Hammond Moore, "Nazi Troopers in South Carolina, 1944–1946," *South Carolina Historical Magazine* 81 (October 1980): 308–9; Merrill R. Pritchett and William L. Shea, "The Afrika Korps in Arkansas, 1943–1946," *Arkansas Historical Quarterly* 37 (Spring 1978): 12; Merrill R. Pritchett and William L. Shea, "The Enemy in Mississippi (1943–1946)," *The Journal of Mississippi History* 41 (November 1979): 362–64; William L. Shea and Merrill R. Pritchett, "The Wehrmacht in Louisiana," *Louisiana History* 23 (Winter 1982): 13–14; Allen W. Paschall, "The Enemy in Colorado: German Prisoners of War, 1943–1946," *The Colorado Magazine* 56 (Summer/Fall 1979): 134–40; Robert D. Billinger, Jr., "With the Wehrmacht in Florida: The German POW Facility at Camp Blanding, 1942–1946," *Florida Historical Review* 58 (October 1979): 167–68.

3. Hermann Jung, *Die Deutschen Kriegsgefangenen in Americanischer Hand/USA*, vol. 10/1, in *Zur Geschichte der deutschen Kriegsgefangenen des*

Zweiten Weltkrieges (Bielefeld, Germany: Verlag Ernst und Werner Gieseking, 1972), 126.

4. U.S. Provost Marshal General's Office, "Prisoner of War Operations," Historical Monograph, vol. 1, 200–206, microfilm, Library of Congress, Washington, D.C.; U.S. War Department, *Enemy Prisoners of War*, Technical Manual, ch. 2, sec. 10, "Discipline and Control," par. 63 (Washington, D.C.: Government Printing Office, 1945).

5. Col. A. M. Tollefson to Chief, Field Liaison Branch, 5 June 1944, Record Group 389, Box 1578, Folder "IX Service Command, Correspondence Transcripts," National Archives, Washington, D.C.

6. Moore, *Faustball Tunnel*, 133.

7. Ibid., 149–51; *Salt Lake Tribune*, 27 December 1944.

8. Moore, *Faustball Tunnel*, 196.

9. Ibid., 188.

10. Russell Kirk to William C. McCann, 26 January 1946, Clarke Historical Library, Central Michigan University, Mt. Pleasant.

11. Capt. DeKoven L. Schweiger, "Report of Visit to Camp Warner," 8–10 March 1944, Record Group 389, Box 2674, Folder "PMGO Inspection Reports, Tooele, Utah," National Archives, Washington, D.C.

12. Lawrence Hood interview by Allan Kent Powell, 18 August 1986, Tooele, Utah; *The Transcript-Bulletin*, 28 March 1944.

13. Wayne Owens interview by Allan Kent Powell, 26 June 1987, Fargo, North Dakota; P. Schnyder, "Camp Ogden, Utah," 30 May 1945, National Archives, Microfilm 365.45, Utah State University; Luis Hortal and Charles C. Eberhardt, "Prisoner of War Camp, Naval Supply Depot, Clearfield, Utah," 14 August 1945, Record Group 389, Entry 461, Box 2658, File "Naval Supply Depot, Clearfield, Utah," National Archives, Washington, D.C.

14. F. D. Lietz, conversation with Allan Kent Powell at lecture, 16 March 1987, Ogden, Utah.

15. Fritz Noack to _____, undated letter.

16. Ernst Luders interview by Allan Kent Powell, 7 May 1987, Bad Oldesloe, Germany.

17. Georg Gaertner with Arnold Krammer, *Hitler's Last Soldier in America* (New York: Stein and Day, 1985).

Chapter 9. WORK

1. Edward John Pluth, "Prisoner of War Employment in Minnesota during World War II," *Minnesota History* 44 (Winter 1975): 290–92.

2. Jake W. Spidle, "Axis Invasion of the American West: POWs in New Mexico, 1942–1946," *New Mexico Historical Review* 49 (April 1974): 112.

3. Hermann Jung, *Die Deutschen Kriegsgefangenen in Amerikanischer Hand/USA*, vol. 10/1, in *zur Geschichte der deutschen Kriegsgefangenen des Zweiten Weltkrieges* (Bielefeld, Germany: Verlag Ernst und Werner Gieseking, 1972), 157, 169–70. For a discussion of the administrative history of the implementation of the contract labor program for prisoners of war by the U.S. War Department see George G. Lewis and John Mewha, *History of Prisoner of War*

Utilization by the United States Army, 1776–1945, U.S. Department of the Army, Pamphlet 10–213 (Washington, D.C.,1955), 101–43.

4. Lewis and Mewha, *Prisoner of War Utilization*, 164.

5. Leonard J. Arrington and Thomas G. Alexander, "Supply Hub of the West: Defense Depot Ogden, 1941–1964," *Utah Historical Quarterly* 32 (Spring 1964): 110; Jung, *Deutschen Kriegsgefangenen*, 174.

6. Ernst Hinrichs interview by Allan Kent Powell, 27 April 1987, Shortens, Germany; Herbert Barkhoff, manuscript history, 58, copy at Utah State Historical Society, Salt Lake City.

7. Jennie M. Thomas, "History of the Prisoner of War Camp, Ogden, Utah," 92, Historical Branch, Headquarters Control Division, Utah Army Service Forces Depot, 1945, Weber State College Library, Manuscript Collection, MS 29, Box 1, Record Group "Defense Depot, Ogden, Chronologies, 1930–1971."

8. Rudolf Fischer, "Prisoner of War Camp, Ogden, Utah, Army Service Forces Depot, Ogden, Utah," 4, 5 April 1945, Record Group 389, Box 2668, Folder "Inspection and Field Reports—Ogden, Utah," National Archives, Washington, D.C.

9. Lewis and Mewha, *Prisoner of War Utilization*, 162–63.

10. Louis S. N. Phillipp, "German Prisoner of War Camp, Naval Supply Depot, Clearfield, Utah," 31 May 1945, Record Group 389, Box 2658, Folder "Naval Supply Depot, Clearfield," National Archives, Washington, D.C.

11. Lewis and Mewha, *Prisoner of War Utilization*, 114; Maj. Edward L. Shannahan, "Report of Visit to POW Base Camp, Tooele, Utah," 20–21 April, 9 May 1944, Record Group 389, Box 2674, Folder "PMGO Inspection Reports—Tooele, Utah," National Archives, Washington, D.C.

12. Quoted in Lewis and Mewha, *Prisoner of War Utilization*, 254–55.

13. U.S. Provost Marshal General's Office, "Prisoner of War Operations," Historical Monograph, vol. 1, 117–18, microfilm, Library of Congress, Washington, D.C.; Jung, *Deutschen Kriegsgefangenen*, 185.

14. U.S. Provost Marshal General's Office, "Prisoner of War Operations," Historical Monograph, vol. 1, 101–2.

15. Rudolf Weltin interview by Allan Kent Powell, 5 May 1987, Frohenleiten, Austria.

16. Anton H. Richter, trans. and ed., "A German P.O.W. at Camp Grant: The Reminiscences of Heinz Richter," *Journal of the Illinois State Historical Society* 76 (Spring 1983): 67.

17. Ibid., 66–67.

18. Shannahan, "POW Base Camp, Tooele, Utah," 4.

19. Richard Boettger interview by Allan Kent Powell, 6 May 1987, Reutlingen, Germany.

20. Lawrence Hood interview by Allan Kent Powell, 18 August 1986, Tooele, Utah.

21. Ernst Luders interview by Allen Kent Powell, 7 May 1987, Bad Oldesloe, Germany.

22. Wesley Andersen interview by Kathy Bradford, 19 February 1987, Brigham City, Utah.

23. Kurt Treiter interview by Allan Kent Powell, 20, 21 February 1984, Mutterstadt, Germany; Paul Hupfner interview by Allan Kent Powell, 12 March 1986, Inzinglen, Germany.

24. Merrill R. Pritchett and William L. Shea, "The Afrika Korps in Arkansas, 1943–1946," *Arkansas Historical Quarterly* 37 (Spring 1978): 16; Stanley W. Hoole, "Alabama's World War II Prisoner of War Camps," *The Alabama Review* 20 (April 1967): 95; Pluth, "Prisoner of War Employment," 290–303; William L. Shea and Merrill R. Pritchett, "The Wehrmacht in Louisiana," *Louisiana History* 23 (Winter 1982): 187.

25. Morris Taylor interview by Allan Kent Powell, 24 March 1987, Hyde Park, Utah.

26. Joseph T. Butler, Jr., "Prisoner of War Labor in the Sugar Cane Fields of LaFourche Parish, Louisiana: 1943–1944," *Louisiana History* 14 (Summer 1973): 283; Director, Western Division of the Agricultural Adjustment Agency of the U.S. Department of the Interior to Senator Elbert D. Thomas, 16 July 1945, *in* Elbert D. Thomas Papers, Utah State Historical Society, Salt Lake City.

27. Extension Service, County Extension Agents, Sevier County, Annual Report, 1945, 51, Special Collections, Merrill Library, Utah State University, Logan.

28. The canneries and the number of prisoners assigned to them included the Blackinton and Son Canning Company, 20 men; California Packing Corporation, 100 men; Kaysville Canning Corporation, 70 men; North Ogden Canning Company, 45 men; Rocky Mountain Packing, 6 men; Royal Canning Company, 50 men; Smith Canning Company, 80 men; Stevens Canning Company, 20 men; Utah Canning Company, 75 men; Varny Canning Incorporated, 40 men; and Woods Cross Canning Company, 45 men. Thomas, "Prisoner of War Camp, Ogden," 100.

29. *Salt Lake Tribune*, 10 January 1945.

30. Lewis and Mewha, *Prisoner of War Utilization*, 131.

31. Extension Service, County Extension Agents, Box Elder County, Annual Report, 1945, 35–37, Special Collections, Merrill Library, Utah State University, Logan.

32. Jung, *Deutschen Kriegsgefangenen*, 184–85.

33. Weltin interview.

34. Extension Service, County Extension Agents, Cache County, Annual Report, 1945, 51, Special Collections, Merrill Library, Utah State University, Logan.

35. Jung, *Deutschen Kriegsgefangenen*, 184–85; Preston Alder interview by Allan Kent Powell, 27 February 1987, Providence, Utah.

36. Taylor interview.

37. Karl Altkruger interview by Allan Kent Powell, 23 April 1987, Hannover, Germany.

38. Colonel Urwiller and Colonel Hannover, Ninth Service Command, conversation, 24 August 1945, Record Group 389, Box 1578, Folder "IX Service Command Correspondence Transcripts," National Archives, Washington, D.C.

39. Frank G. Shelly telegram to Senator Elbert D. Thomas, 25 April 1945, *in* Elbert D. Thomas Papers, Box 117, Folder War 1, General, Utah State Historical Society, Salt Lake City.

40. Floyd Johnson interview by Allan Kent Powell, 1 November 1986, Aurora, Utah.

41. Taylor interview.

42. C. W. Greeno to Elbert D. Thomas, 10 October 1944, *in* Elbert D. Thomas Papers, Box 84, File G-1, General, Utah State Historical Society, Salt Lake City.

43. Mrs. Thomas Rowe to Senator Elbert D. Thomas, 1 November 1945, *in* Elbert D. Thomas Papers, Box 118, Folder R, Utah State Historical Society, Salt Lake City.

44. *Salt Lake Telegram*, 19 March 1945.

45. Boyd H. Ririe to Senator Abe Murdock, 14 December 1945, Record Group 389, Box 1578, File "IX Service Command Correspondence Transcripts," National Archives, Washington, D.C.

46. Maj. Guy E. Matheson to Director of Security and Intelligence, 3 January 1946, Record Group 389, Box 1578, File "IX Service Command Correspondence Transcripts," National Archives, Washington, D.C.

Chapter 10. FREE TIME

1. G. S. Metrauz, "Camp Ogden, Utah," 25 November 1944, Record Group 389, Box 2668, Folder "Other Inspection Reports—Ogden," National Archives, Washington, D.C.; Charles C. Eberhardt, "Prisoner of War Camp, Utah Army Service Forces Depot, Ogden, Utah, Branch Camps: Logan, Tremonton, Orem, Salina," 13 August 1945, Record Group 389, Box 2668, Folder "Other Inspection Reports—Ogden," National Archives, Washington, D.C.; Capt. Walter H. Rapp, Field Service Camp Survey by Office of the Provost Marshal General," 4–5 May 1945, Record Group 389, Box 2668, Folder "Enemy POW Informational Bureau, Inspection and Field Reports," National Archives, Washington, D.C.; Rudolf Fischer, "Prisoner of War Camp, Ogden, Utah, Army Service Forces Depot, Ogden, Utah," 4, 5 April 1945, Record Group 389, Box 2668, Folder "Ogden, Utah, Inspection and Field Reports," National Archives, Washington, D.C.; *Unser Leben*, July 1945. For list of magazines prisoners could subscribe to see Hermann Jung, *Die Deutschen Kriegsgefangenen in Amerikanischer Hand/USA*, vol. 10/1, in *Zur Geschichte der deutschen Kriegsgefangenen des Zweiten Weltkrieges* (Bielefeld, Germany: Verlag Ernst und Werner Gieseking, 1972), 113.

2. Calvin Bartholomew interview by Allan Kent Powell, 14 June 1987, Provo, Utah.

3. Emil Blau interview by Allan Kent Powell, 30 April 1987, Trier, Germany; William L. Shea, ed., "A German Prisoner of War in the South: The Memoir of Edwin Pelz," *Arkansas Historical Quarterly* 44 (Spring 1983): 49; Jake W. Spidle, "Axis Invasion of the American West: POWs in New Mexico, 1942–1946," *New Mexico Historical Review* 49 (April 1974): 103; John Hammond Moore, *The Faustball Tunnel: German POWs in America and their Great Escape* (New York: Random House, 1978), 153.

4. Fischer, "Prisoner of War Camp, Ogden"; Metrauz, "Camp Ogden, Utah," 25 November 1944; Bartholomew interview; Heinz Siegel interview by Allan Kent Powell, 18 February 1984, Niederbierbach by Neuwied, Germany; Jung, *Deutschen Kriegsgefangenen*, 98–99.

5. Rapp, "Field Service Camp Survey."

6. Karl Altkruger interview by Allan Kent Powell, 23 April 1987, Hannover, Germany; Frederick Weber interview by Allan Kent Powell, 26 February, 9, 16, March 1987, Salt Lake City, Utah.

7. Rudolf Weltin interview by Allan Kent Powell, 5 May 1987, Frohenleiten, Austria.

8. Luis Hortal, "Report of Visit to P.O.W. Camp, Camp Warner, Utah," 9, 10 February 1944, Record Group 389, Entry 461, Box 1675, Folder "Inspection and Field Reports, 1942–1946," National Archives, Washington, D.C.; Luis Hortal and Charles C. Eberhardt, "Prisoner of War Camp, Naval Supply Depot, Clearfield, Utah," 14 August 1945, Record Group 389, Entry 461, Box 2658, File "Naval Supply Depot, Clearfield, Utah," National Archives, Washington, D.C.; Ralph A. Busco and Douglas D. Alder, "A History of the Italian and German Prisoner of War Camps in Utah and Idaho," *Utah Historical Quarterly* 39 (Winter 1971): 61.

9. Fischer, "Camp Ogden, Utah"; Luis Hortal, "Report of Visit to Prisoner of War Camp, Ogden, Utah," 13 August 1945, Record Group 389, Box 2668, Folder "Other Inspection Reports—Ogden," National Archives, Washington, D.C.; Rapp, "Field Service Camp Survey"; *Unser Leben*, May 1945. In some camps, German songbooks were available in the camp libraries; the YMCA published a 195-page folksong book for prisoners in the United States under the title *Der Zupfgeigenhansl*. Mr. John Sulich of Salt Lake City made available to me a copy of this book.

10. *Unser Leben*, January 1946, second issue, and September 1945.

11. Ibid, April 1945; Leonhard Mombar interview by Allan Kent Powell, 22 February 1984, Langlau by Gunzenhausen, Germany; Howard Hong, "Report of Visit to Prisoner of War Camp, Douglas, Wyoming," 19–21 December 1944, Record Group 389, Box 2660, Folder "Other Inspection Reports—Douglas, Wyoming," National Archives, Washington, D.C.; Bartholomew interview.

12. Erwin Schott interview by Allan Kent Powell, 6 May 1987, Munich, Germany; Wayne Owens interview by Allan Kent Powell, 26 June 1987, Fargo, North Dakota; Jennie M. Thomas, "History of the Prisoner of War Camp, Ogden, Utah," 89–90, Historical Branch, Headquarters Control Division, Utah Army Service Forces Depot, 1945, Weber State College Library, Manuscript Collection, MS 29, Box 1, Record Group "Defense Depot, Ogden, Chronologies, 1930–1971." Included in the appendix of the Thomas history is a list by artist and title of the fifty paintings.

13. Merrill R. Pritchett and William L. Shea, "The Enemy in Mississippi (1943–1946), *The Journal of Mississippi History* 41 (November 1979): 358. See also Pritchett and Shea, "The Afrika Korps in Arkansas, 1943–1946, *Arkansas Historical Quarterly* 37 (Spring 1978): 11; Arnold Krammer, "When the Afrika Korps Came to Texas," *Southwestern Historical Quarterly* 80 (January 1977): 263.

14. Metrauz, "Camp Ogden, Utah." The shortage of soccer balls was not confined to Ogden alone. In Arkansas, "Soccer must have been the most popular sport, for the game balls were kicked to shreds so rapidly that a chronic shortage of soccer balls existed in Arkansas for the duration of the war," Pritchett and Shea, "Afrika Korps in Arkansas," 9. See also Sture Persson, "Report of Visit to Prisoner of War Camp, Rupert, Idaho," 13–14 March 1946, National Archives, Microfilm 365.45, Utah State University; Hortal, "Prisoner of War Camp, Ogden"; *Unser Leben*, July 1945.

15. Paul Hupfner interview by Allan Kent Powell, 12 March 1986, Inzinglen, Germany; Weltin interview.

16. Weltin interview.

17. Josef Becker interview by Allan Kent Powell, 25 April 1987, Idar-Oberstein, Germany.

18. Ernst Luders interview by Allan Kent Powell, 7 May 1987, Bad Oldesloe, Germany. A more primitive way of making schnapps was explained by Emil Blau, a former prisoner who had been at Salina. Using oranges or preferably grapes, the men would let the fruit ferment for three or four days, then heat it in a cylinder covered by a basin of cold water. The cylinder was placed inside a larger tub so that when the steam created by the heat reached the bottom of the basin (which was cooled by the water), it would condense and fall into the tub to be collected as alcohol. Blau interview.

19. Herbert Barkhoff, manuscript history, 55, copy at Utah State Historical Society, Salt Lake City.

20. John H. Ortner, "Camp Warner, Utah," 11 May 1944, National Archives, Microfilm 365.34, Utah State University.

21. Karl Gustav Almquist, "Report of Visit to Prisoner of War Camp, Camp Clearfield, Utah," 12 July 1945, Record Group 389, Box 2658, Folder "PMGO Inspection Reports, Clearfield, Utah," National Archives, Washington, D.C.

22. Edward L. Shannahan, "Report of Visit to POW Base Camp, Tooele, Utah," 24 May 1944, Record Group 389, Box 2674, Folder "PMGO Inspection Reports, Tooele, Utah," National Archives, Washington, D.C.; Jung, *Deutschen Kriegsgefangenen*, 105.

23. Eberhardt, "Branch Camps," 13 August 1945.

24. Jung, *Deutschen Kriegsgefangenen*, 109.

25. Leroy E. Cowles to Dr. George F. Zook, 30 August 1944, Record Group 389, Box 2668, Folder "Ogden, Utah," National Archives, Washington, D.C.

26. Col. Francis E. Howard to President L. W. Cowles, 28 September 1944, Record Group 389, Box 2668, Folder "Ogden, Utah," National Archives, Washington D.C.; Arthur L. Beeley to Francis G. Howard, 14 October 1944, Record Group 389, Box 2668, File "Ogden, Utah," National Archives, Washington D.C.

27. Denzel S. Curtis to Commanding General, Ninth Service Command, 17 August 1945, Record Group 389, Box 2668, Folder "Clearfield, Utah," National Archives, Washington, D.C.

28. Rapp, "Field Service Camp Survey."

29. Owens interview.

30. Bartholomew interview.

31. *Unser Leben*, January 1946, second issue.

32. Ibid., October 1945.

33. E. Tomlin Bailey, "Ogden Prisoner of War Camp Report," 21 October 1944, Record Group 389, Box 2668, Folder "Other Inspection Reports—Ogden," National Archives, Washington, D.C.

34. *Ogden Standard Examiner*, 16 August 1944.

35. Ernst Hinrichs interview by Allan Kent Powell, 27 April 1987, Shortens, Germany.

36. U.S. Provost Marshal General's Office, "Prisoner of War Operations," Historical Monograph, vol. 1, 90, microfilm, Library of Congress, Washington, D.C.

37. Almquist, "Prisoner of War Camp, Camp Clearfield"; Karl Gustav Almquist, "Report of Visit to Prisoner of War Camp, Camp Douglas, Wyoming," 5 July 1945,

Record Group 389, Box 2668, Folder "Other Inspection Reports—Douglas, Wyoming," National Archives, Washington, D.C.

38. Quoted in Stanley W. Hoole, "Alabama's World War II Prisoner of War Camps," *The Alabama Review* 70 (April 1967): 109–10.

39. Kurt W. Boehme, *Geist und Kultur der Deutschen Kriegsgefangenen im West* (Bielefeld, Germany: Verlag Ernst und Werner Gieseking, 1968), 14.

40. Quoted in Hoole, "Alabama's Prisoner of War Camps," 110.

41. Karl Gustav Almquist, "Report of Visit to Prisoner of War Camp, Ogden, Utah," 10 July 1945, Record Group 389, Box 2668, Folder "Inspection and Field Reports," National Archives, Washington, D.C.

42. Letter from Clemens S. Harms to Ralph A. Busco, 26 July 1966, quoted in Busco and Alder, "Italian and German Prisoner of War Camps," 69–70, 79–80.

43. Almquist, "Prisoner of War Camp, Ogden."

44. Jung, *Deutschen Kriegsgefangenen*, 150–53.

45. Metrauz, "Camp Ogden, Utah"; Owens interview.

46. Quoted in Edward John Pluth, "The Administration and Operation of German Prisoner of War Camps in the United States during World War II" (Ph.D. diss., Ball State University, 1970), 218.

Chapter 11. GERMAN AND AMERICAN RELATIONS

1. Edward J. Pluth, "The Administration and Operation of German Prisoner of War Camps in the United States during World War II" (Ph.D. diss., Ball State University, 1970), 245; Jennie M. Thomas, "History of the Prisoner of War Camp, Ogden, Utah," 75, Historical Branch, Headquarters Control Division, Utah Army Service Forces Depot, 1945, Weber State College Library, Manuscript Collection, MS 29, Box 1, Record Group "Defense Depot, Ogden, Chronologies, 1930–1971."

2. U.S. War Department, *Enemy Prisoners of War*, Technical Manual 19–500, ch. 5, sec. 66, Instructions to Contractor (Washington, D.C.: Government Printing Office, 1945).

3. Arnold Krammer, *Nazi Prisoners of War in America* (New York: Stein and Day, 1979), 3.

4. Gordon Reeves interview by Kathy Bradford, 17 February 1987, Brigham City, Utah; Georg Hirschmann interview by Allan Kent Powell, 23 February 1984, Puelheim by Altdorf, Germany.

5. Gerhard Graenitz interview by Allan Kent Powell, 17 February 1984, Minden, Germany.

6. Lawrence Hood interview by Allan Kent Powell, 18 August 1986, Tooele, Utah.

7. Anton H. Richter, trans. and ed., "A German P.O.W. at Camp Grant: The Reminiscences of Heinz Richter, *Journal of the Illinois State Historical Society* 76 (Spring 1983): 64.

8. Paul Hupfner interview by Allan Kent Powell, 12 March 1986, Inzinglen, Germany.

9. Interview with Jim B. *in* Joseph Frederick Doyle, "German Prisoners of War in the Southwest United States during World War II: An Oral History" (Ph.D. Diss., University of Denver, 1978), 127; Dieter Lampe interview by Allan Kent Powell, 28 April 1987, Grossensee, Germany.

10. Hupfner interview.

11. Herbert Barkhoff, manuscript history, 72–73, copy at Utah State Historical Society, Salt Lake City.

12. Ernst Hinrichs interview by Allan Kent Powell, 27 April 1987, Shortens, Germany.

13. Karl Altkruger interview by Allan Kent Powell, 23 April 1987, Hannover, Germany.

14. Hupfner interview.

15. Xerox copy of the document and card provided to the author by Mr. Wayne Owens, Fargo, North Dakota.

16. *Unser Leben*, December 1945.

17. P. Schnyder, "Camp Ogden, Utah," 30 May 1945, National Archives, Microfilm 365.45, Utah State University.

18. Sture Persson, "Report of Visit to Prisoner of War Camp at the Naval Supply Depot, Clearfield, Utah," 21 March 1946, National Archives, Microfilm 365.45, Utah State University.

19. Charles C. Eberhardt, "Prisoner of War Camp, Utah Army Service Forces Depot, Ogden, Utah, Branch Camps: Logan, Tremonton, Orem, Salina," 13 August 1945, Record Group 389, Box 2668, Folder "Other Inspection Reports—Ogden," National Archives, Washington, D.C.

20. Leath Christensen interview by Allan Kent Powell, 16 June 1986, Salina, Utah.

21. William L. Shea, ed., "A German Prisoner of War in the South: The Memoir of Edwin Pelz." *Arkansas Historical Quarterly* 44 (Spring 1983): 51.

22. Cobie Van der Puhl Wilson interview by Allan Kent Powell, 1 June 1987, Clearfield, Utah.

23. Altkruger interview.

24. Willi Klebe interview by Allan Kent Powell, 28 April 1987, Hannover, Germany.

25. Floyd Johnson interview by Allan Kent Powell, 1 November 1986, Aurora, Utah.

26. Excerpt from Dorothy J. Buchanan, diary, which is in her possession.

27. F. Rulon Nicholes, "The Story of a Painting," copy at the Utah State Historical Society, Salt Lake City.

28. Barkhoff, manuscript history, 34.

29. Maj. Edward L. Shannahan, "Report of Visit to POW Base Camp, Tooele, Utah," 20–21 April, 9 May 1944, Record Group 389, Box 2674, Folder "PMGO Inspection Reports, Tooele, Utah," National Archives, Washington, D.C.

30. Hood interview; William Lawler conversation, 6 September 1988.

31. Beatrice Gappmayer Pyne interview by Allan Kent Powell, 25 September 1986, Orem, Utah.

32. Wayne Owens interview by Allan Kent Powell, 26 June 1987, Fargo, North Dakota.

33. Allen W. Paschal, "The Enemy in Colorado: German Prisoners of War, 1943–1946," *The Colorado Magazine* 56 (Summer/Fall 1979): 130.

34. Ernst Hinrichs, history, 3, copy at the Utah State Historical Society, Salt Lake City.

35. Herbert Barkhoff interview by Allan Kent Powell, 9 November 1988.

36. Faun Earl, conversation, 13 April 1987.

37. Fritz Enders to Lorraine Nielson, 26 January, 26 February 1946, 30 January, 10 March, 10 November 1949, 8 January 1950, copies at the Utah State Historical Society, Salt Lake City. Copies of letters provided by Mrs. Lorraine Nielson Nelson of Salina, Utah.

38. Fritz Noack to _____, undated letter and letter dated 29 May 1946.

39. Audrey Godfrey letter to Allan Kent Powell, 19 February 1987.

40. Delbert J. Olsen letter to Allan Kent Powell, 18 February 1987, copy at Utah State Historical Society, Salt Lake City.

41. Ed Cooper, remarks at North Sevier High School, Salina, Utah, 9 November 1988.

42. Hyrum Olsen letter to Allan Kent Powell, 18 June 1987.

43. *The Hill Fielder*, 3 May 1945.

44. *Unser Leben*, January 1946.

45. Klebe interview; Altkruger interview.

46. Barkhoff, manuscript history, 75–76.

47. Stanley W. Hoole, ed. *And Still We Conquer: The Diary of a Nazi Unteroffizer in the German African Corps Who Was Captured by the United States Army May 9, 1943, and Imprisoned at Camp Shelby, Mississippi* (Tuscaloosa: Confederate Publishing, University of Alabama, 1968), 41.

48. Rudolf Weltin interview by Allan Kent Powell, 5 May 1987, Frohenleiten, Austria.

49. H. Moosmann to the Boettger family, 23 November 1946, copy at Utah State Historical Society, Salt Lake City. Copy of the letter provided by Richard Boettger.

50. Weltin interview.

51. Kaspar J. Fetzer to Elbert D. Thomas, 22 June 1945; Elbert D. Thomas to Kaspar J. Fetzer, 26 June 1945, *in* Elbert D. Thomas Papers, Box 108, Folder For-7 Germany, Utah State Historical Society, Salt Lake City.

52. Mrs. James Isenhour to Elbert D. Thomas, 19 November 1945; Mrs. Gustave Dantel to Elbert D. Thomas, 16 December 1945, *in* Elbert D. Thomas Papers, Box 118, Folder I, Box 117, Folder Immigration and Naturalization Service, Utah State Historical Society, Salt Lake City.

53. Hinrichs interview.

54. Werner Lohner conversation with Allan Kent Powell, 18 June 1987.

55. Weltin interview; Lampe interview.

56. Richard Boettger interview by Allan Kent Powell, 6 May 1987, Reutlingen, Germany; Altkruger interview; Josef Becker interview by Allan Kent Powell, 25 April 1987, Idar-Oberstein, Germany; "Acht Sarge fuer Salina," in *PW, Die Wahre Geschichte der deutschen Kriegsgefangenen*, undated article. Copy provided by Dieter Lampe.

57. Leonhard Mombar interview by Allan Kent Powell, 22 February 1984, Langlau by Gunzenhausen, Germany; Kurt Treiter interview by Allan Kent Powell, 20, 21 February 1984, Mutterstadt, Germany.

58. Pyne Interview.

59. Dorothy J. Buchanan interview by Allan Kent Powell, 2 November 1986, Richfield, Utah.

60. Pyne interview.

61. Johnson interview; Sol S. interview *in* Doyle, "German Prisoners of War," 145.

62. Arnold Krammer, "When the Afrika Korps Came to Texas," *Southwestern Historical Quarterly* 80 (January 1977): 270.

63. Johnson interview.

Chapter 12. THE SALINA TRAGEDY

1. Dieter Lampe, "The Salvo from Salina," copy at the Utah State History Society, Salt Lake City. Salina was not the only camp in which German prisoners were shot. Werner Fredrich Meier was shot and killed after refusing to stop on command while trying to escape from a woodcutting detail in Fort Sutton, North Carolina. In a more tragic instance in Camp Concordia, Kansas, a guard shot and killed a prisoner, Adolph Huebner, as he approached the fence to retrieve a soccer ball during a game among the prisoners. In Colorado, an American soldier shot and killed three German prisoners whom he thought were about to rush him. Apart from Salina, the only other account of an unprovoked shooting which has come to light occurred at a branch camp near West Helena, Arkansas, when two shotgun blasts were fired into the camp. No prisoners were seriously injured and officials were unable to identify any suspects or motives for the incident. Sixteen German prisoners were killed on October 31, 1945, when an accident occurred near Fort Custer, Michigan. The truck in which they were riding was struck by a New York Central Railroad train. Robert D. Billinger, Jr., "Behind the Wire: German Prisoners of War at Camp Sutton, 1944–1946," *The North Carolina Review* 61 (October 1984): 493; Patrick G. O'Brien et al., "Stalag Sunflower: German Prisoners of War in Kansas," *Kansas History* 7 (Autumn 1984): 186; Merrill R. Pritchett and William L. Shea, "The Afrika Korps in Arkansas, 1943–1946," *Arkansas Historical Quarterly* 37 (Spring 1978): 21; John Hammond More, *The Faustball Tunnel: German POWs in America and Their Great Escape* (New York: Random House, 1978), 241; *New York Times*, 1 November 1945; Col. A. M. Tollefson, Director, Prisoner of War Operations, to Special Projects Division, Department of State, 10 December 1945, Record Group 389, Box 1340, National Archives, Washington, D.C.

2. *Deseret News*, 9 July 1945.

3. Wilma Nielsen interview by Allan Kent Powell, 16 June 1986, Salina, Utah. Floyd Johnson gave one variation of the account of Bertucci's being drunk. According to Johnson, there were stories going around that Bertucci had been drinking, fell asleep, and had a dream that the German prisoners were trying to overpower him; he awoke and started shooting at them. Floyd Johnson interview by Allan Kent Powell, 1 November 1986, Aurora, Utah.

4. *New York Times*, 10 July 1945; *Salt Lake Tribune*, 10 July 1945. In interviews with Salina residents in June 1986, the story of the dead brother or friend was always mentioned. Rumors that Bertucci's brother was killed by Germans also circulated among the prisoners of war. Emil Blau maintained that Bertucci's brother was killed during the Ardennes offensive in December 1944. Dieter Lampe speculated that the shooting was a calculated step by Bertucci to avoid being sent to Japan, where he would have to fight. Lampe surmised that Bertucci concluded,

"Go ahead, shoot into the camp. They are the Krauts. There will be a few dead and you will be treated as a psychotic. But soon the war will be over and you will be released and you will still be alive." Emil Blau interview by Allan Kent Powell, 30 April 1987, Trier, Germany; Dieter Lampe interview by Allan Kent Powell, 28 April 1987, Grossensee, Germany.

5. Wayne Owens interview by Allan Kent Powell, 26 June 1987, Fargo, North Dakota.

6. Maj. Stanley L. Richter to Special War Problems Division, Department of State, 20 July 1945, Record Group 389, Box 1340, Folder "704 General P/W, 1 July 1945–13 December 1945," National Archives, Washington, D.C.

7. Col. A. M. Tollefson to Special War Problems Division, Department of State, 28 August 1945, Record Group 389, Box 1513, File "4.1 October 1944 through 1946," National Archives, Washington, D.C.

8. W. Nielsen interview; Sharp Rasmussen interview by Allan Kent Powell, 17 June 1986, Salina, Utah.

9. *Salina Sun*, 22 June 1945.

10. Ibid., 15 June 1945.

11. S. Rasmussen interview.

12. Willi Klebe interview by Allan Kent Powell, 28 April 1987, Hannover, Germany.

13. Blau interview.

14. Herbert Barkhoff, manuscript history, 39, copy at Utah State Historical Society, Salt Lake City.

15. Karl Altkruger interview by Allan Kent Powell, 23 April 1987, Hannover, Germany.

16. *Salina Sun*, 13 July 1945.

17. Wesley Cherry interview by Allan Kent Powell, 1 November 1986, Salina, Utah.

18. Klebe interview.

19. Mrs. Theressa Rasmussen recalled that Anthony Willardson, a member of the North Sevier (Mormon) Stake Presidency, had shared the story with her and several other people sometime before his death. Theressa Rasmussen interview by Allan Kent Powell, 16 June 1986, Salina, Utah.

20. *Salina Sun*, 13 July 1945.

21. Barkhoff, manuscript history, 41.

22. *Deseret News*, 9 July 1945; *Salt Lake Tribune*, 10 July 1945.

23. *Deseret News*, 9 July 1945.

24. Barkhoff, manuscript history, 41.

25. Ibid., 37; *Deseret News*, 9 July 1945.

26. Biographical information on the nine men killed at Salina was compiled from their POW personnel files, which are maintained by the Dienst Stelle fuer die Benachrichtigung der naechsten Angehoerigen von Gefallenen der ehemaligen deutschen Wehrmacht in Berlin, Germany.

Otto Bross (single). Age: 25. Hometown: Pforzheim. Religion: Lutheran. Occupation: Blacksmith. Date and place captured: 5/11/43, Tunisia.

Ernst Fuchs (single). Age: 21. Hometown: Kirchberg/Hunsruck. Religion: Lutheran. Occupation: Electrician. Date and place captured: 7/5/43, Tunisia.

Gottfried Gaag (single). Age: 29. Hometown: Frauenthal by Bayreuth. Religion: Catholic. Occupation: Metal worker. Date and place captured: 5/9/43, Tunisia.

Georg Liske (married, wife Antonie, 1 child). Age: 31. Hometown: Dortmund. Religion: Catholic. Occupation: Soldier. Date and place captured: 5/11/43, Tunisia.

Hans Meyer (single). Age: 24. Hometown: Messenthin/Pomerania. Religion: Lutheran. Occupation: Office clerk. Date and place captured: 5/13/43, Tunisia.

Adolf Paul (single). Age: 28. Hometown: Hussingsen. Religion: Catholic. Occupation: Metal worker. Date and place captured: 5/9/43, Tunisia.

Friedrich Ritter (married, wife Berta, 3 children). Age: 48. Hometown: Frankfurt am Main. Occupation: Clerk. Date and place captured: 3/30/45, Germany.

Fritz Stockmann (married, wife Jutta, 1 child). Age: 24. Occupation: Druggist. Date and place captured: 7/44, France.

Walter Vogel (married, wife Emma, 1 child). Age: 32. Hometown: Boetzingen/Freiburg. Religion: Lutheran. Occupation: Soldier. Date and place captured: 8/29/44, France.

27. *Salt Lake Tribune*, 10 July 1945.

28. *Deseret News*, 13 July 1945; Karl Gustav Almquist, "Report of Visit to Prisoner of War Camp, Ogden, Utah," 10 July 1945, Record Group 389, Box 2668, Folder "Inspection and Field Reports," National Archives, Washington, D.C.

29. Barkhoff, manuscript history, 48.

30. Altkruger interview.

31. Barkhoff, manuscript history, 46–47.

32. Lampe interview.

33. Barkhoff, manuscript history, 50–52.

34. Blau interview.

35. Kurt Treiter interview by Allan Kent Powell, 20, 21 February 1984, Mutterstadt, Germany.

36. Almquist, "Prisoner of War Camp, Ogden."

37. *Salt Lake Tribune*, 10 July 1945.

38. Eric Kososik interview by Allan Kent Powell, 18 March 1987, Ogden, Utah.

39. Richard Boettger interview by Allan Kent Powell, 6 May 1987, Reutlingen, Germany.

40. Rudolf Weltin interview by Allan Kent Powell, 5 May 1987, Frohenleiten, Austria.

41. Correspondence in the Georg Liske file, Dienst Stelle fuer die Benachrichtigung der naechsten Angehoerigen von Gefallenen der ehemaligen deutschen Wehrmacht, Berlin, Germany.

42. Correspondence in the Hans Meyer file, Dienst Stelle . . . , Berlin, Germany.

43. Correspondence in the Gottfried Gaag file, Dienst Stelle . . . , Berlin, Germany.

44. Altkruger interview.

45. Lampe, "Salvo From Salina."

46. Lampe interview.

47. Barkhoff, manuscript history, 43.

48. Altkruger interview.

49. Lampe interview.

Chapter 13. HOME

1. P. Schnyder, "Camp Ogden, Utah," 30 May 1945, National Archives, Microfilm 365.45, Utah State University.

2. Frederick Weber interview by Allan Kent Powell, 26 February, 9, 16 March 1987, Salt Lake City, Utah.

3. Quoted in Edward John Pluth, "The Administration and Operation of German Prisoner of War Camps in the United States during World War II" (Ph.D. diss., Ball State University, 1970), 224.

4. William L. Shea, ed., "A German Prisoner of War in the South: The Memoir of Edwin Pelz," *Arkansas Historical Quarterly* 44 (Spring 1983): 51.

5. Eric Kososik interview by Allan Kent Powell, 18 March 1987, Ogden, Utah.

6. Ernst Hinrichs, "History," 4, copy at the Utah State Historical Society, Salt Lake City.

7. Copy of poem provided by Ernst Hinrichs.

8. Fritz Poes to Annchen Poes, 1 April 1946, copy at the Utah State Historical Society, Salt Lake City.

9. *Unser Leben*, April 1945.

10. Ibid., September 1945.

11. Ibid., August 1945.

12. Herbert Barkhoff, manuscript history, 60, copy at Utah State Historical Society, Salt Lake City.

13. Karl Gustav Almquist, "Report of Visit to Prisoner of War Camp, Bushnell General Hospital, Utah," 13 July 1945, Record Group 389, Box 2657, Folder "Other Inspection Reports—Bushnell," National Archives, Washington, D.C.

14. Mrs. Barkhoff to Herbert Barkhoff, 26 December 1944, copy at Utah State Historical Society, Salt Lake City.

15. Quoted in Ralph Spencer, "Prisoners of War in Cheyenne County, 1943–1946," *Nebraska History* 63 (Fall 1982): 445.

16. *Unser Leben*, November 1945.

17. Ibid., January 1946.

18. Georg Hirschmann interview by Allan Kent Powell, 23 February 1984, Puelheim by Altdorf, Germany.

19. David A. Foy, *For You the War Is Over: American Prisoners of War in Nazi Germany* (New York: Stein and Day, 1984), 150.

20. From the Fort Robinson, Nebraska, camp newspaper, *Neuer Horizon*, quoted in Spencer, "Prisoners of War in Cheyenne County, 1943–1946" *Nebraska History* 63 (Fall 1982): 445.

21. Ernst Hinrichs interview by Allan Kent Powell, 27 April 1987, Shortens, Germany.

22. Hermann Jung, *Die Deutschen Kriegsgefangenen in Amerikanischer Hand/USA*, vol. 10/1, in *Zur Geschichte der deutschen Kriegsgefangenen des Zweiten Weltkrieges* (Bielefeld, Germany: Verlag Ernst und Werner Gieseking, 1972), 257.

23. Anton H. Richter, trans. and ed., "A German P.O.W. at Camp Grant: The Reminiscences of Heinz Richter," *Journal of the Illinois State Historical Society* 76 (Spring 1983): 68.

24. Pluth, "German Prisoner of War Camps," 406.

25. Richard Boettger interview by Allan Kent Powell, 6 May 1987, Reutlingen, Germany.

26. Jung, *Deutschen Kriegsgefangenen*, 251.

27. Kososik interview; Weber interview.

28. Paul Hupfner interview by Allan Kent Powell, 12 March 1986, Inzinglen, Germany.

29. U.S. Provost Marshal General's Office, "Prisoner of War Operations," Historical Monograph, vol. 1, 225–26, microfilm, Library of Congress, Washington, D.C.

30. Hinrichs interview; Josef Becker interview by Allan Kent Powell, 25 April 1987, Idar-Oberstein, Germany; Gerhard Graenitz interview by Allan Kent Powell, 17 February 1984, Minden, Germany.

31. Becker interview.

32. Willi Klebe interview by Allan Kent Powell, 28 April 1987, Hannover, Germany.

33. Hinrichs, "History," 5.

34. The Haimbock letter was found in the Max Zimmer Letter Collection, Manuscript 234, Folder no. 2, Church of Jesus Christ of Latter-day Saints Archives, Salt Lake City, Utah.

35. On September 24, 1946, Bishop J. H. Kirby of Pittsburg, California, wrote to Bartholomew to report that five German prisoners had been baptized in the Mormon church before they left California for England, then Germany. Bishop J. H. Kirby to Calvin Bartholomew, 14 September 1946, copy at the Utah State Historical Society, Salt Lake City.

36. Arnold Krammer, *Nazi Prisoners of War in America* (New York: Stein and Day, 1979), 266.

37. Weber interview; Golden A. Buchmiller, "Artist Makes Statue of Christ Whole Again," *Deseret News*, Church News Section, 16 January 1983.

38. Walter Koch, personal history, 19, in Koch's possession; comments by Walter Koch to Cache Valley Historical Society, 13 May 1987, Logan, Utah.

39. Kososik interview.

40. Otto Liebergesell interview by Allan Kent Powell, 19, 25 April 1988, Salt Lake City, Utah.

41. Ernst Luders interview by Allan Kent Powell, 7 May 1987, Bad Oldesloe, Germany.

42. Cobie Van der Puhl Wilson interview by Allan Kent Powell, 1 June 1987, Clearfield, Utah; Edith Cannon interview by Allan Kent Powell, 17 November 1987, Salt Lake City, Utah; Boettger interview.

43. Hinrichs, "History," 5.

44. Dieter Lampe interview by Allan Kent Powell, 28 April 1987, Grossensee, Germay; *Richfield Reaper,* 29 September 1977; *Salt Lake Tribune,* 30 September 1977. Lampe also recalled the newspaper headlines at the time of the shooting. The *Salina Sun*, 13 July 1945, proclaimed, "American Guard Shoots Sleeping Nazi PW's." Others were not so sensitive to the Nazi label. Herbert Barkhoff, also wounded at Salina, wrote: "I did not take as evil that the newspapers talked about the dead Nazis. How could they tell the difference when it was not easy for us to tell the difference." Gerhard Graenitz recalled he was upset when he was called

a Nazi by the Americans, but when he was told that the word was simply a substitute for "German," such as "Yankee" for "American," and that nothing derogatory was meant by it, he accepted the explanation. Barkhoff, manuscript history; Graenitz interview.

45. *Deseret News*, 10, 11 November 1988; *Salina Sun*, 16 November 1988.

Chapter 14. CONCLUSION

1. Georg Hirschmann interview by Allan Kent Powell, 23 February 1984, Puelheim by Altdorf, Germany.

2. Karl Groeger to Mr. Hoffmann, 23 June 1947, Max Zimmer Letter Collection, Manuscript 234, Folder no. 2, Church of Jesus Christ of Latter-day Saints Archives, Salt Lake City, Utah.

3. Douglas Botting, *From the Ruins of the Reich: Germany 1945–1949* (New York: Crown Publications, 1985), 104.

4. Arthur A. Durand, *Stalag Luft III: The Secret Story* (Baton Rouge: Louisiana State University Press, 1988), 376. Durand's book contains an excellent appendix, "History of Prisoners of War."

5. Ibid., 199.

6. Ibid, 238. Durand illustrates this problem with two examples. A wife wrote to her prisoner husband, "I love you darling, although you are a coward." In the second instance, a prisoner of war received a pair of knitted wool socks in a Red Cross parcel. The name and address of the contributor was included with the socks. In reply to the prisoner's letter of thanks, the woman wrote back, "Sorry, but I made the socks for a member of the armed forces, not a prisoner of war."

Bibliography

Two major sources for this study have been the National Archives and interviews with former German prisoners of war and Utahns who associated with them. Tapes, transcripts, interview notes, correspondence, and other documents collected during this project have been deposited at the Utah Division of State History (Utah State Historical Society) Library in Salt Lake City.

At the National Archives, Record Group 389—records of the U.S. Provost Marshal General's Office, Prisoner of War Division—and Record Group 407—records of the U.S. Army Adjutant General's Office, Operation Branch—have yielded a treasure of reports and correspondence. During research trips to the National Archives, I was able to locate most of the documents cited in the Bibliography. I have benefited greatly from the work of two other scholars, Raymond Kelly Cunningham, Jr., and Ralph A. Busco, who mined the National Archives for their Masters theses in the 1960s and 1970s. Both scholars deposited in Utah libraries the National Archives documents they collected, and in those collections I found documents that I had overlooked or had been unable to find during my own research at the National Archives. Consequently, for those National Archives documents for which I am unable to give box and folder information but which were located in the collections available in Utah, I have cited the appropriate collection and identified the document as originating in the National Archives. The Raymond Kelly Cunningham, Jr., collection in the Western Americana Section, Marriott Library, University of Utah, Salt Lake City, Utah, is the first one. According to Cunningham, the records in his collection for the World War I period are from Record Group 407, with boxes 184–212 relating to enemy aliens at Fort Douglas and boxes 218–224 covering the administration of Fort Douglas in Salt Lake City, Utah. Another source used by Cunningham was the U.S. State Department Decimal Files which contain reports of the Swiss Legation inspections of Fort Douglas. The second collection made by Ralph A. Busco is contained on two rolls of microfilm, number 365.45, "Provost Marshal General's Office, Idaho and Utah Prisoner of War Camp Inspection Reports and Labor Reports," which is available in the Special Collections, Merrill Library, Utah State University, Logan, Utah. For the sake of brevity in the Bibliography, these two sources are identified as "Cunningham Collection, University of Utah," and "Microfilm 365.45, Utah State University."

"Acht Sarge fuer Salina." Undated article published in *PW, Die Wahre Geschichte der deutschen Kriegsgefangenen*. Copy provided by Dieter Lampe.

Adjutant General. Correspondence to Captain Sheriden, 29 September 1917. National Archives, Cunningham Collection, University of Utah.

————. Correspondence to Chief, Military Intelligence Branch, Executive Division General Staff, 26 July 1918. Record group 407, Box 74, Folder 28 "Escapes." National Archives, Washington, D.C.

————. Correspondence to the Commander, War Prison Barracks, Fort McPherson, Georgia, "Naturalization of Prisoners of War," 14 June 1919. Record Group 407, Box 79, Folder 25 "Naturalization." National Archives, Washington, D.C.

————. Correspondence to Hon. James H. Brady, United States Senate, 18 July 1917. Record Group 407, Box 79, Folder 27, "Parole, Releases, Transportation on Release, Exchange War Prisoners and Enemy Aliens." National Archives, Washington, D.C.

————. Correspondence to Secretary of War, 13 March 1918, National Archives, Cunningham Collection, University of Utah.

————. Correspondence to Secretary of War, 13 March 1918. Record Group 407, Box 79, Folder 27, "Parole, Releases, Transportation on Release, Exchange War Prisoners and Enemy Aliens." National Archives, Washington, D.C.

————. Memorandum for the Chief of Staff, 1 February 1918. National Archives, Cunningham Collection, University of Utah.

Alder, Preston. Interviewed by Allan Kent Powell, 27 February 1987, Providence, Utah.

Almquist, Karl Gustav. "Report of Visit to Prisoner of War Camp, Bushnell General Hospital, Utah," 13 July 1945. Record Group 389, Box 2657, Folder "Other Inspection Reports—Bushnell." National Archives, Washington, D.C.

————. "Report of Visit to Prisoner of War Camp, Camp Clearfield, Utah," 12 July 1945. Record Group 389, Box 2658, Folder "PMGO Inspection Reports, Clearfield, Utah." National Archives, Washington, D.C.

————. "Report of Visit to Prisoner of War Camp, Camp Douglas, Wyoming," 5 July 1945. Record Group 389, Box 2660, Folder, "Other Inspection Reports, Douglas, Wyoming." National Archives, Washington, D.C.

————. "Report of Visit to Prisoner of War Camp, Ogden, Utah," 10 July 1945. Record Group 389, Box 2668, Folder "Inspection and Field Reports." National Archives, Washington, D.C.

Altkruger, Karl. Interviewed by Allan Kent Powell, 23 April 1987, Hannover, Germany.

Andersen, Wesley. Interviewed by Kathy Bradford, 19 February 1987, Brigham City, Utah.

Arndt, John, ed. *Microfilm Guide and Index to the Library of Congress Collection of German Prisoner of War Newspapers Published in the United States from 1943–1946*. Worcester, Massachusetts: Clark University, 1965.

Arrington, Leonard J. *The Price of Prejudice: The Japanese-American Relocation Center in Utah during World War II*. Logan, Utah: Utah State University, 1962.

Arrington, Leonard J., and Thomas G. Alexander. "Supply Hub of the West: Defense Depot Ogden, 1941–1964." *Utah Historical Quarterly* 32 (Spring 1964): 99–121.

————. "They Kept 'Em Rolling: The Tooele Army Depot, 1942–1962." *Utah Historical Quarterly* 31 (Winter 1963): 3–25.

————. "Sentinels of the Desert: The Dugway Proving Ground (1942–1963) and Deseret Chemical Depot (1942–1965)." *Utah Historical Quarterly* 34 (Winter 1964): 32–43.

————. "The U.S. Army Overlooks Salt Lake City: Fort Douglas, 1862–1965." *Utah Historical Quarterly* 33 (Fall 1965): 344.

Arrington, Leonard J. and Archer L. Durham. "Anchors Aweigh in Utah: The U.S. Naval Supply Depot at Clearfield, 1942–1962." *Utah Historical Quarterly* 33 (Spring 1963): 109–26.

Bailey, E. Tomlin. "Ogden Prisoner of War Camp Report," 21 October 1944. Record Group 389, Box 2668, Folder "Other Inspection Reports—Ogden." National Archives, Washington, D.C.

Bailey, Ronald H. *Prisoners of War.* Alexandria, Virginia: Time-Life Books, 1981.

Baptiste, Joseph C. "The Enemy among Us: World War II Prisoners of War." Ph.D. diss., Texas Christian University, 1976.

Barkhoff, Herbert. Interviewed by Allen Kent Powell, 9 November 1988.

————. Manuscript history. Copy at Utah State Historical Society, Salt Lake City.

Barkhoff, Mrs. (Herbert Barkhoff's mother). Letter to Herbert Barkoff, 26 December 1944. Copy at Utah State Historical Society, Salt Lake City.

Bartholomew, Calvin. Interviewed by Allan Kent Powell, 14 June 1987, Provo, Utah.

Bear River Valley Leader. 9 August 1945. Tremonton, Utah.

Becker, Josef. Interviewed by Allan Kent Powell, 25 April 1987, Idar-Oberstein, Germany.

Beeley, Arthur L. Correspondence to Francis G. Howard, 14 October 1944. Record Group 389, Box 2668, File "Ogden, Utah." National Archives, Washington, D.C.

Bethell, Nicholas. *The Last Secret.* New York: Basic Books, 1974.

Bierstadt, Francis E. Correspondence to Army Service Forces, Office of the Provost Marshal, 9 February 1944. National Archives, Microfilm 365.45, Utah State University.

Billinger, Robert D., Jr. "Behind the Wire: German Prisoners of War at Camp Sutton, 1944–1946." *The North Carolina Review* 61 (October 1984): 481–509.

————. "With the Wehrmacht in Florida: The German POW Facility at Camp Blanding, 1942–1946." *Florida Historical Review* 58 (October 1979): 160–73.

Billington, Ray Allen. *Land of Savagery, Land of Promise: The European Image of the American Frontier.* New York: W.W. Norton, 1981.

Blackhurst, Stanley Davis. Interviewed by Allan Kent Powell, 13 November 1987, Salt Lake City, Utah.

Blau, Emil. Interviewed by Allan Kent Powell, 30 April 1987, Trier, Germany.

Boehme, Kurt W. *Geist und Kultur der deutschen Kriegsgefangenen im West.* Bielefeld, Germany: Verlag Ernst und Werner Gieseking, 1968.

Boettger, Richard. Interviewed by Allan Kent Powell, 6 May 1987, Reutlingen, Germany.

The Bombshell. Hill Air Force Base, Utah, 1945.

Botting, Douglas. *From the Ruins of the Reich: Germany 1945–1949.* New York: Crown Publications, 1985.

Box Elder News Journal. 6, 29 March 1945. Tremonton, Utah.

Brandeis, Erich. "Birds in a Barbed Cage." Record Group 407, Box 79, Folder 22. National Archives, Washington, D.C.

Brickhill, Paul. *The Great Escape.* New York: Crest Book, 1950.

Buchanan, A. Russell. *The United States and World War II.* 2 vols. New York: Harper Torchbooks, 1964.

Buchanan, Dorothy J. Interviewed by Allan Kent Powell, 2 November 1986, Richfield, Utah.

————. Diary. In possession of Mrs. Buchanan.

Buchmiller, Golden A. "Artist Makes Statue of Christ Whole Again." *Deseret News,* Church News Section, 16 January 1983. Salt Lake City, Utah.

Busco, Ralph A. "A History of the Italian and German Prisoner of War Camps in Utah and Idaho during World War II," M.A. thesis, Utah State University, 1967.

Busco, Ralph A., and Douglas D. Alder. "A History of the Italian and German Prisoner of War Camps in Utah and Idaho during World War II." *Utah Historical Quarterly* 39 (Winter 1971): 55–72.

Butler, Joseph T., Jr. "Prisoner of War Labor in the Sugar Cane Fields of LaFourche Parish, Louisiana: 1943–1944." *Louisiana History* 14 (Summer 1973): 283–96.

Butterfield, Wallace. Interviewed by Allan Kent Powell, 28 May 1987, Salt Lake City, Utah.

Bybee, Kennard. Interviewed by Allan Kent Powell, 14 April 1987, Salt Lake City, Utah.

Byram, George L. Correspondence to the Adjutant General of the Army, 15 February 1918. Record Group 407, Box 74, Folder 28. National Archives, Washington, D.C.

Caldwell, F. M. Correspondence to the Adjutant General, "Investigation of Complaints of War Prisoners, Fort Douglas, Utah," 15 February 1918. National Archives, Cunningham Collection, University of Utah.

Caldwell, John LeRoy. "German Prisoners of War in Utah during World War II." Unpublished paper, 11 December 1969. Western Americana Collection, Marriott Library, University of Utah, Salt Lake City.

Cannon, Edith. Interviewed by Allan Kent Powell, 17 November 1987, Salt Lake City, Utah.

Centerville Newsetter. May 1945. Centerville, Utah.

Cherry, Wesley. Interviewed by Allan Kent Powell, 1 November 1986, Salina, Utah.

Christensen, F. Dean. "The Day Salina Spilled Nazi Blood." *Utah Holiday* 16 (October 1986): 54–58.

Christensen, John E. "The Impact of World War II." *In* Richard D. Poll et al. *Utah's History.* Provo, Utah: Brigham Young University Press, 1978.

Christensen, Leath. Interviewed by Allan Kent Powell, 16 June 1986, Salina, Utah.

Church of Jesus Christ of Latter-day Saints. Archives. Max Zimmer Collection, Manuscript 234, Folder Number 2. Salt Lake City, Utah.

Clements, Ernest, Chief of Welfare Committee. Correspondence to U.S. War Department, 27 November 1918. National Archives, Cunningham Collection, University of Utah.

Cooper, Ed. Remarks at North Sevier High School, Salina, Utah, 9 November 1988.

Cowles, LeRoy E. Correspondence to Dr. George F. Zook, 30 August 1944. Record Group 389, Box 2668, Folder "Ogden, Utah." National Archives, Washington, D.C.

Cunningham, Raymond Kelly, Jr. "Internment 1917–1920: A History of the Prison Camp at Fort Douglas, Utah, and the Treatment of Enemy Aliens in the Western United States." M.A. thesis, University of Utah, 1976.

Curtis, Denzel S. Correspondence to Commanding General, Ninth Service Command, 17 August 1945. Record Group 389, Box 2668, Folder "Clearfield, Utah." National Archives, Washington, D.C.

Daniels, Roger, Sandra C. Taylor, and Harry H. L. Kitano, eds. *Japanese Americans from Relocation to Redress*. Salt Lake City: University of Utah Press, 1986.

Davis, F. B. Correspondence to Commandant, Fort Douglas, 4 June 1919. National Archives, Cunningham Collection, University of Utah.

Deseret News. 10, 12 June 1917, 9, 13 July 1945, 10, 11 November 1988. Salt Lake City, Utah.

Doyle, Joseph Frederick. "German Prisoners of War in the Southwest United States during World War II: An Oral History." Ph.D. diss., University of Denver, 1978.

Durand, Arthur A. *Stalag Luft III: The Secret Story*. Baton Rouge: Louisiana State University Press, 1988.

Earl, Faun. Telephone conversation with Allan Kent Powell, 13 April 1987.

Eberhardt, Charles C. "Italian Prisoners of War Camp, Tooele Ordnance Depot," 15 August 1945. Record Group 389, Box 2674, Folder "Other Inspection Reports—Tooele, Utah." National Archives, Washington, D.C.

_____. "Prisoner of War Camp, Ogden, Utah," 14 February 1944. Record Group 389, Box 2668, Folder "Other Inspection Reports—Ogden." National Archives, Washington, D.C.

_____. "Prisoner of War Camp, Camp Rupert, Idaho, Branch Camps," 6–7 August 1945. Record Group 389, Box 2671, Folder "Other Inspection Reports—Rupert, Idaho." National Archives, Washington, D.C.

_____. "Prisoner of War Camp, Utah, Army Service Forces Depot, Ogden, Utah, Branch Camps: Logan, Tremonton, Orem, Salina," 13 August 1945. Record Group 389, Box 2668, Folder "Other Inspection Reports—Ogden." National Archives, Washington, D.C.

Eberhardt, Charles C., and Luis Hortal. "Prisoner of War Camp, Fort Douglas, Salt Lake City, Utah," 14 August 1945. Record Group 389, Box 2660, Folder "Other Inspection Reports—Fort Douglas." National Archives, Washington, D.C.

Edwards, Earl L., Assistant Director, Prisoner of War Division. Correspondence to the Commanding General, Ninth Service Command, Fort Douglas, Utah, 7 January 1943[44]. National Archives, Microfilm 365.45, Utah State University.

Enders, Fritz. Correspondence to Lorraine Nielson. Xerox copies provided by Mrs. Nielson and are at the Utah State Historical Society, Salt Lake City.

Englebrecht, Walter, and Erich Fratzscher. Correspondence to Commandant, War Prison Barracks #1, Fort McPherson, 13 May 1919. Record Group 407, Box 83, Folder 20, "Release of German Prisoners—Naturalization." National Archives, Washington, D.C.

Ericsson, Arthur J. Letter to prisoner of war Erwin Schott, 4 October 1945. Copy provided by Mr. Schott and is at the Utah State Historical Society, Salt Lake City.

Extension Service. Annual Reports of County Extension Agents, Cache County, 1945, Box Elder County, 1945, and Sevier County, 1945. Special Collections, Merrill Library, Utah State University, Logan.

Farrand, Stephen, Prisoner of War Operations, Provost Marshal General's Office. Correspondence to Special War Problems Division, n.d. Record Group 389, Box 1340, Folder Number 13. National Archives, Washington, D.C..

Faulk, Henry. *Group Captives: The Re-education of German Prisoners of War in Britain, 1945–1948.* London: Chatto and Windus, 1977.

Fischer, Rudolph. "Bushnell General Hospital, Brigham City, Utah," 15 April 1945. Record Group 389, Box 2657, Folder "Other Inspection Reports—Bushnell." National Archives, Washington, D.C.

————. "Prisoner of War Camp, Ogden, Utah, Army Service Forces Depot, Ogden, Utah." Record Group 389, Box 2668, Folder "Ogden, Utah, Inspection and Field Reports." National Archives, Washington, D.C.

Fischer, W. P. Correspondence to Commanding General, Fort Douglas, Utah, 4 April 1945. Record Group 389, Box 1578, Folder "IX Service Command Correspondence." National Archives, Washington, D.C.

Foy, David A. *For You the War Is Over: American Prisoners of War in Nazi Germany.* New York: Stein and Day, 1984.

Fredricksen, Mary K. "Some Thoughts on Prisoners of War in Iowa, 1943 to 1946." *The Palimpsest* 65 (March/April 1984): 68–80.

Gabaldon, Benjamin. Interviewed by Allan Kent Powell, 25 November 1987, Salt Lake City, Utah.

Gaertner, Georg, with Arnold Krammer. *Hitler's Last Soldier in America.* New York: Stein and Day, 1985.

Gansberg, Judith M. *Stalag U.S.A.* New York: Thomas Y. Crowell, 1977.

Gappmayer, Leland. Interviewed by Allan Kent Powell, 1 March 1988, Salt Lake City, Utah.

Gewinner, Albert. Correspondence to Commanding Officer, Prisoner of War Branch Camp, Tremonton, Utah, 23 June 1945. Record Group 389, Box 2483, File "Ogden, Utah, 1942–46." National Archives, Washington, D.C.

Glander, Herwig. Interviewed by Allan Kent Powell, 9 September 1983, Salt Lake City, Utah.

Glasgow, Brunhilde Poes. Interviewed by Allan Kent Powell, 24 March 1987, Logan, Utah.

Glidden, William B. "Internment Camps in America, 1917–1920." *Military Affairs* 37 (December 1973): 137–41.

Godfrey, Audrey. Letter to Allan Kent Powell, 19 February 1987.

Graenitz, Gerhard. Interviewed by Allan Kent Powell, 17 February 1984, Minden, Germany.

Griffith, L. E. Correspondence to Mrs. Josef Paul, n.d. Record Group 389, Box 1513, Folder 3. National Archives, Washington, D.C.

Groeger, Karl. Correspondence to Mr. Hoffmann, 23 June 1947. Max Zimmer Letter Collection, Manuscript 234, Folder no. 2. Church of Jesus Christ of Latter-day Saints Archives, Salt Lake City, Utah.

Hahn, Walter. Telephone conversation with Allan Kent Powell, 13 April 1987.

Hillfielder. 1 March, 3 May 1945. Hill Field Air Force Base, Utah.

Hinrichs, Ernst. "History." Copy at the Utah State Historical Society, Salt Lake City.

_____. Interviewed by Allan Kent Powell, 27 April 1987, Shortens, Germany.

Hirschmann, Georg. Interviewed by Allan Kent Powell, 23 February 1984, Puelheim by Altdorf, Germany.

History of Ogden Air Technical Service Command. CY 1945, vol. 2. Hill Field History Office, Ogden, Utah.

Hong, Howard. "Report of Visit to Prisoner of War Camp, Douglas, Wyoming," 19–21 December 1944. Record Group 389, Box 2660, Folder "Other Inspection Reports—Douglas." National Archives, Washington, D.C.

Hood, Lawrence. Interviewed by Allan Kent Powell, 18 August 1986, Tooele, Utah.

Hoole, Stanley W. "Alabama's World War II Prisoner of War Camps." *The Alabama Review* 70 (April 1967): 83–114.

_____, ed. *And Still We Conquer: The Diary of a Nazi Unteroffizer in the German African Corps Who Was Captured by the United States Army, May 9, 1943, and Imprisoned at Camp Shelby, Mississippi*. Tuscaloosa: Confederate Publishing, University of Alabama, 1968.

Hortal, Luis. "Prisoner of War Camp, Bushnell Hospital," 11 August 1945. Record Group 389, Box 2657, Folder "Other Inspection Reports—Bushnell." National Archives, Washington, D.C.

_____. "Report of Visit to Prisoner of War Camp, Hill Field, Utah," 12 August 1945. Record Group 389, Box 2663, Folder "Other Inspection Reports—Hill Field." National Archives, Washington, D.C.

_____. "Ogden, Utah, Prisoner of War Camp," 5, 6 October 1943, 6, 1943, 5–7 February 1944. Record Group 389, Box 2668, Folder "Other Inspection Reports—Ogden." National Archives, Washington, D.C.

_____. "Report of Visit to Prisoner of War Camp, Ogden, Utah," 13 August 1945. Record Group 389, Box 2668, Folder "Other Inspection Reports—Ogden." National Archives, Washington, D.C.

_____. "Report of Visit to P.O.W. Camp, Camp Warner, Utah," 9, 10 February 1944." Record Group 389, Entry 461, Box 1675, Folder "Inspection and Field Reports 1942–1946." National Archives, Washington, D.C.

_____. "Report of Visit to POW Camp, Ogden, Utah," 8–9 March 1945. Record Group 389, Box 2668, Folder "Other Inspection Reports—Ogden." National Archives, Washington, D.C.

Hortal, Luis, and Charles C. Eberhardt. "Prisoner of War Camp, Naval Supply Depot, Clearfield, Utah," 14 August 1945. Record Group 389, Entry 461, Box

2658, File "Naval Supply Depot, Clearfield, Utah." National Archives, Washington, D.C.

Howard, Francis E. Correspondence to President L. W. Cowles, 28 September 1944. Record Group 389, Box 2668, Folder "Ogden, Utah." National Archives, Washington, D.C.

Huebecher, Karl P., and Charles Vuillenmier. "Inspection Report of Fort Douglas," 20, 21 November 1917. Record Group 407, Box 76, Folder 6, "Report of the Inspection by the Swiss Commission, Ft. Oglethorpe, Ft. McPherson, and Ft. Douglas." National Archives, Washington, D.C.

Hupfner, Paul. Interviewed by Allan Kent Powell, 12 March 1986, Inzinglen, Germany.

Johnson, Floyd. Interviewed by Allan Kent Powell, 1 November 1986, Aurora, Utah.

Jones, Calvin N. *Views of America and Views of Germany in German POW Newspapers of World War II.* Yearbook of German American Studies, vol. 17. Lawrence: University of Kansas for the Society for German American Studies, 1982.

Jung, Hermann. *Die Deutschen Kriegsgefangenen in Amerikanischer Hand/USA,* vol. 10/1, in *Zur Geschichte der deutschen Kriegsgefangenen des Zweiten Weltkrieges.* Bielefeld, Germany: Verlag Ernst und Werner Gieseking, 1972.

Kennett, Lee. *G.I.: The American Soldier in World War II.* New York: Charles Schribner's Sons, 1987.

Kingsley, J. L. "Proposed Intellectual Diversion Program for PW Camp Douglas, Wyoming," 3 January 1945. National Archives, Microfilm 365.45, Utah State University.

Kirby, J. H. Letter to Calvin Bartholomew, 14 September 1946. Copy at the Utah State Historical Society, Salt Lake City.

Kirk, Russell. Correspondence to William C. McCann, 26 January 1946. Clarke Historical Library, Central Michigan University, Mt. Pleasant.

Klebe, Willi. Interviewed by Allan Kent Powell, 28 April 1987, Hannover, Germany.

Koch, Heinrich. Correspondence to the Adjutant General, 30 April 1919. National Archives, Cunningham Collection, University of Utah.

Koch, Walter. Comments to Cache Valley Historical Society, 13 May 1987, Logan, Utah.

————. Personal history. Manuscript in Mr. Koch's possession. Page 19 provided by Mr. Koch.

Kososik, Eric. Interviewed by Allan Kent Powell, 18 March 1987, Ogden, Utah.

Krammer, Arnold. "German Prisoners of War in the United States." *Military Affairs* 40 (April 1976): 68–73.

————. "Japanese Prisoners of War in America." *Pacific Historical Review* 52 (February 1983): 67–91.

————. *Nazi Prisoners of War in America.* New York: Stein and Day, 1979.

————. "When the Afrika Korps Came to Texas." *Southwestern Historical Quarterly* 80 (January 1977); 247–82.

Lampe, Dieter. Interviewed by Allan Kent Powell, 28 April 1987, Grossensee, Germany.

_____. "The Salvo from Salina," Copy at the Utah State Historical Society, Salt Lake City.

Lau, Merle. Interviewed by Roy Caldwell, 15 November 1969, Salina, Utah.

Lawler, William F. Telephone conversation with Allan Kent Powell, 6 September 1988.

Lewis, George G., and John Mewha. *History of Prisoner of War Utilization by the United States Army, 1776–1945*. U.S. Department of the Army, Pamphlet 20–213. Washington, D.C.: Government Printing Office, 1955.

Liebergesell, Otto. Interviewed by Allan Kent Powell, 19, 25 April 1988, Salt Lake City, Utah.

Lietz, F. D. Conversation with Allan Kent Powell, 16 March 1987, Ogden, Utah.

Lohner, Werner. Telephone Conversation with Allan Kent Powell, 18 June 1987.

Luders, Ernst. Interviewed by Allan Kent Powell, 7 May 1987, Bad Oldesloe, Germany.

Maffeo, M. A. Correspondence to Captain Spencer, 20 January 1945. National Archives, Microfilm 365.45, Utah State University.

Marler, Mrs. V. A. Telephone conversation with Allan Kent Powell, 26 February 1988.

Matheny, Ray T. *Die Feuerreiter: Gefangenen in Fliegenden Festungen*. Munich: Alberecht Knaus, 1987.

_____. Interviewed by Allan Kent Powell, 3 December 1987, Provo, Utah.

Matheson, Guy E. Correspondence to Director of Security and Intelligence, 3 January 1946. Record Group 389, Box 1578, File "IX Service Command Correspondence Transcripts." National Archives, Washington, D.C.

Matthews, Harry T. "Report of Investigation of Escape of Ten (10) German Prisoners from, and General Conditions of, War Prison Barracks No. 1 at Fort McPherson, Georgia," 13 November 1917. Record Group 407, Box 76, Folder 7, "Inspection of War Prison Camps in the United States." National Archives, Washington, D.C.

Maw, Herbert. Papers. Utah State Archives, Salt Lake City.

Mazuzan, George T., and Nancy Walker. "Restricted Areas: German Prisoner-of-War Camps in Western New York, 1944–1946." *New York History* 59 (January 1978): 55–72.

Meek, Frank E. Correspondence to Commanding General, 7 March 1944. Record Group 389, Box 2486, Folder "Tooele." National Archives, Washington, D.C.

Metrauz, G. S. "Camp Ogden, Utah," 25 November 1944. Record Group 389, Box 2668, Folder "Other Inspection Reports—Ogden." National Archives, Washington, D.C.

_____. "Camp Rupert, Idaho," August 1945. Record Group 389, Box 2671, Folder "Other Inspection Reports—Rupert, Idaho." National Archives, Washington, D.C.

_____. "Camp Tooele, Utah," 22 November 1944. Record Group 389, Box 2674, Folder "Other Inspection Reports—Tooele, Utah." National Archives, Washington, D.C.

Miconi, Gene. Interviewed by Allan Kent Powell, 17 June 1986, Ogden, Utah.

Mombar, Leonhard. Interviewed by Allan Kent Powell, 22 February 1984, Langlau by Gunzenhausen, Germany.

Monson, Wells. Interviewed by Kathy Bradford, 12 February 1987, Brigham City, Utah.

Moore, John Hammond. *The Faustball Tunnel: German POWs in America and Their Great Escape.* New York: Random House, 1978.

————. "Hitler's Wehrmacht in Virginia, 1943–1946." *The Virginia Magazine of History and Biography* 85 (July 1977): 259–73.

————. "Italian POWs in America: War Is Not Always Hell." *Prologue: The Journal of the National Archives* 8 (Fall 1976): 141–51.

————. "Nazi Troopers in South Carolina, 1944–1946." *South Carolina Historical Magazine* 81 (October 1980): 306–15.

Moosman, H. Letter to Boettger family, 23 November 1946. Copy at Utah State Historical Society, Salt Lake City.

Munz, John. Correspondence to U.S. War Department, April 1919. National Archives, Cunningham Collection, University of Utah.

Nadeshin, Wadim. Correspondence to Igor Konstanovitsch, n.d. Record Group 389, Box 1578, Folder "IX Service Command Correspondence." National Archives, Washington, D.C.

Neuland, Paul. Correspondence to Director, Prisoner of War Special Projects Division, 17 May 1945. National Archives, Microfilm 365.45, Utah State University.

————. "Report of Visit to Prisoner of War Camp, Douglas, Wyoming," 16–17 February 1945. Record Group 389, Box 2660, Folder "Other Inspection Reports—Douglas, Wyoming." National Archives, Washington, D.C.

Neuland, Paul, and Walter H. Rapp. "Report of Visit to Prisoner of War Camp, Clearfield, Utah," 17 May 1945. National Archives, Microfilm 365.45, Utah State University.

————. "Report on Visit to Prisoner of War Camp, Ogden, Utah," 16 May 1945. Record Group 389, Box 2668, Folder "Other Inspection Reports—Ogden." National Archives, Washington, D.C.

New York Times. 10 July, 1 November 1945. New York City, New York.

Nicholes, F. Rulon. "The Story of a Painting," n.d. Copy at Utah State Historical Society, Salt Lake City.

Nielsen, Arlen. Interviewed by Allan Kent Powell, 16 June 1986, Salina, Utah.

Nielsen, Conrad. Interviewed by Roy Caldwell, 15 November 1969, Salina, Utah.

Nielsen, Duane. Interviewed by Roy Caldwell, 15 November 1969, Salina, Utah.

Nielsen, Wilma. Interviewed by Allan Kent Powell, 16 June 1986, Salina, Utah.

Noack, Fritz. Letters to————, dated and undated.

Notarianni, Philip. Conversation with Allan Kent Powell, 9 August 1986, Salt Lake City, Utah.

Noyes, Helen McArthur. "Unpublished History of Rae Noyes." Copy in Mrs. McArthur's possession.

Noyes, Dr. Rae. Interviewed by Roy Caldwell, 15 November 1969, Salina, Utah.

O'Brien, Patrick G., Thomas D. Isern, and R. Daniel Lumley. "Stalag Sunflower: German Prisoners of War in Kansas." *Kansas History* 7 (Autumn 1984): 182–98.

Oederlen, Frederick, and Louis H. Junod. "Fort Douglas War Prison Camp Inspection," 19, 20, 21 December 1918. National Archives, Cunningham Collection, University of Utah.

Ogden Standard Examiner. 16 August 1944, 27 February 1977. Ogden, Utah.

Olsen, Delbert J. Letter to Allan Kent Powell, 18 February 1987. Copy at Utah State Historical Society, Salt Lake City.

Olsen, Hyrum. Letter to Allan Kent Powell, 18 June 1987. Copy at Utah State Historical Society, Salt Lake City.

Ortner, John H. "Camp Warner," 11 May 1944. National Archives, Microfilm 365.45, Utah State University.

Owens, Wayne. Interviewed by Allan Kent Powell, 26 June 1987, Fargo, North Dakota.

Parnell, Wilma. *The Killing of Corporal Kunze.* Secaucus, New Jersey: Lyle Stuart, 1981.

Paschall, Allen W. "The Enemy in Colorado: German Prisoners of War, 1943–1946," *The Colorado Magazine* 56 (Summer/Fall 1979): 119–42.

Persson, Sture. "Report of Visit to Prisoner of War Camp, Bushnell General Hospital," 16 March 1946. National Archives, Microfilm 365.45, Utah State University.

————. "Report of Visit to Prisoner of War Camp at the Naval Supply Depot, Clearfield, Utah," 21 March 1946. National Archives, Microfilm 365.45, Utah State University.

————. "Report of Visit to Prisoner of War Camp, Rupert, Idaho," 13–14 March 1946. National Archives, Microfilm 365.45, Utah State University.

————. "Report of Visit to Prisoner of War Camp, Utah A.S.F. Depot, Ogden, Utah," 19 March 1946. National Archives, Microfilm 365.45, Utah State University.

Phillipp, Louis S. N. "German Prisoner of War Camp, Naval Supply Depot, Clearfield, Utah," 31 May 1945. Record Group 389, Box 2658, Folder "Naval Supply Depot, Clearfield." National Archives, Washington, D.C.

————. "Italian Prisoner of War Camp, Deseret Chemical Warfare Depot, Tooele, Utah," 26 May 1945. Record Group 389, Box 2660, Folder "Deseret Chemical Warfare Depot, Tooele, Utah." National Archives, Washington, D.C.

————. "Italian Prisoner of War Camp, Fort Douglas, Utah," 25 May 1945. Record Group 389, Box 2660, Folder "Other Inspection Reports—Fort Douglas." National Archives, Washington, D.C.

————. "Italian Prisoner of War Camp, Tooele Ordinance Depot," 26 May 1945. Record Group 389, Box 2674, Folder "Other Inspection Reports—Tooele, Utah." National Archives, Washington, D.C.

————. "Prisoner of War Camp, Camp Rupert, Idaho," 4, 5 June 1945. Record Group 389, Box 2671, Folder "Other Inspection Reports—Rupert, Idaho." National Archives, Washington, D.C.

Phillipp, Louis S. N., and Paul Schnyder. "Prisoner of War Camp, Bushnell General Hospital, Brigham, Utah," 1 June 1945. Record Group 389, Box 2657, Folder "Other Inspection Reports—Bushnell." National Archives, Washington, D.C.

Pluth, Edward John. "The Administration and Operation of German Prisoner of War Camps in the United States during World War II." Ph.D. diss., Ball State University, 1970.

_____. "Prisoner of War Employment in Minnesota during World War II. *Minnesota History* 44 (Winter 1975): 290–303.

Poes, Fritz. Letters to Annchen Poes, 30 June 1944, 1 April 1946. Copies at the Utah State Historical Society, Salt Lake City.

Poll, Richard D., Thomas G. Alexander, Eugene E. Campbell, David E. Miller. *Utah's History.* Provo, Utah: Brigham Young University Press, 1978.

Pritchett, Merrill R., and William L. Shea. "The Afrika Korps in Arkansas, 1943–1946." *Arkansas Historical Quarterly* 37 (Spring 1978): 3–20.

_____. "The Enemy in Mississippi (1943–1946)." *The Journal of Mississippi History* 41 (November 1979): 351–71.

Pyne, Beatrice Gappmayer. Interviewed by Allan Kent Powell, 25 September 1986, Orem, Utah.

Rapp, Walter H. "Field Service Camp Survey by Office of the Provost Marshal General," 4–5 May 1945. Record Group 389, Box 2668, Folder "Enemy POW Informational Bureau, Inspection and Field Reports." National Archives, Washington, D.C.

Rasmussen, Leath. Interviewed by Allan Kent Powell, 16 June 1986, Salina, Utah.

Rasmussen, Maurice. Interviewed by Allan Kent Powell, 16 June 1986, Salina, Utah.

Rasmussen, Sharp. Interviewed by Allan Kent Powell, 17 June 1986, Salina, Utah.

Rasmussen, Theressa. Interviewed by Allan Kent Powell, 16 June 1986, Salina, Utah.

Redington, L. W. Correspondence to General McManus, 25 September 1919. National Archives, Cunningham Collection, University of Utah.

Reeves, Gordon. Interviewed by Kathy Bradford, 17 February 1987, Brigham City, Utah.

Richfield Reaper. 29 September 1977. Richfield, Utah.

Richter, Anton H., trans. and ed. "A German P.O.W. at Camp Grant: The Reminiscences of Heinz Richter." *Journal of the Illinois State Historical Society* 76 (Spring 1983): 61–70.

Richter, Stanley L. Correspondence to Arthur L. Lerch, 17 August 1945. Record Group 389, Box 1513, Folder 4.12, "Telegrams, Cables and Memos." National Archives, Washington, D.C.

_____. Correspondence to Special War Problems Division, Department of State, 20 July 1945. Record Group 389, Box 1340, Folder 704, "General P/W, 1 July 1945–13 Dec 1945." National Archives, Washington, D.C.

Ririe, Boyd H. Correspondence to Senator Abe Murdock, 14 December 1945. Record Group 389, Box 1578, File "IX Service Command Correspondence Transcripts." National Archives, Washington, D.C.

Der Ruf: Zeitung der deutschen Kriegsgefangenen in U.S.A. Faksimile-Ausgabe. Munich: K.G. Sauer, 1986.

Rundell, Walter, Jr. "Paying the POW in World War II. *Military Affairs* 22 (Fall 1958): 121–34.

Salina Sun. 15, 22 June 1945, 13 July 1945, 16 November 1988. Salina, Utah.

Salt Lake Telegram. 2 October, 12, 15 June 1917, 17, 19 March 1945. Salt Lake City, Utah.

Salt Lake Tribune. 10, 11, 13, 20, 21, 22 June 1917, 14 September, 4, 16, 26 October 1917, 25 January 1918, 27 December 1944, 10 January, 10 July 1945, 30 September 1977, 23 January 1984.

Sand Blast. 17 August 1945. Dugway Proving Ground, Utah.

Schnibbe, Karl-Heinz, with Alan F. Keele and Douglas F. Tobler. *The Price: The True Story of a Mormon Who Defied Hitler.* Salt Lake City: Bookcraft, 1984.

Schott, Erwin. Interviewed by Allan Kent Powell, 6 May 1987, Munich, Germany.

Schnyder, P. "Camp Ogden, Utah," 30 May 1945. National Archives, Microfilm 365.45, Utah State University.

————. "Camp Clearfield Report," 31 May 1945. Record Group 389, Box 2658, Folder "PMGO Inspection Report—Clearfield, Utah." National Archives, Washington, D.C.

Schweiger, DeKoven L. "Report of Visit to Bushnell General Hospital, Brigham City, Utah," 21 March 1944. Record Group 389, Box 2657, Folder "PMGO Inspection Reports—Bushnell General Hospital." National Archives, Washington, D.C.

————. "Report of Visit to Prisoner of War Camp, Ogden, Utah," 10–12 December 1943. National Archives, Microfilm 365.45, Utah State University.

————. "Report of Visit to Camp Warner," 8–10 March 1944. Record Group 389, Box 2674, Folder "PMGO Inspection Reports—Tooele, Utah." National Archives, Washington, D.C.

————. "Report of Visit to Prisoner of War Camp, Rupert, Idaho," 20 October 1945. Record Group 389, Box 2671, Folder "PMGO Inspection Reports—Rupert, Idaho." National Archives, Washington, D.C.

Shannahan, Edward L. "Report of Visit to POW Base Camp, Tooele, Utah," 20–21 April, 24 May 1944. Record Group 389, Box 2674, Folder "PMGO Inspection Reports—Tooele, Utah." National Archives, Washington, D.C.

————. "Report of Visit," 20 April 1944. Record Group 389, Box 1578, Folder "IX Service Command Correspondence Transcripts." National Archives, Washington, D.C.

Shannahan, Edward L., and W. J. Bridges, Jr. "Report of Inspection of War Camp Rupert, Idaho and Branch Camps." 5–18 June 1945. National Archives, Microfilm 365.45, Utah State University.

Shea, William L., ed. "A German Prisoner of War in the South: The Memoir of Edwin Pelz." *Arkansas Historical Quarterly* 44 (Spring 1983): 42–55.

Shea, William L., and Merrill R. Pritchett. "The Wehrmacht in Louisiana." *Louisiana History* 23 (Winter 1982): 5–19.

Siegel, Heinz. Interviewed by Allan Kent Powell, 18 February 1984, Niederbierbach by Neuwied, Germany.

Sitnek, William G. Letter to Willi Klebe, 30 April 1956. Copy at Utah State Historical Society, Salt Lake City.

Slavens, Charles A. "Memories of a POW," as told to Thomas P. Slavens. *The Palimpsest* 65 (March/April 1984): 53–67.

Smith, Howard W. Correspondence to Commanding General, Ninth Service Command, 30 October 1944. National Archives, Microfilm 365.45, Utah State University.

Spencer, Ralph. "Prisoners of War in Cheyenne County, 1943–1946." *Nebraska History* 63 (Fall 1982); 438–49.

Spidle, Jake W. "Axis Invasion of the American West: POWs in New Mexico, 1942–1946." *New Mexico Historical Review* 49 (April 1974): 93–122.

————. "Axis Prisoners of War in the United States, 1942–1946: A Bibliographical Essay." *Military Affairs* 39 (April 1975): 61–66.

Sundstrom, Harvey. Interviewed by Allan Kent Powell, 14 January, 13 May 1987, Lewiston, Utah.

Taylor, Morris. Interviewed by Allan Kent Powell, 24 March 1987, Hyde Park, Utah.

Tholmas, L. H., President of Montana Beet Growers Association. Correspondence to Ninth Service Command, 20 December 1945. Record Group 389, Box 1578, Folder "IX Service Command Correspondence Transcripts." National Archives, Washington, D.C.

Thomas, Elbert D. Papers. Utah State Historical Society, Salt Lake City.

Thomas, Jennie M. "History of the Prisoner of War Camp, Ogden, Utah." Historical Branch, Headquarters Control Division, Utah Army Service Forces Depot, 1945. Weber State College Library Manuscript Collection, MS 29, Box 1, Record Group "Defense Depot Ogden Chronologies: 1930–1971." Ogden, Utah.

Thorson, Henry. Interviewed by Allan Kent Powell, 16 June 1986, Salina, Utah.

Tollefson, A. M., Director, Prisoner of War Operations. Correspondence to Special Projects Division, Department of State, 10 December 1945. Record Group 389, Box 1340. National Archives, Washington, D.C.

————. Correspondence to Special War Problems Division, Department of State, 28 August 1945. Record Group 389, Box 1513, File 4.1, October 1944 through 1946. National Archives, Washington, D.C.

————. Correspondence, 5 June 1944. Record Group 389, Box 1578, Folder "IX Service Command, Correspondence Transcripts." National Archives, Washington, D.C.

————. Correspondence to Commanding General, Ninth Service Command, 8 January 1946. Record Group 389, Box 2484, Folder "Rupert, Idaho." National Archives, Washington, D.C.

The Transcript-Bulletin. 28 March, 15 December 1944, 22 July 1986. Tooele, Utah.

Treiter, Kurt. Interviewed by Allan Kent Powell, 20, 21 February 1984, Mutterstadt, Germany.

Tuchman, Barbara W. *The Zimmermann Telegram.* New York: Bantam Books, 1966.

University of Utah, Cunningham Collection (National Archives). Synopsis of telegrams and letters in reference to repatriation move. Salt Lake City.

Unser Leben. 1945, 1946. German POW camp newspaper, Ogden, Utah. Microfilm copy in the Library of Congress, Washington, D.C.

Urwiller, Colonel, and Colonel Hannover. Conversation Transcript, 24 August 1945. Record Group 389, Box 1578, Folder "IX Service Command Correspondence Transcripts." National Archives, Washington, D.C.

U.S. National Archives. List of Seventy Three Men Admitted to the United States. Record Group 407, Box 79, Folder 28. Washington, D.C.

_____. "Prisoner of War Agreement," n.d. Record Group 389, Box 2660, Folder "Camp Douglas." Washington, D.C.

_____. Telegrams, cables, memos. Record Group 389, Box 1513, Folder 4.12. Washington, D.C.

_____. Testimony Expected in the Case of the United States vs. the (28) Interned Aliens Whose Names Appear on the Joint Charge Sheet. Salt Lake City.

U.S. Provost Marshal General's Office. "Fort Douglas, Utah, pt. 3, Remarks." PMG Form #27, Period Ending 15 June 1945. Record Group 389, Box 2530, Folder "Fort Douglas." National Archives, Washington, D.C.

_____. "Prisoner of War Menu and Messing Guide." Prisoner of War Circular #35, 1 July 1944. National Archives, Washington, D.C.

_____. "Prisoner of War Operations." 4 vols. Microfilm. Library of Congress, Washington, D.C.

U.S. War Department. *Enemy Prisoners of War.* Technical Manual 19–500. Washington, D.C.: Government Printing Office, 1945.

Vacha, J. E. "When Wagner Was Verboten: The Campaign against German Music in World War I." *New York History* 64 (April 1983): 171–88.

Van Arsdale, Turner. "Prisoner of War Camp, Rupert, Idaho," 29 August 1945. Record Group 389, Box 2671, Folder "Other Inspection Reports—Rupert, Idaho." National Archives, Washington, D.C.

Van Orsdale, J. T. Correspondence to the Adjutant General, 8 May 1918. Record Group 407, Box 74, Folder 28, "Escape." National Archives, Washington, D.C.

Walker, Richard P. "Prisoners of War in Texas during World War II." Ph.D. diss., North Texas State University, 1980.

Warner, Richard S. "Barbed Wire and Nazilagers: PW Camps in Oklahoma." *The Chronicles of Oklahoma* 64 (Spring 1986): 37–67.

Weber, Frederick. Interviewed by Allan Kent Powell, 26 February, 9, 16 March 1987, Salt Lake City, Utah.

Weltin, Rudolf. Interviewed by Allan Kent Powell, 5 May 1987, Frohenleiten, Austria.

Wenz, Robert. Letter to Allan Kent Powell, 2 January 1988.

Wilson, Cobie Van der Puhl. Interviewed by Allan Kent Powell, 1 June 1987, Clearfield, Utah.

Wilson, Terry Paul. "The Afrika Korps in Oklahoma: Fort Reno's Prisoner of War Compound." *The Chronicles of Oklahoma* 52 (Fall 1974): 360–69.

Wilson, W. B., Secretary of Labor. Correspondence to Newton D. Baker, Secretary of War, 25 January 1918. National Archives, Cunningham Collection, University of Utah.

Zimmermann, Harold. "Harvesting Peaches with German Prisoners of War." *Journal of the Western Slope* 2 (Winter 1987): 18–21.

Index